The Knowledge Base in
Educational Administration

SUNY Series in Educational Leadership

Daniel L. Duke, Editor

The Knowledge Base in Educational Administration

Multiple Perspectives

Edited by

Robert Donmoyer

Michael Imber

James Joseph Scheurich

THE STATE UNIVERSITY OF NEW YORK PRESS

Published by
State University of New York Press, Albany

© 1995 State University of New York

Printed in the United States of America

For information address State University of New York Press, State University Plaza, Albany, NY 12246

Production by Laura Starrett
Marketing by Nancy Farrell

Library of Congress Cataloging-in-Publication Data

Donmoyer, Robert.
    The knowledge base in educational administration : multiple perspectives / Robert Donmoyer, Michael Imber, James Joseph Scheurich.
      p.   cm. — (SUNY series in educational leadership)
    Includes bibliographical references and index.
    ISBN 0-7914-2835-9 : $64.50. -- ISBN 0-7914-2386-7 (pbk.) : $21.95
    1. School management and organization--United States--Philosophy. 2. School management and organization--Social aspects--United States.   3. School supervision--United States.   I. Imber, Michael. II. Scheurich, James Joseph, 1944–   .   III. Title.   IV. Series.
LB2805.D66   1994
371.2′001—dc20   94-25386
                                              CIP

10 9 8 7 6 5 4 3 2

Contents

Introduction:
Knowledge Base Problems in
Educational Administration

During the last ten years, various groups within the field of education have attempted to articulate knowledge bases for their particular subfield. The effort began in teacher education, spearheaded in part by the Holmes group, a consortium of deans of schools of education and the American Association of Colleges of Teacher Education,[1] but educational administration—the subject of this book—soon followed suit. These efforts sought to catalog the knowledge that the practitioners of a particular field ought to possess and employ and, in the process, to legitimate the authority of those who posses, employ, or teach the designated knowledge base.

The impetus to develop a knowledge base in educational administration originated with the National Policy Board for Educational Administration, a consortium of ten national school administration–related organizations.[2] In its report, *Improving the Preparation of School Administrators: An Agenda for Reform*, the National Policy Board recommended that the field rethink and clearly articulate its knowledge base and even suggested seven general categories of knowledge that could be used to frame the discussion: (1) societal and cultural influences on schooling; (2) teaching and learning processes and school improvement; (3) organizational theory; (4) methodologies of organizational studies and policy analysis; (5) leadership and management processes and functions; (6) policy studies and politics of education; and (7) moral and ethical dimensions of schooling.

Subsequently, the University Council of Educational Administration (UCEA), one of the National Policy Board's member organizations, accepted the National Policy Board's challenge and began a ten-year effort to identify "the knowledge essential for school leaders to solve critical contemporary problems of practice" (UCEA 1992, 13). The first phase of the UCEA project has been completed and the products of that first phase have been published by McGraw-Hill in the form of a set of documents called *Primis*.

Primis is organized around seven general categories of knowledge. Each category in *Primis* includes an overview essay, a case study, an annotated bibliography of representative readings, and a number of illustrative papers. Patrick Forsyth (1993), the executive director of UCEA, indicates that the second phase of the ten-year project will be built around seven additional objectives: (1) To review the completeness of the seven domain structure, making adjustments and additions where necessary; (2) expand the knowledge in each domain; (3) analyze each knowledge domain for adequacy; (4) modify the content of each domain; (5) articulate the knowledge of each domain; (6) identify appropriate media for communication to multiple audiences; and (7) search for ways to integrate knowledge across domains (2).

The idea that some sort of knowledge base is needed in education is not new. On the contrary, the utility of a knowledge base for the field of education has been accepted relatively uncritically since the turn of the century, when reformers became intent on turning over educational decision-making to professionals (Tyack 1979). Explicit in their notion of professionalism was an assumption about the existence of a body of knowledge that, when learned and understood, conferred on the knower a level of expertise not available to nonprofessionals. The founding of schools of education and departments of educational administration was part of this effort. Contemporary knowledge base projects, however, differ from earlier ones in that they focus on creating a knowledge for educational subfields, such as teacher education or administration, rather than the field of educational more generally. But the goal of defining a knowledge base that in turn can ground and legitimate professional work has not been altered.

This book looks critically at the assumptions and beliefs that underlie efforts to create a knowledge base in educational administration. Its chapters consider a wide range of fundamental issues concerning the need for a knowledge base in educational administration and the possibility of developing and legitimating such a knowledge base. Also included are a number of chapters that accept the need for a knowledge base but offer suggestions concerning the content, development, and legitimacy of a knowledge base in educational administration that differ significantly from other recent efforts.

While this book project was stimulated by UCEA's initiation of a knowledge base project, the book itself should not be viewed primarily as a criticism of UCEA or its effort. We felt there was a need to address fundamental questions that virtually all knowledge base articulation efforts, not just the UCEA project, left unaddressed. We wanted, in short, to bring some assumptions about the nature of knowledge, and the use of knowledge to legitimate professional control, into the open. Indeed, we believe that any effort to develop a knowledge base in educational administration may be problematic for epistemological and practical reasons.

The Epistemological Problem

The epistemological problem can be stated succinctly: knowledge today is not what it used to be. Contemporary conceptions of knowledge in the social sciences and even, to some extent, in the physical sciences (see, for example, Harding 1991), are radically different from the conception encountered by early twentieth-century medical reformers. Nonetheless, it is this early twentieth-century conception that has served as a model for those intent on bolstering the professional status of various education-related fields, including educational administration. Today, in contrast to that positivist-like conception, there is a growing realization that knowledge—most certainly knowledge of the social world—is never independent of the knower. What we know always has something to do with who we are, where we have been, who has socialized us, and what we believe.

To put the matter another way, there is a growing realization that what we know is always dependent on paradigms and that the paradigms we employ are not so much determined by the data as by determiners of what the data mean and often what the data are. The power of paradigms, perspectives, or epistemologies to influence what we know can be understood by considering the plight of an empirical researcher who sets out to determine whether one form of curriculum organization produces more learning than another.

Before the researcher can answer this question, the term *learning* must be defined and operationalized. The field of psychology provides an array of paradigms that define learning quite differently from each other. The researcher, for example, might look at Piagetian psychology and employ Piaget's concept of conservation as the basis for formulating dependent variables. There is no equivalent concept in Skinnerian behaviorism; indeed,

Skinnerians mean something quite different than Piagetians when they use the term *learning* and, hence, the dependent variables they would employ are also quite different.

In fact, these two schools of psychology tend to view learning—and by implication teaching and curriculum organization—in virtually antithetical ways. For Skinnerians, learning occurs because someone has carefully structured curriculum around incrementally sequenced behavior that is to be mastered and reinforced. For Piagetians, learning is itself a process of structuring that must be engaged in by learners themselves. Teaching cannot be turned into a mechanical process of reinforcement, and schools and school districts cannot choreograph the teaching and learning process. Indeed, in Piagetian thought there is no analog for the Skinnerian concept of reinforcement. The best a teacher can do, from a Piagetian perspective, is to create a rich environment with which students can interact, allow students the freedom to interact with that environment, and then fashion instruction improvisationally to respond—frequently in the form of questions—to what students say or do.

The paradigm the empirical researcher chooses will thus influence the dependent variables employed in a study, the type of validity considered appropriate, aspects of the study design, and, ultimately, the conclusions the study comes to about the relative worth of different forms of curriculum organization. No statistical procedure can mitigate this a priori, paradigmatic influence. No critical experiment can be designed that will provide a final, metaparadigmatic answer.

The situation becomes even more complicated when we turn to paradigms that call into question the fundamental assumptions of experimental design. Philosophers such as Buber (1968) and, to some extent, Dewey (1916; see also Kleibard 1975), and curriculum theorists like Jardine and Clandinin (1987), for example, suggest that teachers should not manipulate students in a classroom the way scientists manipulate variables in a laboratory. Rather than attempting to control students, either directly as Skinnerians recommend or indirectly as suggested by Piagetians, these educational perspectives or paradigms suggest that teachers should engage in dialogue with students. Rather than formally or informally transmitting predetermined objectives to students, teachers should work with students to construct the curriculum for the class.

The empirical assumptions implicit in these prescriptive theories are consistent with views of social action articulated by more descriptively oriented sociological paradigms, such as ethnomethodology and symbolic interactionism. These paradigms portray the social world not as a world of causes and effects but as a world of meanings that must constantly be negotiated and renegotiated. From this perspective, the cause-effect way of thinking that undergirds the process of experimental design distorts, in fundamental ways, what social action is and how it occurs.

Whether or not one accepts the conception of human action articulated in ethnomethodology or symbolic interactionism, these paradigms do provide an alternative to a cause-effect conception of how the social world operates, and, as a consequence, they remind us that the cause-effect conception of the social world is just that, one possible conception among many. In short, these paradigms have reinforced an idea put forth by Kant: It is impossible to talk about the nature of reality with any sense of certainty because we can never know reality independent of the cognitive structures that influence our perceptions of it.

Additional complications arise when such phenomena as ethnicity and gender are considered. Heath (1983), for example, indicates that the low-income African-American children in the school and community she studied did not come to school with limited preschool learning and parental teaching; rather, problems arose because what African-American parents meant by *learning* and *teaching* differed radically from the conceptions of learning and teaching enacted in the school setting. (Ironically, many of the skills these children learned in their homes are highly valued by business.) Similarly, it appears that women sometimes have a different way of knowing (Belenky 1986); they also at times know different things (Tannen 1991). Noddings's (1984) feminist theory of ethics, which is built around the notion of caring, for example, suggests that discussions of the moral and ethical dimension of schooling (Category 7 in the National Policy Board's framework and Domain 6 in the *Primis* document base) that are informed by feminist thought would be quite different from traditional discussions of this topic. Among other things, it is unlikely that someone guided by Noddings's feminist conception of ethics would link an ethics discussion with a discussion of legal matters as is done in the *Primis* database. Indeed, the emphasis on caring and affect in Noddings's feminist paradigm seems to require that we either abandon the knowledge base metaphor entirely or radically redefine what knowledge is.

To summarize, today there is a growing realization that no knowledge is objective and that all knowledge reflects the values, interests and biases of the knower. One implication of this realization is that when we legitimate certain knowledge—when we make it part of an official knowledge base, for instance—we are, in essence, serving the interests of some individuals and groups and thwarting the interests and concerns of others. To state the matter more boldly: We are engaging in a political act. This analysis calls into question the professional/political distinction that has been accepted uncritically throughout most of this century. At a more fundamental level, it calls into question the viability of the very notion of professionalism within an applied, value-oriented field such as educational adminisration.

The Pragmatic Problem

There is a second, more pragmatic problem with traditional and possibly contemporary notions of a knowledge base. For years, many practitioners have described traditional administrative preparation programs as being largely irrelevant and out of touch with practical concerns. Today practitioners who advance this point of view have a growing number of allies among academics both within the field of educational administration (see, for example, Bridges 1992) and in other related fields (see, for esample, Schon 1983). These allies provide powerful theoretical justifications for practitioners' claims because these theoretical justifications often suggest that the knowledge required in action-oriented contexts is fundamentally different from the theoretical knowledge valued in universities. This pragmatic problem, therefore, like the epistemological difficulty discussed above, suggests the need to question traditional assumptions about professionalism and traditional notions about a knowledge base. That is precisely what this book attempts to do.

The Purpose of This Book

The purpose of this book, in fact, is to bring to bring the epistemological and pragmatic concerns articulated above to the center of the knowledge base discussion. Because our wish is to give voice to an array of alternative perspectives rather than to advocate a particular point of view, the reader will encounter considerable diversity within this book. We have intentionally created an intellectual vaudeville rather than a book with a single coherent point of view.

As was noted above, some of our contributors call into question the very notion of a knowledge base; others accept the legitimacy of the notion, but argue for a particular kind of knowledge base, or for the inclusion of content that to date has not been a part of the educational administration knowledge base. Furthermore, the book's diversity is not limited to substance. Because substance and form are often inextricably linked (for example, even such a simple matter as whether one writes in first or third person can suggest something about one's views on the value and/or inevitability of subjectivity), the editors of this volume have consciously tried to limit their editorial role. We have solicited participants, using a concern for diversity as a guiding principle; we have managed the process (serving as a liaison with the publisher, setting deadlines); we have engaged in minimal mechanical editing or "correcting"; we have shared reviewers' comments; and we have organized the selections into three broad, loosely defined parts, and put the selections into what seemed to us to be a sensible order within each part. To the extent possible, however, we have tried to let our contributors speak for themselves, both with respect to form and substance.

The Organization and Content of the Book

The essays in Part I, Framing the Debate, address the two problems articulated in the first part of this introduction. The frst group of essays in Part I focus primarily on the epistemological problem. The lead-off essay, "The Knowledge Base in Educational Administration: Postpositivist Reflections," by James Joseph Scheurich, directly challenges the current UCEA knowledge base project from a postpositivist point of view. In this paper, Scheurich contends that newly emergent perspectives, like critical theory, feminism, race-oriented perspectives, and postmodernism, undermine or, at least, call into question much of what has been considered to be the knowledge base in educational administration. The second essay, Janet Littrell and William Foster's "The Myth of a Knowledge Base in Educational Administration," is written from a similar vantage point but is even more critical of the knowledge base project. Littrell and Foster argue that a science of management, or a science of administration, is a myth that serves to hide the dimensions of power and control that shape contemporary management methods. A third essay, Paul Bredeson's "Building a Professional Knowledge Base in Educational Administration: Opportunities and Obstacles," takes a more neutral stance with respect to the recent knowledge base articulation effort but, nevertheless, poses an important cautionary question for those articulating the knowledge base: Does the articulation of domains of professional knowledge and skills enhance our understanding and inform our practice, or does it tend to perpetuate historic boundaries that separate individuals and groups within teaching and learning communities?

Bredeson's concern with informing practice provides a transition to a second set of essays in Part I, that address pragmatic issues. Joseph Murphy, in his essay, "The Knowledge Base in School Administration: Historical Footings and Emerging Trends," provides a historical perspective on contemporary knowledge articulation efforts. Murphy's essay offers considerable optimism that contemporary efforts will yield a knowledge base rooted in the craft dimensions of the profession and avoid the problem of elitism that plagued past efforts. In the next essay, "A Knowledge Base for Educational Administration: Notes from the Field," Robert Donmoyer, writing from the perspective of an acting principal, develops a position that is considerably less optimistic than Murphy's. Donmoyer's experiences with and reflections on knowledge use in the field has led him to conclude that the search for a knowledge base and the whole knowledge base metaphor may be inappropriate starting points for reforming administrator preparation. According to Donmoyer, we should ask, instead, pedagogical questions: "How do we make preparation programs more 'lifelike?' What should we have future administrators do so they will be prepared for the complexity of their work?"

Rodney Muth's essay, "Craft Knowledge and Institutional Constraints," suggests that those who ask such questions and arrive at sensible answers will confront mammoth implementation problems. Muth describes an array of factors likely to impede efforts to make the academy more responsive to the craft dimensions of our profession. Following Muth's essay is Michael Imber's "Organizational Counterproductivism in Educational Administration," which adopts a skeptical stance similar in many respects to the stance found in preceding articles in this section. Imber contends that practicing administrators possess little of the knowledge that professors of educational administration claim to teach and that these practitioners often act in ways that are inconsistent both with what they have been taught and what they claim to know.

The final essay in this section is Gary Anderson and Bonnie Page's "Narrative Knowledge and Educational Administration: The Stories That Guide Our Practice." Anderson and Page argue that an extensive knowledge base for educational administration can be found within what they refer to as practitioner stories or narratives. These practitioner narratives are themselves contained within larger metanarratives that are based on assumptions about schools, administration, learning, and children. These assumptions, according to Anderson and Page, need to be subjected to critical questioning.

The second part of the book reinforces the critique of Part I but from a different slant. Part II, Hearing Traditionally Excluded Voices, presents perspectives that have historically been under-represented within the field of educational administration. The first essay, Charol Shakeshaft's "A Cup Half Full: A Gender Critique of the Knowledge Base in Educational Administration," examines ways that the traditional knowledge base has systematically ignored gender and demonstrates, through current research on men and women in administration, that a knowledge base built solely on male administrator behavior only tells part of the story.

Flora Ida Ortiz and David Jude Ortiz reach a similar conclusion in "How Gender and Ethnicity Interact in the Practice of Educational Administration: The Case of Hispanic Female Superintendents." As their title suggests, however, their chapter considers how both gender and ethnicity undermine traditional conceptions of the knowledge base in educational administration. Gender and ethnicity concerns remain at the center of the third essay in this part of the book: Vivian Ikpa's "Gender, Race, Ethnicity, and the Quest for a Knowledge Base in Educational Administration" argues that in the quest for an appropriate knowledge base, gender, ethnicity, and race have not been sufficiently considered. Her essay, like others in this section, contends that the knowledge base in educational administration primarily reflects the exclusive concerns of white male administrators. She suggests that efforts to articulate a knowledge base need to be grounded in an inclusiveness that reflects societal diversity.

The fourth essay in Part II, Jayminn Sulir Sanford's "Lessons of Leadership: A Critique of the Knowledge Base in Educational Adminisration," also places race at its center, but Sanford is more pessimistic than Ikpa about the possibility that any resulting knowledge base will be more inclusive than previous ones. She sees little reason to expect that any improvement appreciative of the diverse populations of successful urban educators and people of color will occur. This section concludes with an essay by Rosemary Papalewis, "Fe/Male Voices: Leadership and the Knowledge Base."

Papalewis focuses specifically on differences between female and male patterns of communication and relationship styles that have been traditionally excluded in educational administration. She concludes by advancing a critically important point made by all of the authors of this section: Any knowledge base in educational administration needs to reflect the diverse voices in society and in educational administration.

The third and final part of the book, Adding New Points of View, is a potpourri of positions that range from suggestions for incremental change to suggestions for changes that are more radical. The first four essays would require only slight modifications to the seven-category scheme proposed by the National Policy Board and employed in UCEA's *Primis* project. The first essay in Part III, Joseph Blaze's "The Micropolitics of Education: The State of the Art," accepts the politics and policy category proposed by the National Policy Board and employed by UCEA. He proposes, however, a somewhat different, more "micro" definition of politics. Similarly, Rodney Ogawa, in "Developments in Theory and Practice: An Opportunity to Examine the Impact of the Environment on School Organizations" does not challenge the utility of the organizational theory category; he simply wants to alter the scope of the organizational theory employed. Tyll van Geel's "The Preparation of Educational Leaders and Rational Choice Theory," the third essay in this section, would also fit within the seven-category scheme, but he too wants to alter the scope of the organizational theory category, in his case, by adding rational choice theory and game theory perspectives to the array of possible approaches.

Another contributor, Jane Lindle, proposes an orientation that also does not significantly challenge current efforts to articulate a knowledge base for the field, although her proposal does not fit easily into the seven-category scheme that has served to organize UCEA work to date. Lindle's "Needed: A Knowledge Base that Promotes Creativity—Toward a Rhetorical Knowledge Base for Educational Administration" is reflective of a renewed interest in rhetoric across the social sciences. While her paper begins with a discussion of the importance of classical rhetoric, it ends with a focus on how the "rhetorical art" of humor can serve educational administrators.

The next two authors in this section suggest more global and fundamental changes in our conception of the knowledge base in educational administration, although the changes each recommends are quite different. Nona Prestine roots her recommendations in the perspective of cognitive psychology. Her essay, "A Constructivist View of the Knowledge Base in Educational

Administration," argues that educational administration is an ill-structured domain of knowledge rather than a well-structured one. Consequently, she suggests that from a constructivist viewpoint, any knowledge base articulated for educational administration must be both loosely construed and open to diverse interpretations.

Like Prestine, Coileen Capper criticizes the general orientation of the knowledge-base articulation effort and proposes an entirely different orientation. Capper's "An Otherist Poststructural Perspective of the Knowledge Base in Educational Administration" is developed in comparison to other relatively new perspectives in educational administration, namely, critical theory, feminist theory, and poststructural theory. In fact, her perspective could be said to be one particular integration of these three latter theories. She concludes by supporting the proliferation of a range of perspectives and opposing the very idea of a definitive knowledge base.

The final chapter in the book is particularly important, given our focus and goals. For much of his career, the essay's author was, according to Culbertson (1988), one of the small number of architects of the ascension of positivism within educational administration. It is, thus, much to the point of this book that Daniel Griffiths's essay is entitled "Theoretical Pluralism in Educational Administration." Griffiths argues that organizations, and the activities that occur within them, are complex phenomena, requiring study from many points of view. He then develops a framework for determining how various problems and issues within organizations are to be matched with appropriate theories or perspectives.

Conclusion

Griffiths's endorsement of theoretical pluralism provides a somewhat comforting conclusion to the seemingly chaotic intellectual vaudeville on display in this book. We caution the reader not to feel too comforted, however. Theoretical pluralism—for all of its appeal in the intellectual realm of understanding—may be more problematic at the level of action. When we act, either as administrators or as professors of adminisration, hard choices must be made and contradictions and antithetical points of view must be confronted and somehow resolved. How we go about resolving, at the level of action, what are often incommensurable points of view is not at all obvious.

That issue is beyond the scope of this book which seeks to alert readers to problems or positions that have not been sufficiently addressed and to make sure voices that have traditionally not been heard or even presented in forums like this are presented and, we hope, heard. More fundamentally, we want to open up a debate about what the notion of professionalism should mean in a field such as ours and what role knowledge can legitimately play in grounding and legitimating professional expertise.

Notes

1. See, for example, Holmes 1986, and two recent publications of the Americn Association of Colleges of Teacher Education: *Knowledge Base for the Beginning Teacher* (Reynolds 1989) and *Knowledge Base for Teacher Education* (Murray 1994).

2. The membership includes the American Association of Colleges for Teacher Education (AACTE), the American Association of School Administrators, (AASA), the Association for Supervision and Curriculum Development (ASCD), the Association of School Business Officials, the Council of Chief State School Officers, the National Association of Elementary School Principals (NAESP), the National Association of Secondary School Principals (NASSP), the National Council of Professors of Educational Administration (NCPEA), the National School Boards Association (NSBA), and the University Council for Educational Administration (UCEA).

References

Belenky, M. (1986). *Women's ways of knowing*. New York: Basic Books.

Bridges, E. (1962). Problem based learning for administrators. ERIC Document.

Buber, M. (1968). *Education: Between man and man*. New York: Macmilian.

Culbertson, J. A. (1988). A century's quest for a knowledge base. In *Handbook of research on Educational Administration* (N. J. Boyan, ed.). New York: Longman.

Dewey, J. (1916). *Democracy and education*. New York: Macmillan.

Forsyth, P. (1993). *Educational administration: The UCEA document base*. New York: McGraw-Hill.

Harding, S. (1991). *Whose science? Whose knowledge?: Thinking from women's lives*. Ithaca, New York: Cornell University Press.

Heath, S. (1983). *Ways with words: Language, life, and work in communities and classrooms*. New York: Cambridge University Press.

Holmes Group. (1986). *Tomorrow's teachers*. East Lansing, Mich.: Holmes Group.

Jardine, D., and Clandinin, J. (1987). Does it rain on Vancouver Island? Teaching as storytelling. *Curriculum Inquiry, 17,* 471–81.

Kleibard, H. (1975). Reappraisal: The Tyler rationale. In *Curriculum theorizing: The reconceptualists* (W. Pinar, ed.). Berkeley, Calif.: McCutchan.

Murry, F. (1994). *Knowledge base for teacher education*. New York: Jossey-Bass.

Noddings, N. (1984). *Caring, a feminine approach to ethics and moral education*. Berkeley, Calif.: University of California Press.

Reynolds, M. (1989). *Knowledge base for the beginning teacher.* New York: Pergamon Press.

Schon, D. (1983). *The reflective teacher: How professionals think in action*. New York: Basic Books.

Tannen, D. (1991). *You just don't understand: women and men in conversation*. New York: Ballantine Books.

Tyack, D. (1979). *The one best system*. Cambridge, Mass.: Harvard University Press.

UCEA. (1992). Essential knowledge for school leaders: A proposal to map the knowledge base of educational administration. Unpubiished proposal.

PART I

Framing the Debate: Philosophical, Historical, and Practical Issues

The Knowledge Base in Educational Administration: Postpositivist Reflections

James Joseph Scheurich

In May of 1989, the National Policy Board for Educational Administration published its agenda for the reform of educational administration. The sixth of its nine recommendations was that educational administration training programs should establish a knowledge base or, as they labeled it, "a common core of knowledge and skills," composed of seven subject areas.[1] While this recommendation raises many different questions, I want to focus primarily on two questions that I think are central to any effort to establish a knowledge base in educational administration. First, is it currently possible to codify or catalog a body of knowledge in educational administration that could be called a knowledge base? And, second, if a knowledge base is not possible, where does that leave us? Is there some other approach, besides one based on a "knowledge base," that the National Policy Board could take to reform "the preparation of school administrators"? Before I address those two questions, however, I will briefly comment on the functions of a knowledge base and the University Council for Educational Administration's effort to develop the knowledge base called for by the National Policy Board.

A Knowledge Base

A knowledge base has two major functions, one external and the other internal. The external function of a knowledge base is to prove to those outside the profession that there exists a body of specialized knowledge and skills, the mastery of which confers special status on its practitioners. For example, medicine and law both have specialized knowledge bases that society recognizes as highly valuable, and thus many in these two professions enjoy considerable status and relatively high incomes (Schon 1983). Most of the other professions, predominantly the "minor" professions in Glazer's (1974) schema, do not have knowledge bases that are highly valued by society; nonetheless, almost all professions claim that they do possess a specialized body of knowledge.

Within educational administration, a knowledge base is the core knowledge, or the canon, that every member of the profession should know. A knowledge base standardizes the profession in that all of its members are certified to have mastered this canon. It also standardizes the training necessary to become a member of the profession in such a way that it does not matter in which institution a person receives her or his training; she or he will receive basically the same training, at least within some acceptable range of difference. For example, if the National Policy Board's 1989 recommendations were followed, every educational administration training program in the United States would establish the seven subject areas called for in the board's report. Every subsequent graduate of such programs would thus possess this "common core of knowledge and skills."

UCEA Accepts the Challenge Posed by the National Policy Board

The University Council for Educational Administration (UCEA) assumed the responsibility for developing such a knowledge base. During the presidency of Gail Schneider (1991–92), the UCEA Executive Committee committed to identifying "an appropriate knowledge base for educational administration" (Schneider 1992, 5). Wayne Hoy was chosen to chair a steering committee, and seven study committees were appointed for seven knowledge domains that were only slightly different than the areas identified previously by the National Policy Board.[2]

In the Fall of 1993, UCEA, in cooperation with McGraw-Hill, issued the first phase results of the knowledge base effort. This first phase product, which is called "Educational Administration: The UCEA Document Base," consists of the seven domains, a taxonomy and overview for four of the domains, and exemplary articles (called "illustrative writings") in each domain. The proposed second phase, according to Patrick Forsythe, the Executive Director of UCEA, includes a review of the seven domain structure, an expansion of the knowledge in each domain, a determination of the adequacy of each domain, the identification of ways to communicate the knowledge to other audiences, and the integration of knowledge across the domains (Forsythe 1993).

As the knowledge base project has moved beyond the conceptual stage, it has changed to some degree. There has been a limited revision of the domains, though the domain structure remains primarily unaltered. The fears, expressed in some Plenum sessions (the UCEA governance sessions) and in this book, that the product would be limited to traditional positivist or structural-functional orientations, which continue to dominate preparation programs, have, to some degree, not been realized. One of the domains, "societal and cultural influences on schooling," is clearly dominated by nontraditional views. In addition, there are a smattering of articles in the other domains that represent similar nontraditional views.

Is a Knowledge Base Currently Possible

My first question was, "Is it currently possible to codify or catalog a body of knowledge in educational administration that could be called a knowledge base?" The National Policy Board certainly thinks so, at least in terms of its seven topic areas. Jack Culbertson (1988) appears to agree; he recently concluded in "A Century's Quest for a Knowledge Base" that "there is an extensive body of knowledge available for use" in educational administration (23). This conclusion, though, is somewhat undermined by the fact that he entitled the section on the most recent period, 1967–1985, "Administrative Science as an Embattled Concept." His conclusion is more substantially undermined by the fact that he spends the entire section on the recent period discussing the paradigm wars, especially in terms of the application of positivist science to the study of educational administration and the criticism of that application by interpretivists, such as Greenfield, or critical theorists, such as Foster.

It is clear from Culbertson's (1988) chapter, from Daniel Griffiths' (1988) chapter on administrative theory in the same book, and from Nicolaides and Gaynor's (1989) recent research on textbook usage in educational administration that the "extensive body of knowledge available for use" in educational administration is predominantly positivist or functionalist.[3] It is also clear from Culbertson's chapter, as well as from Griffiths', that the interpretivists and critical theorists, among others, are at odds with the positivists over what is knowledge and how one appropriately obtains it. In fact, Schon (1983) asserts that the very idea of a knowledge base is derived from and is only functional in relation to positivism. Hence, it would be more correct for Culbertson to conclude that we have a positivistic or functionalistic body of knowledge in educational administration and that this knowledge is under serious attack by other paradigms.

Burrell and Morgan (1979), Smith and Heshusius (1986), and Sparkes (1989) have argued that these different paradigms are fundamentally incompatible. They assume different views of humans; they assume different views of the appropriate methods for inquiry; they assume different positions in terms of what reality itself is. A body of knowledge derived from one of these paradigms will, thus, not fit within the theoretical presuppositions of another paradigm. This incompatibility position, however, has been disputed by other scholars (Gage 1989; Howe and Eisenhart 1990; Miles and Huberman 1984). The argument of this latter group is that while at the abstract philosophical level there may be epistemological or ontological incompatibilities, according to "old-fashioned pragmatism" (Gage 1989, 8) or "middle-range epistemologists" (Miles and Huberman 1984, 23), the different paradigms can be treated as complementary tools or strategies "judged relative to given purposes." (Howe and Eisenhart 1990, 3)

While there is not space to adequately address this controversy, I can make my position clear with a few statements. It may be true in some areas that two different paradigms could be applied in a complementary fashion (though even this could be disputed). For instance, an organizational researcher might use Greenfield's (1978) interpretivist orientation to study an organization. The same or a different researcher might also study the same organization from a functionalist point of view like that of Hoy and Miskel (1987). The researcher or researchers could then integrate these two studies into a more comprehensive picture of the organization. While some postpositivists, like Smith and Heshusius (1986), Schon (1983) and even Greenfield (1978) himself would, I think, correctly disagree with this integrative approach, it does have a certain compelling practical logic to it.

Nonetheless, other problems are not so amenable to complementarity. This is particularly evident when a critical theory approach is compared to a positivist or interpretivist approach. Critical theory–based research is value-laden research. It begins with a commitment to emancipatory interests (Lather 1986; Gitlin, Siegel, and Boru 1988). Neither positivism nor interpretivism begins with this kind of axiological stance (Polkinghorne 1983). In addition, critical theory is opposed to research that does not make a similar commitment to emancipation.[4] Schon (1983) makes a similar point from a practice-oriented interpretivist position. He suggests that the practice of professionals has been inappropriately presided over by positivism or, in his terminology, technical rationality. Such paradigmatic opposition would, in my opinion, argue against the practical level of integration supported by some scholars. Whether one agrees with the critical theory position or Schon's position, it can readily be seen that in many cases integration or compatibility or complementarity is not possible.

These kinds of fundamental disagreements make it difficult to understand how we can assume that educational administration could reach a consensus on a body of knowledge, around which the training of new administrators should be standardized. To conclude that there is already such a body of knowledge privileges, intentionally or not, the positivist position at the considerable expense of marginalizing the emergent alternatives of interpretivism and critical theory, among other perspectives. Just on this basis alone, I would have to conclude that there is presently no acceptable justification for supporting a knowledge base in educational administration.

Nonetheless, there is still the possibility, raised earlier, that the National Policy Board's subject areas are broad enough to encompass a pluralistic set of approaches that include positivism, neopositivism, interpretivism, and critical theory, among others, whether they were complementary or not. My first response is that the Board's seven subject areas are themselves a positivist derivation, even if we accept their broad vagueness. I would argue that these subject area categories have historically grown out of the application of functionalism to administrative and organizational theory. While it is certainly possible, in a practical sense, to pour new wine in old bottles by redefining each subject area to fit an interpretivist or critical theory frame, the old functionalist list of seven areas would not be the list that critical theorists would derive from their frame of reference. For instance, from a critical theory position, "moral and ethical dimensions," one of the seven subject areas, would not be categorically separated from the other areas; these dimensions would be redefined as emancipatory interests and would be infused throughout all categories. Also, "leadership and management processes and functions," another of the subject areas, is, according to critical theorists, historically related to hierarchy-oriented, authoritarian control of subordinates (Bates 1980a; 1980b; 1982; 1987). Although a critical theorist might be able to survive within the Board's seven areas, it would be neither an honest survival nor a comfortable one.

There is another theory that I have purposely not yet discussed. This theory is one I think especially important, not just in terms of the demographics of educational administration, but also because, in my opinion, it fundamentally destroys the possibility of a knowledge base in educational administration. This theory is feminism. Feminism is particularly important for educational administration because, much to our detriment as a discipline and contrary to any idea of public schools as models of democracy for students, public education is extremely gender stratified. Public school administrators and professors of educational administration are overwhelmingly male, and public school teachers are predominantly female. As Charol Shakeshaft (1987) concludes in "Women School Administrators: Too Few for Too Long,"

> The percentage of women in school administration in the 1980s is less than the percentage of women in 1905. Women have seldom attained the most powerful and prestigious administrative positions in schools, and the gender structure of males as managers and females as workers [teachers] has remained relatively stable for the past 100 years. [The] Historical record, then, tell[s] us that there never was a golden age for women administrators, only a promise unfulfilled. (51)

Examination of the historical record to date leaves no doubt that the exclusion of women from administrative positions continues as strongly today as it did ten years ago, twenty years ago, or thirty years ago.

The continuing existence of this extreme gender stratification of the professional staff for public schools and of the educational administration professorship is unquestionably a disgrace to a field of inquiry that considers leadership to be its central issue. Unfortunately, there is ample evidence that gender stratification continues to be reinforced by the leadership in educational administration. As recently as two years ago I heard one of the prominent scholars in educational administration give a talk to a group of individuals who were considered to be among the finest doctoral candidates nationally in educational administration. The subject of his talk was the needed reform in our discipline, but not once did he even mention the gender stratification in educational administration. In addition, while the National Policy Board's agenda for reform calls for "vigorous recruitment strategies [to] be mounted to attract the brightest and most capable candidates, of diverse race, ethnicity, and sex," it does not address the fact that numerous bright and capable candidates are excluded from principal and superintendent positions because of their gender.

The idea that feminism undermines the idea of an agreed upon body of knowledge in educational administration is addressed in Charol Shakeshaft's critically important work, *Women in Educational Administration* (1987). She says that

> The underlying assumption [of research in educational administration] is that the experiences of males and females are the same, and thus research on males is appropriate for generalizing to female experience. In developing theories of administration, researchers didn't look at the context in general and, therefore, were unable to document how the world was different for women (148)

In other words, Culbertson's (1988) knowledge base is not only predominantly positivist, it is also "based on observations and assumptions drawn primarily by males from male experiences" (Shakeshaft 1987, 150). To provide evidence, Shakeshaft reviews

> five theories/concepts that are cited most often in educational administration textbooks...[including] Jacob Getzels [whom Culbertson (1988) cites as his chief example of the success of positivism] and Egon Guba's Social Systems model, John Hemphill and Alvin Coon's Leader Behavior Description Questionnaire, Andrew Halperin's Organizational Climate Description Questionnaire, Fred Fiedler's Theory of Leadership Effectiveness, and Abraham Maslow's Theory of Human Motivation and Self-Actualization. (151)

For these five key theories/concepts she shows that male-biased samples, attitudes, methods, and theories have served to create a biased body of knowledge in educational administration.

Consequently, I would argue, in reference to whether the Board's subject areas are broad enough to encompass all possibilities, that pouring feminist wine into these old male bottles would create the same problem as pouring critical theorist wine into functionalist bottles. Yes, it would be possible to teach a feminist perspective within one or all of the categories, but such instruction would not, in my opinion, occur within the categories that feminists would choose on their own. If it were taken seriously that women administrators practice differently than men administrators and that women's administrative ways of knowing are often better for children, one feminist knowledge base category might be teaching men administrators how to act more like women administrators. I, for one, would consider this a strong positive possibility, though I would have sympathy for the person undertaking the task.[5]

Once this point about male-biased knowledge is understood, it takes little additional consideration to see that a similar point can be made with regard to race bias. Although the only work on race and the knowledge base in educational administration that I am aware of is in this book, there have been two relatively recent articles by Afro-Americans that address racial bias in knowledge production in education and the social sciences. In 1985, John Stanfield's "Ethnocentric Basis of Social Science Knowledge Production" appeared in *Review of Research in Education.* Stanfield's essay argues that

> no matter how well tested a theory is and no matter how well constructed social research instruments are, they are *human* constructs and are therefore embedded in the cultural background of social scientists. The social sciences are. . .reflectors and microcosms of the societal hegemony privileges of [white] Euro-Americans. (387)

More recently, Edmund Gordon, Fayneese Miller, and David Rollock (1990) published an article in *Educational Researcher* entitled "Copying with Communicentric Bias in Knowledge Production in the Social Sciences." In this article they assert that, as Afro-American members of the American Educational Research Association (AERA), they are highly concerned about the racial bias embedded in knowledge production in the social sciences in general and in education in specific.

> Although there are some common denominators across all human experiences and groups, there is reason to believe that an overemphasis on the search for universals [which is based in positivism] has been, at the very least, premature, if not mistaken. . . . [I]nsufficient attention has been given to the impact of unique cultural, ethnic, or

gender experiences on the development of. . .the social systems by which behavior is expressed. This neglect is probably the result of androcentric, cultrocentric, and ethnocentric chauvinism in Euro-American and male dominated production of social science knowledge. We refer to this chauvinism as communicentric bias: The tendency to make one's own community the center of the universe and the conceptual frame that constrains all thought. (15)

It is reasonable, then, to conclude that any currently existing knowledge base in educational administration and any current suggestions for the appropriate categories for a knowledge base are also race biased.

I have thus provided three arguments that delineate why constructing a knowledge base in education is not possible at this time. The first was that the knowledge base that does currently exist is thoroughly dominated by only one perspective, the positivist or functionalist paradigm, largely excluding such alternatives as interpretivism or critical theory. Second, as Shakeshaft (1987) has shown, the knowledge in educational administration is biased toward males and thus works to exclude feminism, female perspectives, and the promotion of women within administration. Third, Stanfield (1985) and Gordon, Miller, and Rollock (1990) have asserted that race bias is embedded in knowledge production in the social sciences and by extension in educational administration. I have also suggested that the seven subject area categories recommended by the National Policy Board are derived from functionalism and thus at odds with the categories that might be derived from other paradigms.

The second question I wanted to address was this: if a knowledge base is not currently possible, where does that leave us, what are our alternatives? I am aware, as I pointed out in the beginning, that a knowledge base has been traditionally considered externally useful to a profession because it provides a justification for that profession. I would like to suggest, nonetheless, that the general public is much less concerned about the stature of educational administration, either as a professional discipline in the university or within the context of all professions, than it is concerned about the success of the public schools. Our main responsibility is to improve the condition of the public schools, especially those rural and urban schools where our failure is blatantly obvious on a daily basis. I do not see a concern with the professional standing of our discipline as our main responsibility.

High professional standing should serve as a consequence of our work as educators, not as a goal of our work.

In my opinion, the public will accord our profession more respect than we can imagine if we show the kind of outstanding leadership that risks commitment to the success of all children, regardless of class, race, or gender. Unfortunately, when I look at the suggested reform offered by the National Policy Board, I am sorely disappointed by its lack of vision and its lack of leadership in terms of the problems in many of our nation's schools. I see very little concern for the plight of our children and our schools in this so-called "reform" report. I largely see support for the status quo and efforts to enhance the standing of the profession, both of which will divert our attention away from the very real problems in the public schools.

Rather than our establishing a nationally standardized knowledge base, I advocate virtually the opposite direction. I suggest strong support for widespread experimentation in the training of educational administrators. I would suggest many different approaches. Our current practice, the functionalist status quo, clearly is insufficient in a large number of schools. Since no one has all of the answers, we need instead to explore multiple alternatives, especially where traditional methods are failing. As an example, my vision of a doctoral training program is considerably different from that offered by the National Policy Board.

First, where the National Policy Board urges that "vigorous recruitment strategies be mounted to attract...the brightest and most capable candidates of diverse race, ethnicity, and sex" (p. 5). I would confront directly and explicitly the gender and racial stratification in administration. We already have many fine female and nonwhite teachers who would make excellent professors of educational administration, public school principals, and superintendents, if we would only open up these positions. Second, I would do away with the dissertation in its current form. It is a vast waste of time for practitioners, and it generally serves more as a barrier than an asset. In its place I would develop site-based, collaborative research projects built around student and school interests. The dissertation could then be replaced with this site-based process and a report on these projects.

Third, I would eliminate the full-time residency for practitioners. While I support the use of residency-like cohorts, I would approach them in a very different way. I would take the professors out of the universities and put them in the schools with the graduate students. In my experience, most doctoral students in educational administration will not give up their full-time work positions. This is especially true of the growing infusion of female students and single-head-of-household female students. Rather than waste time and energy fighting this trend and inequitably excluding many highly qualified candidates, I would suggest using the students' employment situation as an active part of their doctoral education. What is happening in the students' schools should become an integral part of an educational process in which the students and the professors learn to think together, critically and reflectively, about the everyday problems that exist in the schools. Graduate students should experience their professors as co-learners in the process of creating good, equitable schools.

Fourth, I would insist that we administrators judge our work and our schools by how well we do with those at the bottom rather than with those at the top. It is all too true that, for the most part, our schools are simply replicating the socioeconomic status (SES) of the students and the race and gender stratification that governs society. This was obvious, for example, when Ohio released its statewide test results. With few exceptions, the ranking of the schools matched the socioeconomic ranking of the schools' communities. If we cannot improve on the SES, gender, and race positions the students bring to the school with them, we can only say that we have reproduced those positions.

While there are several other measures I would include in my approach to training school administrators, these four suggestions show that my vision differs from that of the National Policy Board. I do not mean to imply that my ideas are unique. It is my understanding that the University of Delaware has a somewhat similar program. Nor do I mean to imply that my ideas should dominate; this is exactly the opposite of what I am recommending. We need instead to explore and evaluate a broad range of possibilities, many of which would not easily fit within the subject areas proposed by the National Policy Board. A national knowledge base would, in my opinion, eliminate or, at the least, severely restrict such exploration.

Finally, we need to worry much less about the stature of our profession and worry much more about the condition of our schools. Most of us are educators because we care about learning and we care about children. Somewhere along the way, our concern for our degrees and our titles and our salaries has led us astray, has made us forget why we are educators. I suggest we come back home to what we know is important: that all children, whether black, Hispanic, white, Asian, or Native American, whether poor or rich, need to be loved, appreciated, and educated by teachers and administrators who are committed to successful, equitable schools. We need to remember that since no one has all the answers, no single group should control or dominate the range of possible alternatives. Whatever serves these purposes and this leadership is gold; all the rest is dross.

Notes

1. Those seven areas are 1) societal and cultural influences on schooling, 2) teaching and learning processes and school improvement, 3) organizational theory, 4) methodologies of organizational studies and policy analysis, 5) leadership and management processes and functions, 6) policy studies and politics of education, and 7) moral and ethical dimensions of schooling. (National Policy Board for Educational Administrations 1989 1989, 5–7)

2. When the National Policy Board's recommended seven subject domains were oprationalized by UCEA, the following changes were made to the seven areas: "school improvement" was dropped from "teaching and learning processes and school improvement"; organizational theory was changed to "organizational studies"; "methodologies of organizational studies and policy analyses" was dropped as a domain and "economic and financial dimensions of schooling" added; "leadership and management processes" and "policy and political studies" remained the same; and, "moral and ethical dimensions of schooling" was changed to "legal and ethical dimensions of schooling."

3. Functionalism is the common label for the sociology and the organizational theory that has been derived from a positivist epistemology. For a discussion of functionalism in organizational theory and sociology, see Burrell and Morgan (1979) or Giddens (1984). For a similar discussion on inquiry in general, see Polkinghorne (1983) or Lincoln and Guba (1985). For a critical discussion of the application of positivism to professional practice, see Schon (1983).

4. For examples of critical theory work in educational administration, see Bates (1980a; 1980b; 1981; 1982; 1987); Foster (1980; 1982; 1983; 1986); Scheurich and Imber (1991).

5. A pervasive naiveté among the paradigm integrationists suggests that research as we currently know it will be able to sustain itself against the profound critique that has been developed by feminists. Unfortunately, very few professors in educational administration are thoroughly aware of the incredible range and depth of the feminist critique of the male-dominated academy in all its many guises.

References

Bates, R. J. 1980a. Bureaucracy, professionalism and knowledge: Structures of authority and control. *Educational Research and Perspectives 7*:2.

———. 1980b. Educational administration, the sociology of science, and the management of knowledge. *Educational Administration Quarterly 16*:2.

———. 1981. Educational critique, the new sociology of education, and the work of teachers. *Journal of Education 163*:4.

———. 1982. Towards a critical practice of educational administration. Paper presented at the American Educational Research Association Annual Meeting. New York.

———. 1987. Corporate culture, schooling, and educational administration. *Educational Administration Quarterly 23*:4.

Burrell, G., and Morgan, G. 1979. *Sociological Paradigms and Organisational Analysis.* Portsmouth, N. H.: Heinemann.

Culbertson, J. A. 1988. A century's quest for a knowledge base. In *Handoook of Research on Educational Administration,* ed. N. J. Boyan. New York: Longman.

Foster, W. P. 1980. Administration and the crisis in legitimacy: A review of Habermasian thought. *Harvard Educational Review 50*: 4.

———. 1982. Toward a critical theory of educational administration. Paper presented at the American Educational Research Association Annual Meeting. New York.

———. 1983. Leadership as praxis. Paper presented at the American Educational Research Association Annual Meeting. New York.

———. 1986. *Paradigms and Promises: New Approaches to Educational Administration.* Buffalo, N.Y.: Prometheus.

Gage, N. L. 1989. The paradigm wars and their aftermath: A "historical" sketch of research on teaching since 1989. *Educational Researcher 18*:7.

Giddens, A. 1984. The Constitution of Society: Outline of the Theory of Structuration. Berkeley, Calif.: University of California Press.

Gitlin, A., Siegel, M., and Boru, K. 1988. Purpose and method: Rethinking the use of ethnography by the educational left. Paper presented at the Annual Meeting of the American Educational Research Association. New Orleans.

Glazer, N. 1974. Schools of the minor professions. *Minerva*.

Gordon, E. W., Miller, F., and Rollock, D. 1990. Coping with communicentric bias in knowledge production in the social sciences. *Educational Researcher 14*.

Greenfield, T. B. 1978. Reflections on organization theory and the truths of irreconcilable realities. *Educational Administration Quarterly 14*:2.

Griffiths, D. E. 1988. Administrative theory. In *Handbook of Research on Educational Administration,* ed. N. J. Boyan. New York: Longman.

Howe, K., and Eisenhart, M. 1990. Standards for qualitative (and quantitative) research: A prolegomenon. *Educational Researcher 19*:4.

Lather, P. 1986. Research as praxis. *Harvard Educational Review 56*:3.

Lincoln, Y. S., and Guba, E. G. 1985. *Naturalistic Inquiry.* Beverly Hills, Calif.: Sage.

Miles, M. B., and Huberman, A. M. 1984. Drawing valid meaning from qualitative data: Toward a shared craft. *Educational Researcher 13*.

National Policy Board for Educational Administration. 1989. *Improving the Preparation of School Administrators: An Agenda for Reform.* Charlottesville, VA.

Nicolaides, N., and Gaynor, A. 1989. *The Knowledge Base Informing the Teaching of Administrative and Organizational Theory in UCEA Universities: Empirical and Interpretive Perspectives.* A publication of the National Policy Board for Educational Administration.

Polkinghorne, D. 1983. *Methodology for the Human Sciences: Systems of Inquiry.* Albany, N. Y.: State University of New York Press.

Scheurich, J. J., and Imber, M. 1991. Educational reforms can reproduce societal inequities: A case study. *Educational Administration Quarterly 27*:3.

Schon, D. A. 1983. *The Reflective Practitioner: How Professionals Think in Action.* New York: Basic Books.

Shakeshaft, C. 1987. *Women in Educational Administration.* Newbury Park, Calif.: Sage.

Smith, J. K., and Heshusius, L. Jan. 1986. Closing down the conversation: The end of the quantitative-qualitative debate among educational inquirers. *Educational Researcher 5*:1, 4–12.

Sparkes, A. C. 1989. Paradigmatic confusions of the evasion of critical issues in naturalistic research. *Journal of Teaching in Physical Education 8.*

Stanfield, J. H. 1985. The ethnocentric basis of social science knowledge production. *Review of Research in Education 12.*

The Myth of a Knowledge Base in Administration

Janet Littrell and William Foster

In much of the world, this century has seen the explosion of programs, degrees, and courses in management or administration. Many universities and proprietary schools earn considerable revenue from degree programs designed to induct students into the mysteries of management science, administrative behavior, or other organizational control strategies. There are programs in business administration, health administration, educational administration, sports and recreational administration, and probably a host of others. Each makes a claim that there are significant and important *theories* of administration to guide the novice administrator, that there is considerable and significant *research*, and that there are accepted and exemplary *practices* in the field. In other words, these programs in business, education, health, and the like, essentially argue that there is a *knowledge base* from which we can draw. This knowledge base is founded in the social sciences and provides insight into organizational behavior, ideas on motivation, ideas on human performance and job satisfaction, notions of role, concepts of leadership, and so on.

In contrast, this chapter argues that there is *no* adequate knowledge base for administrative theory or management science, if one takes the term "knowledge base" to mean a definable, acceptable, and testable set of assumptions about organizations and about administration. Rather, we claim that there is no such base, nor is one attainable. Most textbooks, however, in the field of administration or management, whether in education, business, or other fields, make the claim that there is such a thing as an "administrative science," that there is knowledge which supports a compelling analysis of administrative or managerial behavior, and that social science continues to make progress in the development of laws which will predict organizational behavior. We disagree.

Social science in the modern era has been based in a positivist agenda that hopes to achieve reliable, valid, and predictable knowledge about human behavior. The positivist agenda has claimed that certain rules of behavior can be outlined, and that eventually, predictive laws of behavior will emerge. The purpose of social science research has been to discover such laws, and, when applied to administration, to discover laws of administrative behavior. Hoy and Miskel (1982), for example, in a popular text designed as an introduction to the field of educational administration, claim this field can be defined "as both the art and the science of applying knowledge to administrative and organizational problems" (27) and then conclude that "the road to generalized knowledge can lie only in tough-minded scientific research" (28). That there is such a knowledge base or that one can be fully developed is an illusion rooted in the two arguments that follow.

The Lack of Predictability

Management or administration, informed by behavioral science (as in the labels *management science* or *administrative science*), and taken as a means of imposing order and certainty on a fluid and disorderly organizational universe, is a myth of the first order. This is not to say, of course, that administrators do not make certain things happen, or that they are not instrumental in helping to create morale in the school, or that they do not help to impose some form of organization. Administrators accomplish these feats not because of their scientific training and their judicious use of principles of management, but because of their personal and moral presence, their sense of "what's right," and their attention to people's needs. This is an expertise that comes from experience, not from theory. It *is* true that theoreticians and researchers in the administrative/managerial fields do come up with interesting and sometimes useful models and theories. Certainly the work done on the politics of organizing, on the symbolic dimensions of organizations, and on organizational psychology provide notable ways of reconceptualizing the bureaucratic form of organization. But the model (which, we suspect, informs most of the work being done in these areas) of further research leading to generalizable laws of organizational behavior, which can be implemented by administrative experts trained in the science of management, is simply unattainable.

Yet the idea of the administrative expert reigns supreme in Western society. It is an idea that presupposes administrators' abilities to impose order and rationality on what is otherwise an unordered chaos. Administrators and managers, though, are much like the rest of us; sometimes their suasions work and sometimes they doen't. The idea that the administrator is a so-called "expert" is again a moral fiction, because "the kind of knowledge which would be required to sustain it does not exist" (MacIntyre 1984, 75). This means, simply, that the social and administrative equivalent of a physics of administration and management is not now present and virtually unattainable in the future. The nightmare that writers have had of the totally managed state, with its capacity for total control, is only true under principles of coercion, not of science.

Basically, the social sciences, including those concerned with administration, lack any kind of predictability. If a science is to have any legitimacy, then it must be able to say that under certain conditions "X" will happen. The social sciences cannot do this. Their lack of predictability has to do with a the basic truth of human life: people can choose, and with those choices defy what social science might believe. MacIntyre (1984) argues that there are several sources of unpredictability in the social sciences. One is that innovations in social life are themselves unpredictable; to predict the invention of the wheel is indeed to invent it. Thus, prediction of the future—at least a radically new future—is not possible, because to predict it is to in fact invent it.

Other sources of unpredictability lie in the "game" of social life, whereby individuals make choices based on their assessment of current events and previous choices; these events and choices remain unpredictable. Whether to use American or Delta, in my choice of flights, is inherently unpredictable, because certain events could emerge that might make neither carrier the preferred one. Normally, and in the statistical probability of events, it can be shown that I will board one flight because I have made reservations, I like the airline (or hate the other one), and so forth. But this probability can be thrown askew by all kinds of events; in other words, the certainty implied by the observation that water will boil at a certain temperature is a certainty not found in the social sciences.

The unpredictability argument, largely as mounted by MacIntyre (1984), is an important one, in that it brings into question the basic epistemological assumptions of social science, and thus those of administrative or managerial science. If a social *science* cannot approach the avenues of lawlike generalization demanded of other sciences, then its status as a science is considerably undermined, and "the salient fact about those [social] sciences is the absence of the discovery of any law-like generalization whatsoever" (MacIntyre 1984, 89). This means, in essence, that the overlay that management and administrative theorists put on their theory, that it indeed can provide meaningful and predictive generalizations about human behavior in organization, consists of a basically false assumption, one that only shores up the power and status of university professors, highly paid consultants, and other so-called "imagers" of managerial expertise.

The Postmodern Argument

A second approach to the idea of managerial expertise, to the idea of a knowledge base in administration, lies in various postmodern arguments. The postmodernist movement developed primarily, within the fields of literature and philosophy, but has a certain application to the social science. Postmodernism makes the following claims:

1. Knowledge is nonfoundational. This means that we act in our organizational worlds as if we had a solid knowledge base to guide our decisions; indeed, we act as if there is a accepted foundation for what it is that we do. Postmodernists argue the opposite: they insist knowledge is always produced in specific contexts that are dependent on time and space. Thus, what we know is not what we know *universally*; rather it is only what we claim to know in a specific setting, within the parameters defined by our history and culture.

2. The agreement we develop about what constitutes "true" knowledge is intimately related to the distribution of power in a society. The powerful, in other words, support a particular form of knowing (of what counts as knowledge, of what is valued and what is not), which in turn reinforces their position in a society.

3. The resulting outcome is the development of what poststructuralists call "grand narratives," or widely-accepted stories that construct reality for most of us and serve to maintain the existing system of privileges and power. For example, Reed (1992) argues that in poststructuralist organizational theory:

> Belief in an independently existing and objective "organiza-
> tional reality," knowable through scientific reasoning and
> discourse, is replaced by a conception of theories as self-
> justifying representational forms or "intelligible narra-
> tives" which allow groups or communities of researchers
> and scholars to make shared sense of their collective
> engagement with a predefined phenomenon. (11)

Culler (1982) summarizes the argument nicely when he says that
"structuralists are convinced that systematic knowledge is possible;
poststructuralists claim to know only the impossibility of this
knowledge" (22).

Poststructuralist, or postmodernist, thought, then, reflects an
analysis of language and society that accepts their dependence,
acknowledges the fact that power relates to language use, and
which asserts that the many divisions a society accepts—between
classes, races, genders, and so on—are related to the ways in which
the "power elite" dominates the signifiers in a language.

In other words, poststructuralist thought suggests that there
is no final nor ultimate position that one can come to through one's
research or analysis; one's position depends on the power of the
arguments, on the acceptance of these arguments by the power elite,
and on the symmetry of the words with the times.

Postmodern thought, combined with an analysis of modern
social science, thus suggests that there is no foundation or ultimate
position for theories of management or administration. Indeed, such
theories in management science represent attempts to solidify the
power base of those presenting them. Such theories represent the
methods used to initiate the student into the mystifications of
management science or administrative behavior. And such theories
reflect a more basic preoccupation with how economics drive the
social sciences. Such a pessimistic view of administrative science
is not meant to impugn the many people who work in this area;
rather, it is to suggest that they perhaps labor under conditions
of false consciousness, although they do in fact believe in the power
of social science.

Gergen (1992) would place the administrative or managerial
scientist within the period he calls "modernism." He finds that
modernist approaches to organization include a belief in the power
of reason and observation, a belief in foundations or essentials, faith
in progress and development, and "absorption in the machine
metaphor" (211). Postmodernism, however, exposes these concepts
as weapons in the fight for organizational control, not as neutral

signifiers of one organizational reality. Postmodernists, particularly in their analysis of power and language, show "that the 'rational sayings' available to the individual are of indeterminate meaning" (Gergen 1992, 219) and thus susceptible to multiple interpretations and many rationalities.

Why, then, do we continue to believe in the myth of managerial expertise, despite evidence to the contrary? Perhaps we believe the myth because we have few or no other meaning systems to sustain us. Bureaucracy demands that we acquiesce to the idea of expertise, as well as to the idea that we can in fact control events to our liking. But what if we cannot? What alternatives remain?

The Reconstruction of Administration

Many texts about administration talk about administrative "behavior" in much the same way as they talk about animal behavior, social behavior, or any other kind of behavior imaginable. Such terminology conjures up images of stimulus-response situations, of administrators responding to inputs in a somewhat mechanistic fashion. A more accurate definition might be found in the term "administrative action," which suggests that human agents can, in fact, influence and control events through the *actions* that they take, and that human agents do indeed make a difference in the conduct of local affairs. Such actions, performed by human agents, can be meaningful or meaningless.

Giddens's (1978) theory of structuration suggests that human agents both create and are dominated by structures. No organizational structure is created out of natural necessity; each represents human intervention and the historical organization of power, influence, and control. Material resources, as they are distributed in various fashions, combine to restrict the access to power, to allow access by some, and to generally reinforce the traditional ways through which social power is assigned.

Both the non-predictability argument and that of postmodernism suggest that the structures we do create tend to support the dominant relationships in a society. The language used, the images evoked, and the metaphors that result all tend to recreate the kind of society that rewards those in power and disenfranchises those without power. In educational administration, or in management science, the images of power and control, of the ability to make sense of organization, and of the talent required to shape the organizational future all contribute to a myth of performance unsupported by results. Yet the myth continues, unabated. The reason for our pervasive belief must lie more in a generalized cultural myth, carefully built up and reinforced over generations, than in palatable results.

We hope to display these theoretical concerns by looking at an actual case, one that shows how administrators basically eschew administrative science in favor of making decisions on a moral basis, on a basis of the best "feel" for the situation, and on a basis where they make judgments rooted not in science, but in their own *reading* of a situation. This reading, we will show, is driven more by power and economic interests than it is by any foundational knowledge of the field. We will also try to show how their decision-making process generally tends to ally itself against change and to re-create pathways to power.

Eastern Community College: A Case Example

Eastern Community College is located in a predominantly white, affluent suburb of Southern California, where it serves approximately 18,000 students. Like all community colleges, Eastern has two primary agendas: (1) to provide the first two years of a four-year college education by transferring students to four-year universities and (2) to provide certificate and two-year degree programs in vocational education and employment training. All community colleges serve educationally, economically, socially and physically disadvantaged students; millions of dollars of federal funding are available every year in support of such programs. Eastern has carved out a niche for itself in serving disadvantaged students, via a program that helps individuals on welfare become computerized-office specialists, insurance specialists, and account clerks. We will examine one such program.

Eastern's employment training program, like all other federally-funded training programs nationwide, must meet the needs of four diverse special-interest groups. First, it must meet state and local governments' needs to decrease the amount paid out in public assistance. Second, the program is required to meet the needs of the local business community by increasing the available skilled worker pool. Third, it must be sensitive to the needs of Eastern Community College's district for additional sources of funding. Finally, it must meet the needs of the participants themselves by preparing them to make the transition from welfare to work.

In this case study, we will look at Eastern's one-semester, federally-funded program to retrain displaced workers who are on welfare. We will examine the underlying assumptions of each of the special-interest groups involved and ask the following questions: How do underlying assumptions about management and administration contradict or conflict with the assumptions of the other groups? What theories and what kind of research and management knowledge base inform administrative agendas? How is access to power affected by the choice of administrative knowledge base?

The Knowledge Base for Federal Policy Makers

Federal policy for such employment training programs appears to hold these assumptions: (1) Educational institutions must produce quantifiable measures of accountability for the federal funding they receive; accountability is best measured by the number of students placed into jobs. (2) Sixteen weeks of training is sufficient time to move people off welfare and into jobs; the only barrier to employment for individuals on welfare is lack of marketable skills. (3) Legislators (most of them white, male, affluent attorneys) understand and should decide what individuals on welfare need. (4) A good training provider will be able to bring a student to completion in one semester, regardless of the student's level of education upon entering the program.

Federally-funded employment training programs emphasize *performance*; training providers (schools) are paid only if students meet competencies and are placed into jobs. This so-called "performance-based" model for employment training is widely touted as a no-nonsense, outcome-driven training program for disadvantaged students, one that is efficiently funded and reliant on the increased involvement of the private sector to keep it focused on the bottom line.

Eastern Community College, the training provider, competitively bid for and was awarded a federal training contract six years ago. Since then, it has implemented a federally-funded program, that trains for low-income individuals in three employment areas: secretary/word processing, insurance clerk, and account clerk. Eastern has consistently met the requirements of its federal contract by training and placing at least 75% of its completers, and is well-known by the local community as a leader in the war against unemployment.

Assumptions Driving
Eastern Community College

In contrast to Federal policy makers, Eastern's staff seem to make these assumptions: (1) In these uncertain economic times, schools must look for funding anywhere they can get it. (2) The primary responsibility of the federally-funded employment training program is to continue to meet contract so it can continue to bring federal revenues into the college. It must consistently produce completers to continue to get funding; therefore, completion competencies must be kept low and students should be encouraged not to be selective about job placements. (2) Students must complete the program and be placed into jobs in as short a time as possible so that federal payments can be made more frequently. (3) As the training provider, it is Eastern's responsibility, not the students', to see the students through the program to completion. (4) Students with skills, experience, personal attractiveness, and charisma should be given preference over students without these qualities, because the former will be easier to place into jobs.

Community colleges are the most common training providers for federal training contracts. These contractual relationships tend to be quite stable and subject to renewal year after year. As a federal service provider, Eastern Community College recruits and assesses clients, determines eligibility, and determines measures of competency for completers.

Because it is a provider of federally-funded employment training, Eastern Community College receives more than just federal money; it also receives state ADA (funds based on average daily attendance), based on enrollment numbers. This is quite a significant source of additional revenue for Eastern, since the community college district that Eastern is part of is "at cap". In other words, the district has enrolled all the students it has room for; districts cannot collect additional ADA over the capped amount *unless the student is on welfare*. Therefore Eastern's enrolling of welfare clients in a federally-funded employment training program is an effective way for the college to receive additional state funding for which it would otherwise be ineligible.

Most federally-funded programs (including Eastern's) are short-term (six months or less), in order to move students into jobs quickly, minimize school-related child care and transportation costs, and minimize the costs required to bring each student to the performance standard. Even though the ordinary full-time load for students is 12–15 units, the students in Eastern's federally-funded employment training program (who are defined as educationally under-prepared and, therefore, more challenged by college coursework) are required to take 18–21 units per semester.

Because Eastern's federally-funded employment training program is performance-based and measures success solely in terms of numbers of placements, other outcomes (such as long-term placement numbers or qualitative aspects of job placement—higher wages and/or benefits) are almost entirely unexamined. Information about how students in this program do beyond the 90 days that they are required to remain on the job—if they are still working, whether they have bounced back to welfare or pursued further education—is virtually unknown by Eastern Community College administrators.

Federally-funded programs are required to provide educational services for under-prepared students who have barriers to employment. However, these programs are widely criticized for "creaming," the practice of selecting participants who already have skills and experience and are, therefore, more likely to complete and get placed into jobs. Since students have to be placed, they must enter the program with the potential to make a positive impression on employers. Students with high skills make a good impression; so do students who are attractive and who come across well in a job interview. The intake process at Eastern seeks to determine how much students know coming in. Students who are considered a "good risk" are admitted into the program; students who have a long way to go in terms of their appearance and their skills are termed "high-risk" and, typically are not accepted into the program.

Eastern enjoys a stable relationship with the local Private Industry Council and anticipates continued federal funding for the foreseeable future. Administrators of the program are proud of their record of placements, since they have always "made contract." The federal funding the county receives is the mainstay of its entire Business Office Technology program and it is often said that the federal funding supports the entire department. The federal employment training program boasts about the individual attention it gives to students, especially with regard to helping them find jobs. Since records are only required for 90 days beyond the training, finding out what happens to students after that period is not on the agenda.

And the Students. . .

Students function under yet another set of assumptions, which are rooted in *their* knowledge base: (1) The federally-funded employment training program at Eastern Community College will train them and help them get a job; (2) they will have a better life if they get off welfare and get a job; and (3) they will feel better about themselves and be better role models for their children if they get off welfare.

Most students in Eastern's employment training program, both men and women, are the sole wage-earners for their families. Child care, transportation, and health care are the financial obstacles to employment most frequently mentioned by individuals who enroll in Eastern's employment training programs.

Most of the students are women; not only are they a lot more likely than men to meet low-income eligibility requirements, but they are also more likely to qualify according to other modes of eligibility, such as being displaced homemakers, AFDC recipients, and teenage parents. In addition to getting all of their school expenses paid for, women in Eastern's program who receive welfare are assured of a continuation of their previous levels of welfare payments (approximately $663/month for one adult and one child), food stamps ($95/month), and Medicaid. Students are encouraged (and helped) to apply for Pell grants and other federal or state financial aid, and many of them receive student loans. While they are in school (and for the first year of employment), they also receive Greater Avenues of Independence (GAIN) funds to pay for child care services for children under age 13, public transportation (for them and for their children to go to daycare), and up to $450 for any other school-related expense, such as clothing. GAIN funds can also be used for vocational assessment and counseling for school- and/or employment-related difficulties. Students who take advantage of all of these resources may put together a remarkably substantial support package while they are in school.

Upon completion of the program, however, the story changes. After training, students make five to seven dollars per hour and have to give up all welfare support, food stamps, health insurance, and student financial aid; they are expected also to start paying back student loans.

At Eastern, students sign a statement saying that they understand they are expected to get a job and stay in that job for 90 days in exchange for free schooling, books, and support services, such as counseling and advising for placement. The students are tracked very closely while in school, during the placement period, and during the 90 days they are required to work. At this point, the final billing is done.

The Knowledge Base Here:
Why It Is a Myth

Eastern emphasizes that its employment training program increases students' self esteem and confidence and makes them feel better about themselves. A closer look at the program, however, reveals contradictory agendas and theories of administration. The behavior, motivation, and assumption of rules by individuals within the system of education begins to make more sense. By and large, an instrumental "human capital" orientation is applied to the concept of employment training, and performance standards are commonly used as measures of educational program effectiveness. Eastern Community College gets paid approximately $4,500 for each student who completes the training program; completion is determined according to the competency criteria Eastern established for its own students. The general feeling among Eastern's administrators is that if standards are too low, they will erode motivation to excel, yet if they are set too high, too few students pass the course. However, upon closer examination, it can be seen that measuring student competencies at the end of a program encourages Eastern to "cream" applicants—not to enroll students who have the most to learn, but to enroll those who have the *least* to learn. Students entering Eastern's program with high levels of mastery may complete their training with little or no assistance from the staff and faculty and are much more likely to find jobs at the end, appreciably reducing the Eastern's contractual risk in enrolling them. The performance-based nature of federal employment training contracts also drives Eastern (as well as all other similar training providers) to provide these students with shorter-term, less expensive services. Students who are most likely to find employment are those who have skills upon entering the program, as well as those whom prospective employers will find attractive and who will perform well in job interviews.

This distinctly discriminatory attitude about who to train and who not to train is easily justified by Eastern's administrators and faculty. They say that it is the reality of having to meet the performance standards of the federal contract that makes it important to "counsel out" students who are considered "not ready" for employment training. But again, on closer examination, it is clear that a contradictory logic is operating. Policymakers fault administrators for creaming, even when administrators are required to place students after five months of training. It is important that they either acknowledge that programs have to cream, or drop the requirement to place completers; the two requirements are logically contradictory. Programs cannot be simultaneously praised and vilified for attempting to meet both requirements.

Another example of a contradictory agenda and seeing different things through different eyes is the tendency of policymakers and schools to view individuals who voluntarily withdraw or fail to complete as so-called "by-products" of an "otherwise successful" training program. Administrators at Eastern blame the very individuals they are mandated to serve for failure to complete the program. They do not ask themselves "Why is this educational intervention not serving the very population it was designed to serve?"

Federally-funded employment training programs are designed to meet the needs of business and government, not those of individuals. The language of federal employment training legislation is clearly framed around the needs of the employers and the federal budgets, not the needs of individuals. Recurrent use of the terms "investment in human," "basic return on investment," and "measured by increased. . .earnings" clearly indicate this bias. Consider the following excerpt from federal JTPA legislation:

> The Congress recognizes that job training is an investment in human capital. In order to determine whether that investment has been productive, the Congress finds that. . .
> the basic return on the investment is to be measured by the increased employment and earnings of participants and the reduction of welfare dependency. (Section 1-4a and 2, Job Training Partnership Act: Public Law 97–300, October 13, 1982).

Performance contracting is a management tool for the federal government, a straightforward, easily measured, quantitative measure of program effectiveness that can be operated from Washington, D.C. These performance standards, however, drive Eastern to serve those within the general eligibility categories who are most liksly to find employment, and then to provide them with shorter-term, less expensive services. Given the serious skill deficiencies of this group of students, it is doubtful that very short training periods can adequately prepare them for employment. Skilled positions at higher pay require longer periods of education, but program length is not determined by the needs of individuals. It is determined more by Eastern's need to move students through training quickly and to receive federal payments more frequently.

It is a tendency among well-meaning educators, who truly want to help, to reduce the problem of widespread educational and societal disadvantage to a remedy that they can singlehandedly implement. By adopting a "human capital" view of work education, educators and administrators at Eastern are allowed to feel that they are helping. In applying simple remedies to long-term problems, they are prevented from having to look at the systemic underlying social inequalities that they may, in fact, be perpetuating.

Many Eastern students have very little incentive to leave the welfare rolls, even after training. It is common to see marginally persistent students who eke by without making a commitment to do well, but who don't want to give up either. Often, students have little more than the vaguest notion of why they are in school and where it will all lead. Their goals are sketchy, not clearly defined and inconsistent with what they are told their goals and aspirations should be. After the training is over, they find they cannot afford to leave welfare for the low-wage jobs available to them. Students, in theory, become employable after the Eastern training, but the kinds of jobs they become eligible for leave them teetering on the brink of poverty. Wages after training are only 45¢ per hour higher (on average) than before training for women ($4.33 to $4.78) and 19¢ higher for men ($5.31 to $5.50). Training administrators at Eastern persistently assert, however, that low wages were inevitable in view of the pressure for short-term training imposed by the cost-per-placement performance standard and because of a persistent recessionary economy. They emphasize that student gains in self-confidence make the training worthwhile.

It is clear that no knowledge base adequately explains or describes more than a portion of the entire system of education for all its players. Assumptions about the administration of human behavior are not universal, testable or definable. Administrators do what they do because they seek to secure their own positions, from a desire to keep a program going, out of a genuine wish to do the right thing, or simply because it's all they know. They are operating reactively, not on the basis of theoretical knowledge. Sometimes the greater good is served, and sometimes the good of the individual is improved. Very often, however, the layers in administration simply push and pull against each other, spending large sums of federal money in the process, and never really move very far from where they started.

The unpredictability of the social sciences requires that the physics of administration keep special interests balanced and opposite of each other, separated by power relations that are generally unexamined by administrative players, rather than opening up access to greater numbers of participants in educational systems. This case example, then, was designed to show that in the so-called "real world" of administrative behavior there is no satisfactory knowledge base, but rather only competing actors, resources and power.

References

Culler, J. D. 1982. *On Deconstruction: Theory and criticism in the 1970s.* Ithaca, New York: Cornell.

Gergen, K. J. 1992. Organization theory in the postmodern era. In M. Reed and M, Hughes, eds., *Rethinking organization: New directions in organization theory and analysis.* Newbury Park, Calif.: Sage.

Giddens, A. 1984. *The constitution of society.* Berkeley, Calif.: University of California Press.

Hoy, W., and C. Miskel. 1982. *Educational administration: Theory, research, and practice.* 2nd ed. New York: Random House.

MacIntyre, A. 1984. *After virtue.* 2nd ed. Notre Dame, Ind.: University of Notre Dame Press.

Reed, M. 1992. Introduction. *Rethinking organization: New directions in organization theory and analysis.*

Building a Professional Knowledge Base in Educational Administration: Opportunities and Obstacles

Paul V. Bredeson

Something there is that doesn't love a wall.

In "Mending Wall," Robert Frost invites his neighbor and the reader to rethink the rationale for and purposes of maintaining walls that clearly mark the boundaries and thus separate the interests and properties each from the other. The neighbor replies:

Good fences make good neighbors.

Yet, the speaker wonders,

Why do they make good neighbors?
Isn't it where there are cows? But here there are no cows.
Before I built a wall I'd ask to know
what I was walling in or walling out,
and to whom I was like to give offence.

Like the neighbors in the poem who go through the perennial task of mending sundered stone walls, each keeping to his own side while picking up stones and restacking them, educational reformers, practitioners, policy makers and administrators are going about rebuilding their own walls.

There are many walls, conceptual, structural, and professional, which stretch across the contours of the field of educational administration. They exist in the forms of licensure and certification standards, content specializations and academic programs in universities, educational support structures (public and private), institutional type and level, professional associations, and various governmental agencies (federal, state and local). Another wall that influences and likewise is influenced by those listed above is the professional knowledge base in educational administration. The construction of a knowledge base in educational administration is but one example of conceptual, academic and professional wall-building.

My purpose is not to question the intent or the motivations behind such an activity. However, a knowledge base, by definition, marks off the territory of a given field of study and practice. Thus, there are reverberations throughout the educational system that affect all stakeholders. I would want to know: What's being walled in and what's being walled out? And do the purposes and products of this mapping best serve our needs, goals and aspirations for education?

In this chapter I will examine boundary-building written documents developed by two major educational professional groups interested in redefining the professional knowledge base for educational administration. The first is *Principals For Our Changing Schools: The Knowledge Base*, developed under the auspices of the National Commission for the Principalship (1992) and sponsored by the National Association of Secondary School Principals and the National Association of Elementary School Principals. The second is the University Council for Educational Administration *Steering Committee on Knowledge and Research in Educational Administration*. Just as the wall mender ponders the purpose of rebuilding the old wall and wonders just what he is walling in and walling out, this chapter asks whose voices, whose expertise and what processes contributed to these recent conversations about the establishment of newly configured boundaries of professional knowledge. Does the articulation of domains of professional knowledge and skills enhance our understanding and inform our practice, or does it tend to perpetuate historic boundaries that separate individuals and groups within teaching and learning communities?

Mapping the Professional Knowledge Base: Historical Context

The redefinition of a knowledge base is not a new professional activity among educational administration professors and practitioners. Jack A. Culbertson (1988) provides an excellent historical description of this perennial quest for more adequate theoretical and practical frameworks to describe and prescribe the work of administrators in educational settings: "After a century's pursuit of knowledge, scholars of educational administration still look to science, with its multifaceted and changing definitions for a legitimatizing cloak, facilitator of inquiry, and a tool to be used in the continuing quest for knowledge about the ends, means, and settings of a very complex social process" (24).

The quest for a knowledge base in educational administration according to Culbertson, has been influenced by many forces. Changes in schools, in social/economic/political conditions and in the realities of professional practice trigger calls for reexamination of educational administration theory and practice and the professional knowledge base that defines them.

> The National Commission For The Principalship, recognizing a mismatch between preparation programs and job requirements, decided to develop a new framework for preparing principals based on the realities of the work place. While the social sciences would not be ignored, the new framework would focus upon programs and operations within today's changing school environment. The new knowledge base, therefore, would reflect the outcomes of a task analysis of the principalship as well as a conceptual model of the principalship. (17)

Another force is the desire by professors of educational administration to legitimate their own place in the academy alongside of other disciplines of inquiry by specifying and codifying core content for the preservice preparation of school administrators. Professors want to be key players in setting the direction for changes in the knowledge base in their academic field. Following ten years of educational reform initiatives from nearly every educational stakeholder group, UCEA, through the direction of its Executive Committee, determined that attempts by other groups to define the professional knowledge base for the field lacked credibility, and thus decided that "the identification of an appropriate knowledge base for educational administration" (1992, 11) would be the consortium's primary program goal. Within a dynamic reform environment, professional associations such as UCEA, NASSP and NAESP have seized the reigns of the galloping reform roan. Through their knowledge-base projects they are attempting to bridle the energies and resources of reform initiatives and at the same time protect their primary constituents from the perils of runaway reform.

Philosophic disagreements and debates concerning the nature of reality in teaching and learning have persisted throughout the history of schools. Changes in philosophic orientations regarding inquiry and knowledge also have influenced definitions of core content in educational administration. Culbertson (1988) cites the shift from speculative abstractions and laws derived from moral disciplines to a knowledge base grounded in empirical, scientific, fact-based generalizations. Another shift is apparent in the work of Tom Greenfield (1975). He argues that the very character of the knowledge in educational administration is one that is socially constructed and grounded more in temporal values, preferences and human intentions than it is in objectified universal laws or principles. Culbertson (1988) notes that Greenfield's argument against positivistic science, if used as a model for an educational administration knowledge base, supports Harris's position from a century earlier.

> Organizations cannot be equated with such objective phenomena as planets and stars. Rather, organizations are social inventions, which humans construe in diverse ways. Organizations do not think, choose, or act as theories claim; rather, individuals do. Nor are organizations regulated by scientific laws; rather, they are guided by human intentions and decisions. (20)

Throughout the 1970s and 1980s, paradigm shifts offered multiple frameworks for creating new meanings and understandings of educational administration. Anchored in particular methods of disciplined inquiry, these new lenses suggested new ways in which researchers could think about and construct curriculum and pedagogy to prepare educators for effective practice in today's schools.

Borrowing theory from social science disciplines has also directed research attention to the boundaries and body of professional knowledge in educational administration. Theoretical lenses from economics, sociology, political science, psychology, anthropology and management sciences have proved to be particularly influential intellectual tools for inquiry and organizers for maps of core content. As valuable as these disciplines have been, however they have limited use within the arena of education. John Dewey believed in the value of science to inform education, but not in a science of prediction, precision and universally generalizable laws. Dewey's notion of educational science was one grounded in practice and the realities of schools. Whether the analogue derives from physical science or social science, Dewey argued that educational sciences that become isolated, by design or default, from everyday practice inevitably lead to educational specializations that are "barren and susceptible to loose speculation" (1929, 41). The domains shaping the current knowledge base projects are examples of the enduring impact social science methods of inquiry have on conceptual maps for codifying educational administration knowledge.

Another force influencing knowledge base examination in educational administration is the natural human inclination to seek order and rules to explain and to help deal with the complexities and paradoxes of practice in teaching and learning. The promise of specific rules of thumb, the right model and generally applicable laws of human behavior, all of which inform professional practice, is very alluring. However, as Dewey noted, "The final reality of educational science is not found in books, nor in experimental laboratories, nor in classrooms where it is taught but in the minds of those engaged in directing educational activities" (32).

Two Knowledge Base Projects

Educational reform energies of the 1980s and 1990s have spawned countless initiatives to improve what is generally perceived to be an ailing public enterprise. What perhaps distinguishes this reform movement from previous ones is that schools and education tend to be viewed more as the root of various social, economic and political problems than as solutions to these societal concerns. Within this reform environment, the National Association of Secondary School Principals and the National Association of Elementary School Principals agreed to jointly sponsor the National Commission for the Principalship, stating, "the roots of this initiative come from a conviction that preparation programs have failed to move ahead with the times, and that most licensing requirements are unrelated to current job demands" (1990, 3). Similarly, UCEA, through its governing Plenum and its Executive Committee, determined that attempts by other groups to define the professional knowledge base for the field lacked credibility and thus decided that "the identification of an appropriate knowledge base for educational administration" (UCEA Plenum Agenda 1992, 11) would be the consortium's primary program goal. UCEA established a Steering Committee on Knowledge and Research charged with the task of planning "a series of events and activities aimed at defining the knowledge base and propos[ing] ambitious curriculum goals for the field of school administration by October 1994" (11).

A primary task in each of these projects has been to map the existing knowledge domains of educational administration and to produce documents that provide descriptions of what is known in the field. For the National Commission for the Principal, the exploratory map outlined a taxonomy of 21 performance domains organized into four areas—functional, programmatic, interpersonal and contextual. These areas

> blend the traditional content-driven curricula with leadership and process skills to create a new framework for preparing principals. This framework recognizes the functional leadership skills and interpersonal competencies required of principals to succeed in today's school environment as well as the precedence of the educational program and the changing nature of the context within which schools live." (19)

Specific performance domains were assigned to specialists whose task was "to define the knowledge and skills essential to informed practice within the boundaries of separate domains" (31). A full description of the performance is contained in *Principals for Our Changing Schools: The Knowledge Base* (The National Commission for the Principalship 1992).

UCEA identified seven knowledge domains, which are "currently recognized as comprising the field" (5) and serve as organizers for mapping educational administration. The domains are as follows: 1) societal and cultural influences on schooling; 2) teaching and learning processes; 3) organizational studies; 4) leadership and management processes; 5) policy and political studies; 6) legal and ethical dimensions of schooling; and 7) economic and financial dimensions of schooling (UCEA Plenum Report 1992, 13–14). *Essential Knowledge for School Leaders: A Proposal to Map the Knowledge Base of Educational Administration* contains a description of the rationale for this project.

> Although there have been many efforts to list the elements of knowledge for school administration by various governments and associations, there has been no comprehensive effort to map and integrate that knowledge since the fragmentation and paradigm shifts of the 1970s and 1980s. In brief, the history of curriculum in educational

administration is a story of drift. Our curriculum is the product of buffeting by social, historical, and political winds; it has never been the product of deliberate, systematic, or consensual shaping by practitioners and scholars. (3)

The sequencing of the knowledge base projects is predicated on the idea that "the knowledge domains are a reasonable beginning because they represent the areas in which the knowledge of the field is codified and individuals acquire expertise. They are the current state of the field" (6). The process parallels the wall-mending in the Frost poem that began this chapter. The proposals suggest that, once built, that knowledge base is only a starting point. Expanding the territory within the codified knowledge base remains a goal. Interestingly, the walls bounding these knowledge domains will be erected first, then tested for conceptual and pragmatic sufficiency.

The list of knowledge base builders is a who's who in educational administration. UCEA relies exclusively on professors, while The National Commission and National Jury, charged with the development of performance domains, include a much more diverse group in terms of position and institutional representation. The issue I raise is not about the quality of these scholars and practitioners. They are indeed distinguished professionals who are committed to enhancing the quality of educational experiences for all learners by specifying and clarifying the content of the field.

However, if the intention truly is to expand the boundaries of knowledge domains, the process that defines the new knowledge base and the criteria to judge its adequacy must be considered. At least four considerations are relevant: First, the definition and assessment of an appropriate knowledge base requires the inclusion of multiples voices and perspectives, especially across disciplines, roles and institutions. Second, the identification and integration of extant professional knowledge and requisite competencies for informed practice are important components of knowledge base projects. As with any project, however, once significant amounts of energy are invested in setting up the boundaries and substance of knowledge domains, it is likely that there will be few substantive changes. Further refinement of these domains will most likely be limited to tinkering with the boundaries. Third, the processes used to define a new knowledge base become crucial to its implementation. Unless the projects are nurtured in collaborative work environments characterized by shared professional values and goals, it is unlikely that the ideas and domains themselves will be mutually valued by other educational stakeholders. Finally, norms of collegiality are promising markers for mapping a professional knowledge base and for implementing it successfully.

Rethinking the Knowledge Base: Curriculum Reform at the University

The meaning of change in the knowledge base in educational administration became apparent to me during the approval process for a new set of courses at our university. Most educators tend to agree that greater collaboration is essential to meaningful change in the preparation of educators for successful professional practice in today's schools. The task of enacting such collaboration across specific territorial boundaries of education, however, can be daunting. Deliberations about the boundaries and terrain of an educational administration knowledge base can be quite abstract and many times a distant reality for most professors. As I noted earlier in the paper, changes in the professional knowledge base have reverberations throughout the field of education. A brief description of the ripples across my small pond, the university, illustrates the impact of knowledge base activities and their anticipated and unanticipated outcomes when the four considerations described above are not central to knowledge base assessment and program revision.

Recent waves of educational reforms triggered academic program soul-searching in our department. Part of the context necessary to understand our particular experience is that our request for new course approval was concurrent with a larger issue, namely, approval of our certification programs by the Department of Public Instruction. In response to reform initiatives in general and to new administrator certification standards promulgated by our state, our faculty worked over a four-year period to rethink and reconceptualize a core experience for all students in our program. A major goal was to cut across intellectual, conceptual and pedagogical boundaries to provide a highly rigorous, integrative experience for all of our students, not just those seeking administrative certification. The Danforth Foundation supported our program revision efforts for three years. I might add that prior to seeking external approval for these course changes, nearly all of the planning was done by professors in our department. Despite the creativity and innovative designs built into this new core experience, the ideas emerged in a very traditional form. Our new core would consist of two three-credit graduate courses titled *Administration of Teaching and Learning Communities I and II.* For a department serving primarily part-time graduate students, many factors including university timetables, scheduling requirements, graduate school regulations, faculty work load, and curriculum sequencing pressed for maintenance of the status quo. Even with accommodations to structural limitations, however, the new core still represented a significant reformulation of the foundations of our administrator preparation program.

Changes in courses at our university are reviewed at departmental, school and university levels. Since the new educational administration core experience was designed as a prerequisite for further study in our department for all students, approval at each level of program review was essential. University approval was required in order for our certification program to be accepted by the Department of Public Instruction. Without such approval, we were without an administrator certification program.

Similar to the organizational structure of many colleges of education, my own, the University of Wisconsin-Madison, has separate, autonomous academic departments for curriculum and instruction, educational psychology, counseling, administration, policy studies, special education and a number of content specific units. Typically, each department is responsible for preparing and certifying its clientele—teachers, counselors, psychologists, special educators and administrators. What became readily apparent in our situation was that the walls of academic specialization, as well as those of institutional and personal histories, would put up formidable barriers to professional collegiality during the course approval process.

As noted earlier, the approving bodies for these new courses were not part of the earlier conversations and work sessions that created the new core curriculum. The process for new course approval looks much like an iceberg: nine tenths of the real substance lies beneath the surface. A number of latent issues were embedded in this course review process. They were proprietary in nature and were played out in terms of resource allocation—courses, students, funds and faculty positions. When we reviewed the approval process, the questions raised, diversions created and delays experienced, it became clear that the traditional walls defining program areas and academic departments were major obstacles not only to course approval, but more broadly, to building a culture of shared professional norms and goals across departments.

At times the strategies employed by representatives of specific program units became so proprietary that particular words within the course descriptions and syllabi, (even lay terms such as policy, history, curriculum and foundations) became hostages of particular program units. By exploiting strategic advantage through endless delays, requesting many revisions, and mostly by not acting to secure the required approval, the curriculum review committee could easily starve out educational administration supplicants in terms of content and language in core courses. Subsequent certification changes in our program could not be approved by the state without consent of the university curriculum review committees.

One might describe the resolution of the conflicts embedded in this course approval process as one steeped more in pragmatism than in principle. The courses were finally approved, but at a cost. The boundary markers and terrain that were highlighted by such words as "policy," "history," "curriculum," and "foundations" were within the confines of units, other than that of educational administration. Rather than using this opportunity to begin an important conversation among highly expert academic units and personalities about the professional preparation of educators, in this case school administrators, as distant neighbors we simply restacked the stones of traditional, academic program walls. Our new courses attempted to reconfigure knowledge base boundaries. Regrettably, those external to the original planning and designing of these new courses saw them as infringements on their territory. Unfortunately, this incident simply provided the means to maintain preexisting walls among college academic units and program specializations.

Over a century ago, William T. Harris (1886) argued that schools and their educative functions were integrally linked to society's "cardinal institutions": the family, state, civil society and the church. He warned against studying education as only a school phenomenon and stated that, when viewed too narrowly through endless subdivision and specializations of interest, such study might result in "false and injurious tendencies" (492). The prescience of this assessment can be seen in the hyperspecialization legitimated today in knowleclge bases undergirding preparation programs, licensure and certification requirements for educators. Specializations represented by academic departments and professional certifications are double-edged realities. The primary purpose of these specialized academic units is to enhance the preserve preparation of educators through high quality, focused instruction of core professional knowledge, skills, attitudes and values. However, this purpose often becomes subservient to the conflicting interests of various players in teaching and learning communities. A similar critique was offered recently at an invitational conference, "Tomorrow's Schools of Education," sponsored by the Holmes Group. Among the proposals highlighted, one recommended that "all prospective educators-classroom teachers, counselors, administrators, and other specialists—should learn together collaboratively in the ed school, all studying a common core of professional knowledge" (*Forum* 1992, 2–3). Based on the details in the case described above, building an integrative core learning experience through collaboration seems a remote possibility, unless norms of collegiality and shared educational goals precede redefinitions of requisite knowledge bases and preparatory experiences.

On Walls, Knowledge Domains and Professional Work

My intent in this chapter has been to discuss the possibilities as well as the endemic problems that attend any knowledge base project. Meeting to survey and map the territory of existing knowledge in educational administration and concomitantly examining the conditions of existing walls bounding that body of professional knowledge are important activities. However, when limited to cooperative rituals of maintaining and mending broken walls, they risk becoming Harris's "false and injurious tendencies." The tasks of knowledge base projects can provide opportunities for important conversations among educational stakeholders about the relationship of various boundaries and domains to current realities in education.

Are the original purposes that guided prior conceptual maps of educational administration and the construction of existing boundaries still salient? Names, boundary lines, and shapes of various entities on geographical surface maps need periodic updating because of political, social and economic changes. Similar adjustments are necessary in maps of the conceptual domains and territories of practice in educational administration. The mapping analogy, however, is limited, in that it presupposes a fixed terrain with adjustments in the naming and outlining, not in the existence of the surface area itself. Fixing the boundaries and naming the contours of the field of educational administration present real difficulties, in that not only are the names and boundaries of the knowledge domains changing, but the actual surface area being mapped out is dynamic. Thus, the challenge is to provide frameworks for charting a course to inform and guide professional practice through the complexities, paradoxes and multiple possibilities in teaching and learning communities.

In *Improving Schools from Within*, Roland Barth (1990) maintains that the foundation upon which school improvement must be built is collegiality. Based on Judith Warren Little's work (1981), Barth describes collegiality as the presence of four specific behaviors of professional educators in schools. They *talk* about professional practice, *observe* each other and reflect on those observations, *collaborate* in planning, designing, researching and evaluating curriculum, and *teach* each other by sharing craft knowledge. Barth states

> Collegiality is nice—but it is extremely difficult to introduce into the persistent cultures of schools. As we all know, enormous risks and frequent costs are associated with observation, communication, mutual visibility, sharing knowledge, and talking openly about the work we do. Collegiality requires that everyone be willing to gave up something without knowing in advance just what that may be. But the risks and costs of interdependence are nothing compared to the risks and costs of sustaining a climate of emotional toxicity, of working in isolation, in opposite corners of the sandbox. (32–33)

By extension, I would argue that improvement in the preparation and practice of educational administrators asks for more than another redefinition of the professional knowledge base. Attention to core content in our field is important. However, in order for the processes and products of knowledge base activities to be successful and ultimately meaningful sources that inform theory and practice, they need to be grounded in the risky behaviors of establishing professional norms of collegiality across the multiple walls that separate us. If collegiality is the key, why don't we engage more in collegial practices? What factors work against us?

We are all quite familiar with the boundaries that mark off particular areas of interest and proprietorship in education. Historically, as schools became more complex social institutions, specializations in content area, in function and in responsibility evolved. Expertise and specialization were responses to the needs of students, demands of diverse populations and realities of work in complex organizations. Clearly, all educators could not be doing the same thing. Thus, the issue of specialization, often emulating the industrial metaphor, played itself out across the field of education. The creation of state licensure standards for individual specializations in teaching and administration, specific academic preparation programs within colleges and universities to prepare these educational specialists, research units primarily housed in universities or policy centers separated from schools, professional associations dedicated to promoting and protecting the interests of their clientele, and governmental agencies at local, state and federal levels with particular jurisdictional responsibilities all emerged to meet specific needs. Over time these specialized areas became defined by walls of professional demarcation. Just as the neighbors in Frost's poem accept the stone walls, there has been a tendency to accept various walls of specialization as givens and to mend them rather than rethink their utility. The latter would require a great deal of work, energy, and above all, the risky practice of collegiality.

The maintenance of existing walls, whether conceptual, structural, programmatic or professional only requires periodic visits to the boundaries to check for breaches, such as the example of program revision and course approval described above. Based on this example, rethinking and replacing long-standing walls requires something quite different in terms of relationships and norms among professional educators; it requires us to create and sustain norms of professional collegiality. Part of the work involves our taking the risk to question the existence of the boundaries in the first place. As the narrator in the poem questions the necessity of mending walls because their original purposes no longer exist, educators need to question the multiple walls that separate them from one another.

The creation of norms of professional collegiality provides a promising environment in which educators and policy makers can raise prickly questions about the boundaries and domains of professional knowledge. My own discomfort is not with the two knowledge-base projects but with various unintended outcomes. Like any educational stakeholder, teacher, administrator, policy maker or client, I want answers to the following questions regarding the value and worth of a redefined knowledge base in educational administration, regardless of who sponsors, supports or participates in such an activity. Do our efforts at reexamining and fortifying the boundaries of our professional knowledge base enhance opportunities for us as educators to engage in important conversations about teaching and learning frequently, continuously, concretely and precisely? Or does the quest for a knowledge base perpetuate professional fragmentation, isolation and competition? Will these knowledge-base projects provide sufficient opportunities for meaningful interactions among educational professionals? What possibilities are there to observe each others' work so that reflective conversations about our goals and our work are grounded in mutual understandings and shared meanings? In what ways do these knowledge-base initiatives provide possibilities for educational stakeholders to collaborate on issues of substance through collaborative planning, designing, researching and evaluating curriculum? Are our professional energies being used to further separate us, or do they enable us to teach and learn from each other what we know?

As each of us in education considers the content and delivery of our professional knowledge we might consider Frost's lines:

Before I built a wall I'd ask to know
what I was walling in or walling out,
and to whom I was like to give offense.

References

Barth, R. 1990. *Improving schools from within.* San Francisco: Jossey-Bass.

Culbertson, J. A. 1988. A century's quest for a knowledge base. N. Boyan, ed., *Handbook of research on educational adminis- tration.* New York: Longman.

Dewey, J. 1929. *The sources of a science of education.* New York: Liverright.

Essential knowledge for school leaders: A proposal to map the knowledge base of educational administration. 1992. University Park, Pa.: The University Council for Educational Administration.

Greenfield, T. B. 1975. Theory about organization: A new per- spective and its implications for schools. In M. Hughes, ed., *Administering education: International challenge.* London: Athlone.

Harris, W. T. 1886. Method of pedagogical inquiry. *The Journal of Proceedings and Addresses of the National Education Association*, 493–503.

Principals for our changing schools: The knowledge base. 1992. Fairfax, V.I.: The National Commission for the Principalship.

Principals for our changing schools: Preparation and Certification. 1990. Fairfax, V.I.: National Commission for the Principalship.

Tomorrow's schools of education: New mission? New structures? 1992. *The Holmes Group Forum.* 6(3):1–23.

UCEA Agenda for the 1992 Plenum. 1992. The University Council for Educational Administration.

The Knowledge Base in School Administration: Historical Footings and Emerging Trends

Joseph Murphy

Throughout its brief history, the knowledge base undergirding school administration has been subjected to periodic reviews. In two previous eras—in the early 1900s and from 1947 to 1957—the crescendo of criticism was so pronounced that fundamental changes in the intellectual scaffolding of the profession resulted. It is the belief of many analysts that we are now in the midst of a third period of great ferment in educational administration (Murphy 1993b), one from which the profession of school administration will emerge with a significantly reconstructed knowledge base. The goal of this chapter is both to portray the evolution of the cognitive foundations of the field and to provide some insights into the shape and texture of the emerging intellectual underpinnings of the profession.

The Evolution of the Knowledge Base

Before 1900, not much had been written about school administration. Indeed, a school leadership role separate from the teaching function did not emerge to any significant degree until after the Civil War. It is not surprising, therefore, that in the era of ideology in school leadership (1820–1900), the knowledge base undergirding administration was not greatly different from the one informing teaching. Influential historical analyses provided by Callahan and Button (1964) and Button (1966) reveal that what little training school administrators received focused on curricular and instructional issues, applied philosophy, and descriptions of outstanding school leaders.

The Prescriptive Era (1900–1946)

Starting at the turn of the twentieth century, the field of school administration—and its defining knowledge base—began to take on a new form. As has been the case during each of the three eras of ferment, basic alterations in the fabric of the field were fueled by harsh attacks on the status quo and by the emergence of a new vision for a reconfigured profession. Thus, in the early 1900s, a good deal of muckraking literature about the deficiencies of practicing administrators was available. Concomitantly, a new perspective on management—the captain of commerce role—that reflected dominant social and cultural forces was held up as an appropriate model for school leaders.

The knowledge base for the profession, especially its preparation programs, followed suit. Shaped significantly by the scientific management revolution in industry, the foundation of the field increasingly underscored the business ideology of the time. In his influential volume, *Educational Administration as Social Policy*, Newlon (1934) completed a variety of analyses to ascertain the nature of the knowledge base of his era. After one examination of topics viewed as important by professors and school superintendents, Newlon concluded that the field was oriented toward "the spheres of finance, business management, physical equipment, and the more mechanical aspects of administration, organization, personnel management, and the like" (259). In analyzing the content of textbooks in school administration, Newlon discovered that over 80 percent of the material focused on the "purely executive, organizational, and legal aspects of administration" (93). In still a third review, this time of the actual courses available in educational administration programs, he uncovered a similar bias toward the "technical and factual" dimensions of the profession and the mechanics of administration" (99). Equally noteworthy is what Newlon failed to see in the knowledge base. He reported that attention "to the fundamental social and economic problems of school administration and to the social methods and techniques which their solution requires" (262) was conspicuous by its absence. Newlon also discovered that "there was virtually no discussion of the 'why', [and] little critical examination of educational and social implications of the structures and procedures discussed" (93). Following a similar strategy of defining the knowledge base in the field by examining the content of preparation programs, Callahan and Button (1964) found the intellectual base to be a mixture of "finance, business management, public relations, and plant management (86)."

Beginning in the 1930s, the knowledge base in educational administration underwent a modest expansion. In particular, as the business ideology of scientific management fell into disfavor during the Great Depression, consideration of the social foundational aspects of leadership was significantly enhanced. The so-called "human" dimension began to find its way into the knowledge base shaping research agendas and preparation experiences. According to Guba (1960), it was the era in which "the industrial engineer had to become a human engineer as well" (117).

Still, by the end of the prescriptive era the knowledge base in school administration was not particularly robust. Even with renewed emphases on the human aspects of the profession, the educational and moral foundations of the ideological era had largely been lost. The mechanical, technical, and prescriptive dimensions of the profession were highlighted. Equally distressing, most of the existing knowledge base of the time was neither theoretically nor conceptually grounded. As we have reported elsewhere:

> The knowledge base was comprised of: "folklore, testimonials of reputedly successful administrators, . . .the speculation of college professors" (Griffiths 1959, v); "personal success stories and lively anecdotes" (Marland 1960, 25); "personal accounts or 'war stories', and prescriptions offered by experienced practitioners" (Silver 1982, 51); "experiences of practicing administrators as they managed the various problem areas of school administration" (Gregg 1969, 996); "maxims, exhortations, and several innocuous variations on the theme of the Golden Rule" (Halpin 1960, 4); and "preachments to administrators about ways in which they should perform" (Goldhammer 1983, 250). (Murphy 1992a, 32)

The Behavioral Science Era (1947–1985)

The post–World War II era brought devastating attacks on the exising knowledge base and severe criticisms of preparation programs employing prescriptive content and of the administrators who had been trained therein. Based on these criticisms and renewed hope about the possibility of developing stronger cognitive foundations for educational leadership, new ideas about the appropriate knowledge base began to take form. The quest began for a science of administration. Prescriptions from practice were increasingly supplanted with theoretical, conceptual, and empirical material drawn from the various social sciences. "Technique-oriented substance based on practical experience" (Culbertson and Farquhar 1971, 9) fell into disfavor as scholars set about trying "to produce a foundation of scientifically supported (hypothetico-deductive) knowledge" (Crowson and McPherson 1987, 47).

> The behavioral science movement led to a view of admin-istration as "an applied science within which theory and research are directly and linearly linked to professional practice [and in which] the former always determine the latter, and thus knowledge is superordinate to the principal and designed to prescribe practice" (Sergiovanni 1991b, 4); the acceptance of a heavy reliance on social science content "as an indicator of a high quality program" (Miklos 1983, 160); "the borrowing and adopting of research techniques and instruments from the behavioral sciences" (Culbertson 1965, 7) and an interdisciplinary—or at least multi-disciplinary—approach to training (Culbertson 1963; Farquhar and Piele 1972; C. Hodgkinson 1975). (Murphy 1992a, 52)

And despite periodic warning signals and occasional major assaults on the science of administration, by the middle of the 1980s the knowledge base in school administration—as reflected in the course content of preparation programs and faculty specializations—was firmly anchored in the social science disciplines.

> The content of these courses of study [was] basically the same. The programs typically focus[ed] on the study of administration, leadership, and supervision, and include[d] an introduction to school law, planning, politics and negotiation, finance and budgeting, and some gesture at research methods and evaluation. These courses generally rel[ied] on a small number of rather similar textbooks, cite[d] articles from the management and educational administration journals, and [were] taught by professors from this same tradition. . . .The programmatic content of the One Best Model [rested] on an intellectual paradigm borrowed from social psychology, management, and the behavioral sciences. The philosophical base of the One Best Model, one that evolved alongside the programmatic com-ponent, [was] an abiding belief in empiricism, predictability,

and 'scientific' certainty, taught by professors steeped in this approach. (Cooper and Boyd, 1987, 4)

The Dialectic Era (1986–)

As noted earlier, "it is our contention that we are now enmeshed in a third era of turmoil in educational administration, one which promises to reorient the knowledge base as radically as have the proceeding two periods of ferment, which resulted in the respective appearances of the prescriptive and behavioral science eras. All of the trends that defined these earlier periods of ferment have surfaced again over the last decade. To begin with, the existing knowledge base has been roundly criticized for being weak and inappropriate. A lengthy list of deficiencies has been accumulated, including, most importantly: (1) a lack of concern for organizational outcomes—"the tendency to neglect the careful tracing of connections between organizational variables and student outcomes" (Erickson 1979, 12); (2) the neglect of the moral and ethical dimensions of the knowledge base (Beck and Murphy, in press; Farquhar 1981); (3) an absence of attention to educational issues (Murphy and Hallinger 1987), what Bates (1984) labels "a deafening silence concerning the fundamental message systems of school: curriculum, pedagogy, and evaluation" (261); (4) gaps in the intellectual scaffolding of the profession due to the failure to adequately consider issues of diversity (Shakeshaft 1988; Valverde and Brown 1988); and (5) inattention to the craft dimensions of leadership, resulting in a knowledge base that "does not provide the kind of experiences or knowledge that practitioners feel they need" (Muth 1988, 5). All in all, the picture is one in which there is considerable room for improvement in the cognitive foundations of the profession (Murphy 1990; 1992a).

At the same time, an extensive thrashing about for a more appropriate knowledge base is occurring, and it is widely believed that a new vision for the field will emerge from these struggles. The most important events providing form for this reconstructed knowledge base include: (1) the work of the National Commission on Excellence in Educational Administration (NCEEA), captured in the 1987 report *Leaders for America's Schools,* in Griffiths' influential address at the AERA (subsequently published as a UCEA paper) (Griffiths, 1988), and in an edited volume containing most of the background papers commissioned by the NCEEA (Griffiths, Stout, and Forsyth 1988); (2) reports from the National Policy Board for Educational Administration, particularly the 1989 document *Improving the Preparation of School Administrators: An Agenda for Reform*; and (3) two national efforts to flush out ideas about the cognitive infrastructure contained in these earlier reports, namely, the 1990 National Commission for the Principalship and the 1993 National Policy Board for Educational Administration's efforts to unpack the needed kowledge base into 21 functional areas, and work by the University Council for Educational Administration to define six cognitive domains for the profession. In addition to the reports and volumes noted above, four books have also exerted important influence in helping to deepen our understanding of the cognitive foundations of school administration in the dialectic era: *The Handbook of Research on Educational Administration* (Boyan 1988); *Under Scrutiny: The Educational Administration Professoriate* (McCarthy, Kuh, Newell, and Iacona 1988); the 1990 National Society for the Study of Education Yearbook, entitled *Educational Leadership and Changing Contexts of Families, Communities, and Schools* (Mitchell and Cunningham 1990); and *Cognitive Perspectives on Educational Leadership* (Hallinger, Leithwood, and Murphy 1993).

Emerging Trends in the Knowledge Base

Driven by critiques of the past and an emerging vision of education and leadership for tomorrow's schools, the knowledge base that will define the dialectic era of school administration is beginning to crystalize. Judging from a review of the commissioned reports and volumes noted above and from preliminary analyses of preparation programs engaged in reform efforts, three major trends appear to be taking root, namely, increased attention to ethics and values, the social context of schooling, and the craft dimensions of the profession. Below, we offer a brief discussion of each of these trends.

Ethics and Values

In 1981, Farquhar reported that in approximately 75% of the training programs he surveyed, attention to the subject of ethics was conspicuous by its absence. Over the years—both before and after Farquhar's report—there have been regular critiques of this deficiency. Yet, throughout the behavioral science era, little headway was made in addressing the problem. There is considerable evidence today, however, that in the currently forming era of school administration ethics will occupy a more central place in the knowledge base of the profession (Slater 1991; Willower 1988). Efforts to develop a heightened role for ethics in educational leadership parallel an emerging focus on values in education in general. These endeavors are reinforced by a growing acceptance of critical perspectives within the field of education.

Demands for a knowledge base infused with values fill the pages of some of the most influential reform documents of the late 1980s. For example, the NPBEA (1989) lists the moral and ethical dimensions of schooling as one of the seven key areas of study for school leaders. They go on to argue that the "curriculum should be designed to provide frameworks and tools to assist students in assessing the moral and ethical implications of administrative decisions in schools (21)." Reviews of alterations in the content of preparation programs reveal that action is somewhat in line with the rhetoric. For example, Murphy (1993a) concludes that ethical issues are prominently featured in the reconstructed intellectual foundations of nine representative universities engaged in restructuring their training programs. In their work, Beck and Murphy (in press) also find considerably more attention to issues of ethics across UCEA preparation programs in 1992 than Farquhar did a decade earlier.

Social Context of Schooling

"For the most part, the social and cultural context of education has received only cursory attention in administrative preparation programs" (Cambron-McCabe 1993, 164), a condition that has changed little since Newlon (1934) first brought it to light nearly 60 years ago. While we have known for some time that "the heart of the matter [educational leadership] seems to be how one behaves toward people," and that it is "far more important. . .that [the leader] have a reasonably adequate conception of the human condition than he have at his fingertips the most recent work in 'the politics of education,' 'the economics of education,' or 'organizational change' " (Hill 1975, 12), attempts to address this understanding have not been particularly vigorous. Education during the behavioral science era was grounded in the soil of behavioral psychology. Organizations were established on the principles of bureaucracy and hierarchy. Both phenomena promoted a focus on the structural dimensions of education. As behavioral views of learners are replaced by cognitive, social perspectives and as bureaucracy is supplanted by more communal and professional understandings of schooling (Murphy 1991; 1993c), a focus on the human dimension of schooling is emerging (Murphy 1991). Again, there is support for the claim that the knowledge base in educational administration is changing to reflect these realities of restructured schools (Murphy 1993a). This shift is being buttressed by a significantly enhanced focus on issues of equity and diversity (Murphy in press).

Craft Dimensions of the Profession

It will come as a surprise to no one to learn that during the behavioral science era, insights from the social sciences were epistemologically privileged. Partly in response to the abuses of the prescriptive era and partly in deference to the allure of science, the craft foundations of the knowledge base in educational administration atrophied. Knowledge was something that was created at the university and applied in the field. It was a nonrecursive relationship. As a result of this academic self–conceit, a distinct breach developed between the university and field dimensions of the profession, one incorrectly and arrogantly labeled the theory-practice gap. The officially sanctioned knowledge base became increasingly less useful to practitioners. Worse yet, the processes and procedures employed to transmit this knowledge were often diametrically opposed to conditions that characterize the workplace in which school administrators found themselves (Bridges 1977; Mann 1975; Murphy and Hallinger 1987). The knowledge base in the dialectic era offers hope of re-legitimizing the craft aspects of the profession. There are a variety of efforts underway to ground preparation programs in the world of practice and to anchor scholarship in the problems of the field (see Murphy 1993d).

References

Bates, R. J. 1984. Toward a critical practice of educational administration. In T. J. Sergiovanni and J. E. Corbally, eds. *Leadership and organizational culture: New perspectives on administrative theory and practice*: 260–74. Urbana: University of Illinois Press.

Beck, L. G., and J. Murphy. (in press). *Preparing educational leaders for ethical practice.* Newbury Park, Calif.: Corwin/Sage and the University Council for Educational Administration.

Boyan, N. J., ed.. 1988. *Handbook of Research on Educational Administration.* New York: Longman.

Bridges, E. M. 1977. The nature of leadership. In L. L. Cunningham, W. G. Hack, and R. O. Nystrand, eds. *Educational Administration: The Developing Decades*: 202–30. Berkeley: McCutchan.

Button, H. W. 1966. Doctrines of administration: A brief history. *Educational Administration Quarterly* 2(3): 216–24.

Callahan, R. E., and H. W. Button. 1964. Historical Change of the Role of the Man in the Organization: 1865–1950. In D. E. Griffiths, ed. *Behavioral science and educational administration*: 73–92. Chicago: University of Chicago Press.

Cambron-McCabe, N. 1993. Leadership for democratic authority. In J. Murphy, ed. *Preparing tomorrow's school leaders: Alternative designs*: 157–75. University Park, Pa.: University Council for Educational Administration.

Cooper, B. S., and Boyd, W. L. 1987. The evolution of training for school administrators. In J. Murphy and P. Hallinger, eds. *Approaches to administrative training in education*: 3–27. Albany: State University of New York Press.

Crowson, R. L., and McPherson, R. B. 1987. The legacy of the theory movement: learning from the new tradition. In J. Murphy and P. Hallinger, eds. *Approaches to administrative training in education*: 45–64. Albany: State University of New York Press.

Culbertson, J. A., and Farquhar, R. H. 1971. Preparing educational leaders: Content in administration preparation. *UCEA Newsletter 12*(3): 8–11.

Erickson, D. A. 1979. Research on educational administration: The state-of-the-art. *Educational Researcher 8*: 9–14.

Farquhar, R. H. 1981. Preparing educational administrators for ethical practice. *The Alberta Journal of Educational Research 27*(2): 192–204.

Griffiths, D. E. 1988. *Educational administration: Reform PDQ or RIP.* Occasional paper 8312. Tempe, Ariz.: University Council for Educational Administration.

Griffiths, D. E., Stout, R. T., and Forsyth, P. B., eds. 1988. *Leaders for America's schools: The report and papers of the National*

Commission on Excellence in Educational Administration. Berkeley: McCutchan.

Guba, E. G. 1960. Research in internal administration: What do we know? In R. F. Campbell and J. M. Lipham, eds. *Administrative theory as a guide to action*: 113–41. Chicago: University of Chicago, Midwest Administration Center.

Hallinger, P., Leithwood, K. A., and Murphy, J., eds. 1993. *Cognitive perspectives on educational leadership.* New York: Teachers College Press.

Hill, J. 1975. The preparation of school administrators: Some observations from the "Firing Line". *Educational Administration Quarterly 11*(3): 1–20.

Mann, D. 1975. What peculiarities in educational administration make it easy to profess: An essay. *The Journal of Educational Administration 13*(1): 139–47.

McCarthy, M. M., Kuh, G. D., Newell, L. J., and Iacona, C. M. 1988. *Under scrutiny: The educational administration professoriate.* Tempe, Ariz.: The University Council for Educational Administration.

Mitchell, B., and Cunningham, L. L., eds. 1990. *Educational leadership and changing contexts of families, communities, and schools.* Chicago: University of Chicago Press.

Murphy, J. 1990. The reform of school administration: Pressures and calls for change. In *The reform of American public education in the 1980s: Perspectives and cases*: 277–303. Berkeley: McCutchan.

———. 1991. *Restructuring schools: Capturing and assessing the phenomena.* New York: Teachers College Press.

———. 1992a. *The landscape of leadership preparation: Reframing the education of school administrators.* Newbury Park, Calif.: Corwin/Sage.

———. 1992b. School effectiveness and school restructuring: contributions to educational improvement. *School Effectiveness and School Improvem ent 3*(2): 90–109.

———. 1993a. Alternative designs: New directions. In J. Murphy, ed. *Preparing tomorrow's school leaders: Alternative designs*: 225–53.

———. 1993b. Ferment in school administration: Rounds 1–3. In J. Murphy, ed. *Preparing tomorrow's school leaders: Alternative designs*: 1–17.

———. 1993c. Restructuring: In search of a movement. In J. Murphy and P. Hallinger, eds. *Restructuring schooling: Learning from ongoing efforts*: 1–31. Newbury Park, Calif.: Corwin/Sage.

———. 1993d. *Preparing tomorrow's school leaders: Alternative designs*. University Park, Pa.: University Council for Educational Administration.

———. 1993e. Restructuring schooling: The equity infrastructure. *School Effectiveness and School Improvement 4*(2): 111–30.

Murphy, J., and Hallinger, P. 1987. Emerging views of the professional development of school administrators: A synthesis with suggestions for improvement. In J. Murphy and P. Hallinger, eds. *Approaches to administrative training*: 245–281. Albany: State University of New York Press.

Muth, R. 1988. *Reconceptualizing training for educational administrators and leaders*. Charlottesville, Va.: National Policy Board for Educational Administration.

National Commission for the Principalship. 1990. *Principals for our changing schools: Preparation and certification*. Fairfax, Va.: Author.

National Commission on Excellence in Educational Administration. 1987. *Leaders for America's schools*. Tempe, Ariz.: University Council for Educational Administration.

National Policy Board for Educational Administration. 1989. *Improving the preparation of school administrators: The reform agenda*. Charlottesville, Va.: Author.

———. 1993. *Principals for our changing schools: Knowledge and skill base*. Fairfax, Va.: Author.

Newlon, J. H.. 1934. *Educational administration as a social policy*. New York: Scribner.

Shakeshaft, C. 1988. Women in educational administration: Implications for training. In D. E. Griffiths, R. T. Stout, and P. R. Forsyth, eds. *Leaders for America's schools*: 403–16. Berkeley, Calif.: McCutchan.

Slater, R. O. April 1991. On some recent developments in educational administration. *Organizational Theory Dialogue*: 1, 18–21.

Valverde, L. A., and Brown, F. 1988. Influences on leadership development among racial and ethnic minorities. In N. J. Boyan, ed. *Handbook of research on educational administration*: 143–57. New York: Longman.

Willower, D. J. 1988. Synthesis and projection. In N. J. Boyan, ed. *Handbook of research on educational administration*: 729–47.

A Knowledge Base for Educational Administration: Notes from the Field[1]

Robert Donmoyer

Recent concern with articulating a knowledge base in educational administration (see, for example, National Policy Board for Educational Administration 1989; University Council for Educational Administration 1992) and related fields (see, for example, Murray 1994; Reynolds 1989) can be examined and critiqued from various perspectives. Elsewhere, I have examined the notion of a professional knowledge base from the vantage point that knowledge is inevitably political, a view informed by a variety of theoretical perspectives including the philosophy of science, critical theory, feminist thought, the sociology of knowledge and the postmodern critique (Donmoyer 1994). Here, however, I want to look at the knowledge base issue in general—and the National Policy Board for Educational Administration's recommendations in particular— from a perspective that is unusual for an academician: I will examine the knowledge base question from the perspective of a practitioner. My mode of discourse will also mimic the discourse mode of many practitioners in that I will tell stories.

Background

I had an opportunity to revisit the practitioner role recently when I took a one-quarter leave of absence from my university position and served as the acting principal of a middle school located in a suburban school district near the university in which I work. The school had 570 students and 30 faculty members. The school's

---

1. An earlier version of this paper was presented at the 1991 Annual Meeting of the American Educational Research Association in Chicago.

population came primarily from middle and upper middle class homes, although new, relatively inexpensive apartments had been built in the school's attendance area in recent years and, as a result, the school's population had become more heterogeneous both economically and ethnically.

Since there was no assistant principal, I had responsibility for all discipline beyond the classroom level and for all teacher evaluation. Also, during my tenure, ten percent had to be cut from the existing budget and a budget for the next academic year had to be prepared; a decision was made to not renew the contract of one certificated staff member (I participated in but did not have to make the decision; I did, however, have to manage the aftermath in the building with a staff that was divided about the wisdom of this action); and I also helped one noncertificated staff member decide to resign.

There were other ongoing issues. As indicated above, a new type of student and a new type of parent had moved into the district. This created a series of problems at the classroom and community-relations levels, which often landed at my door. Even before demographics began to change, staff members had a reputation for being talented but volatile—"all chiefs, no Indians" was the ethnically insensitive way one of the district's other principals put it. One staff member commented, about a month into my tenure, "I thought you were just going to be a figurehead. You've been anything but that."

The Experience as Action Research

At the outset I decided I was simply going to do the job, not attempt to use my experience on the job as a means of doing research. Old habits die hard, however. I have had a longstanding theoretical interest in questions related to knowledge utilization; at a more pragmatic level, I have often wondered whether the knowledge my colleagues and I disseminate in our administrative preparation courses has any utility in the real world. Therefore, I found myself unable to resist reflecting on questions of knowledge use as I played the role of principal and kept notes (albeit sometimes cryptic) on my experiences and reflections. This paper is an attempt to bring some sort of ex post facto order and coherence to this work.

Some individuals, of course, will not want to call what I did research. They will undoubtedly point out that I was an actor in the situation, not an observer of it; that consequently my findings are subjective rather than objective; that the sort of storytelling in which I will engage may be popular among practitioners but is not considered a legitimate form of discourse by academicians; and that this study is only the study of a single case and therefore has at best only heuristic value.

At the risk of sounding defensive, let me anticipate these charges and respond to each in turn. First, the observer-as-participant role is well established within the fields of anthropology and sociology. Harry Wolcott's (1987) study, "The Teacher is Enemy," is an example of an observer-as-participant study within the field of anthropology; Gertrude McPherson's (1972) book, "Small Town Teacher," is an example of a sociological work built around the researcher playing the observer-as-participant role. Anthropologists and sociologists know that any research strategy and any research stance has advantages and disadvantages. I would be the first to acknowledge that there are disadvantages to playing the observer-as-participant role. There are also significant advantages, however, particularly if one wants to study what a social role looks like from an insider's subjective perspective.

Second, the whole subjective/objective distinction has been called into question in recent years. Various scholars have suggested that objective knowledge is impossible; that the notion of objectivity should be rejected even as a regulative ideal (Barone 1990; Lincoln and Guba 1987); that what empirical researchers report always tells as much about the subjective, a priori assumptions of researchers and the research community of which they are a part as about the empirical reality being studied (Donmoyer 1991); and that the subjective experience of the researcher provides a useful and unique source of data (Peshkin 1988). Sometimes the magician example is used to demonstrate the value of the subjective perspective and the limits of intersubjective agreement. What would be a better source of information about what happened during a magician's act? The magician's subjective account of what he did or audience members' intersubjectively validated accounts of what they saw him doing?

Third, it is no longer the case that academicians do not value storytelling and do not recognize it as a legitimate form of academic discourse. The respected scholar Jerome Bruner (1986), for instance, has distinguished between narrative and paradigmatic forms of knowing and has argued that the former type of knowledge cannot be translated into the latter type without losing a great deal in the translation. Similarly, within our own field of education, Connelly and Clandenin (1990) and a host of other academicians have argued that teachers and other practitioners lead storied lives and that the best way to capture these lives on paper is in story form.

Finally, let me respond to the charge that this work represents a study of only a single case and, therefore, has only heuristic value. I cannot deny this charge, nor would I want to. Those who study research utilization—I am thinking in particular of people like Carol Weiss (1982)—indicate that all research, even research that works with large, randomly selected samples, must always be used heuristically. Because of the idiosyncracies that shape people, places, and events, research can never provide prescriptions for practice. Rather, as Weiss notes, it serves a problem-posing function, not a problem-solving one. Research can raise new and interesting questions, provide novel perspectives, and suggest issues that may not have come into focus before. These are my goals in reporting findings from an admittedly subjective, observer-as-participant, narrative-based, n of 1 study. I will organize the presentation of findings and reflections around three topics: (1) academic knowledge used and functions served; (2) "knowing that," "knowing how," and "knowing what"; and (3) visceral knowing.

Academic Knowledge Used and Functions Served

The title of this section, "Academic Knowledge Used and Functions Served," begs an important question: Was any academic knowledge used and, if so, did this knowledge serve any useful function? This is not simply a rhetorical question. The literature on administrative preparation programs has raised questions about the utility of the academic knowledge dispensed in such programs, and I, personally, have been concerned that the skepticism evidenced by the literature on administrative preparation may be justified. So I attempted to monitor the technical knowledge, research, and theories I employed in the course of doing my job. I assumed that if I—someone in the academic knowledge business—did not consciously employ academic knowledge on the job, it was doubtful that anyone would.

My findings provide both good news and bad for those of us involved in administrative preparation programs. Let me get some of the bad news out of the way right off. First, I found I needed very little in the way of specialized technical knowledge to do my job. Lest anyone believe that my specialized technical knowledge had become so ingrained, so unconscious after years of training and teaching in educational administration that I was simply unaware that I knew what I knew, I should note the following: (1) neither my Ph.D. nor either of my two masters degrees is in educational administration; (2) although I have taught in an educational administration program area, my teaching has been limited to the topics of instructional leadership research and methodology and knowledge use; (3) I received my administrative certificate after an exceedingly generous and creative reading of my transcript by State Department of Education personnel at a time when certification requirements in the state were both small in number and vaguely defined (under current requirements, it would take me at least a year of full time classwork to qualify for a principal certificate in my state). Despite my lack of specialized technical knowledge, I encountered very little difficulty on the job. Indeed, since so much of what happened in the district from a technical standpoint was idiosyncratic to the district, it may have been advantageous to come to the job with a conceptual blank slate. For instance, we were told to engage in zero-based budgeting in certain areas, but because the operational meaning of the term was so unique to the district, it was better to learn how to do zero-based budgeting in this context from my fellow principals than from a generic textbook description.

There was one exception to what I have just said: knowledge related to special education. The costs of making a mistake in this area are so great and the legal requirements are so complex that general intelligence, experience in and around schools, and good intuition are not sufficient to ensure success on the job. My school, in fact, was involved in an arbitration proceeding, which, even if the district won, would cost the district $50,000. Although the blunders that led to this proceeding occurred before I assumed the acting principal position, the situation made me painfully aware of my inadequacies and, I might add, of an inadequacy in the administrative preparation program in which I participated.

I should add that in the educational rather than in the legal domain of special education, I believe I did a reasonably good job without specialized technical knowledge. For example, I worked with special education tutors and teams of teachers to develop procedures to insure communication about students they had in common. This heightened communication allowed tutors to focus tutoring sessions on the skills and knowledge students needed to master course content, rather than on generic skills, which often did not transfer to specific classes. I needed no specialized technical knowledge either to recognize this problem or work with staff to generate solutions. The legal domain of special education, however, was a very different story.

Let me turn now to a second bit of bad news for academics in the field of educational administration: I cannot recall, and my notes do not indicate, ever thinking about a particular research study at any point during my tenure as acting principal. There is also some good news here, however: The general constructs that guide research studies and/or are built from the results of such studies were very much a part of my reflections.

I would frequently, for example, find myself labeling my leadership style as an Argyris and Schön (1985) Model II–democratic one. Like an Argyris Model II leader, I attempted to make my reasoning public, encouraged criticism and alternative suggestions, and happily altered my position and adopted others' alternative proposals if my reasoning was not sound or others came up with a better suggestion.

Employing the Argyris and Schön label, I believe, served several functions. First, the label reassured me that I indeed had a leadership style, that there was a label for what I was doing, and that others—many of whom were considered experts in the field—had endorsed my approach to leadership. In organized anarchies (Cohen and March 1974), the importance of such emotional support should not be underestimated. Second, the ability to name what I was doing, I believe, created a more consistent performance. The label conjured up a template for action, which I used—with significant variations, of course—time after time after time.

Third, because I had a name for what I was doing, I was in a better position to stop what I was doing when it did not work. Although my Argyris and Schön Model II-democratic style served me well in most situations with most people, it was not particularly effective with one teacher who was also the school's basketball coach. The only concern board of education members expressed when they approved my appointment was that I would be at the school during basketball season. Midway through my tenure, I realized the reason for what I perceived initially as a rather shallow, insignificant concern.

Problems arose when one of the coach's star players received two F's and therefore, because of state athletic association rules, became ineligible to play. The coach was very upset. He was particularly upset because one of the teachers who gave the student an F had not followed the fairly elaborate warning procedures that the coach had established and that the staff had previously endorsed. The teacher had followed the procedures earlier in the quarter, had continued to warn the student informally, and in fact both the student and his father indicated that the F was no surprise. She had not followed the letter of the law, however.

I attempted to find a solution to the coach's difficulty and find a way that the student could continue to play, not because I wanted the coach's team to win basketball games, but because I was convinced by other teachers in the school that the student's academic effort had actually improved over the past several months and that this improvement was attributable, in large part, to being on the basketball team. I investigated whether the one teacher's failure to follow through with the school's warning system might be a loophole to exempt the student from the eligibility requirement. I discovered, however, that the warning system was an intrabuilding procedure and, therefore, had no bearing on state athletic association rules. I also talked with the teacher who had failed to follow procedures. She expressed regret for her inaction and indicated that, in the future, she would abide by the letter of the law even though she felt the procedures were cumbersome, unnecessary, and an intrusion on her academic focus.

All the while I kept playing the role of the Argyris and Schön Model II–democratic leader with the coach. I kept him informed about what I was doing and what I was thinking. I invited him to critique my plans and suggest alternative possibilities. When, after working on virtually nothing else for two days and concluding that there was nothing I could do, I reiterated, at great length, what I had done and why it had not worked. I once again invited suggestions about another tack I might take, another strategy I might explore, another possibility I might consider. I was acting out the Argyris and Schön script as written.

The problem was that the coach was playing, at this point, a very different sort of scene. He was not interested in collaborative reasoning. Rather, he needed to vent frustration and anger, and I became a convenient target. One of his favorite tactics when upset was to say negative things about a person to a third party within earshot of the person being criticized. The coach had a reputation for using this tactic on students and other staff members. He now began using it on me. On two occasions, within a ten-minute time, span he made his move. I realized I had to respond, and not in the guise of an Argyris and Schön Model II leader.

Indeed, I realized that, to the coach, my Argyris and Schön "lets reason together" stance was probably taken as a sign of weakness and ineffectiveness. Therefore, I decided to abandon my Model II–

democratic leader role briefly and transform myself, temporarily, into the very model of a domineering, top-down, assertive leader. I told the coach, with voice controlled but raised and finger jabbing in his face, that I did not appreciate his tactics; that I would not tolerate them; that I had done all I could do to solve his problem; and that as far as I was concerned, the matter was closed.

The coach quite literally backed away from me with his mouth open. It was only a matter of minutes before I would return to my more comfortable leadership style with the coach. I am convinced, however, that for a brief period, it was necessary to move out of my typical mode of operating. I am convinced that the only reason I won the coach over (in fact, he became one of my strongest supporters in the school), was because I did alter my style when necessary. I am also convinced that the only reason I realized that an Argyris and Schön way of operating was not working was because I could label it in the first place. The label alerted me to the fact that my way of doing things was only one of many ways of operating in the world—one of many scripts that might be acted out—and, consequently, when things were not working, that I should probably choose another leadership stance and scenario.

One other example of a body of literature that was very useful to me is the literature on school culture. Writings by people such as Deal and Kennedy (1982) and Firestone and Wilson (1985) suggested to me that it would be useful to go into the school with a very limited number of key ideas to promote. I decided to focus on two goals: (1) to nudge the organization back to focusing on academics, a focus which, I believe, had been lost in this resource-rich district, and (2) to try to make staff members more sensitive to the needs of the culturally different kids who were beginning to come to the school.

The literature on school culture also suggested how I should promote my agenda. Rather than relying on formal staff development programs or bureaucratic rules and regulations, the organizational culture literature suggested the need to tell stories and get the message out informally. So I spent lots of time in the teachers' room talking with people.

For example, when I thought it might be a good idea to have a Martin Luther King Assembly to signal to our minority students that we cared about them and respected their heritage, I spent much of the morning in the teachers' room in informal conversation, giving my reasons and also expressing my concern that a special assembly might, in fact, intrude on academic time in a school where I already saw a lot of such intrusion going on. Part of my reason for being in the teachers' room and getting people's reactions to my ideas was to play an Argyris Model II democratic game. I sincerely wanted feedback. I wanted to be certain the assembly would not duplicate what was already happening in class, and I wanted to know whether people would see the assembly as tokenism or thought students might view it as such. I was certainly willing to abandon my plan if there were good reasons to do so.

I remained in the teachers' room and continued to talk with people, however, long after I had sufficient evidence that staff members supported the assembly idea. I remained to tell stories about students experiencing culture clash and, in the process, hopefully get others to accept my stories as legitimate. I remained, also, to discuss my dilemma about intruding on class time and, in so doing, to begin to model that intruding on class time should never be done lightly.

One staff member commented at one point during my tenure, "You are always in the teachers' room; you must really like us!" In fact, I really did like the staff members and that was one reason I spent a lot of time with them. But I also spent time with them because (1) I wanted to be an Argyris Model II leader and (2) the literature on school culture suggested that informal interaction was the best way of nudging the organization in the directions in which I believed it should head.

So there is good news for those of us who teach in administrative preparation programs: I, at least, used many of the theories that are taught in such programs and found them to be functional in helping me act intelligently on the job. Once again, however, good news is balanced by bad: I relied as much on theoretical knowledge from other academic disciplines as I did on theories that are normally taught in educational administration programs. Anthropological explanations for minority students' school failure, for example, were invaluable in analyzing why certain students were continually in my office for disciplinary reasons and habitually on failure lists. My master's degree in political science provided heuristics to understand decision'making processes and human motivation. And sociologists' discussions of the social construction of reality reminded me that I could not discount the interpretations of students, parents, and teachers, even when I believed them to be wrong. Indeed, if I were forced to choose between my general liberal arts education (I took no courses in education as an undergraduate) and special training in educational administration or even education generally, I would certainly choose the former rather than the latter.

Furthermore, some of my most useful knowledge came from sources that were nonacademic. I constantly reminded myself, for example, of journalists' accounts of decision-making processes in the Carter and Reagan presidencies to check my academician's inclination to complicate issues and muddle matters that needed to be simplified. Even the arts provided grist for my intellectual mill. I found the image of Louise Fletcher portraying Nurse Ratchet in *One Flew Over the Cuckoo's Nest* popping into my head whenever I struggled with the seemingly conflicting desires to be both open and honest with my staff and strategic and political.

Finally, one of the most interesting findings about knowledge use to come out of this study was the realization that some of the theory I found most useful was theory emerging from what I considered bad (or at least questionable) social science. For example, I had always been somewhat skeptical of personality-type theory, in part because personality types are ideal types and ideal types are really not that much different from stereotypes. I found the Myers-Briggs personality type theory (see Myers and McCaulley 1981); however, the most useful theory I employed during my tenure in the school. For instance, during one of my conversations with the basketball coach I talked about earlier, I tried to convince him that he had acted inappropriately when he talked with a friend of the teacher who had given his star player an F and said nothing when the friend indicated he would go back to the teacher and ask about changing the grade. I was trying to make the point that while the coach had not violated the letter of the rule about not putting pressure on teachers to change grades for athletes, he certainly had violated the rule's spirit. We went on for some time. I finally realized this person was probably such a strong sensing and judging type, a strong SJ in Myers-Briggs parlance, that it was unlikely, no matter what I said, we would ever have a meeting of the minds on this issue. For strong SJ's, the letter of the law is the law's spirit. Therefore, at one point I simply said, "Let's just agree to disagree on this one," and we moved on to another topic.

Another example—an even more dramatic one because the theory is even more problematic than the theory on personality type—involves theory about dysfunctional families (see, for example, LaMar 1992). At best this theory is based on clinical knowledge that grossly oversimplifies social phenomena. At worst it is so general—so capable of applying to everyone—that it functions much as a horoscope does. Nevertheless, dysfunctional family theory's notion of enabling—the idea that some people, in an effort to protect a person, may inadvertently support the person's dysfunctional behavior—was a very useful notion for me in analyzing what I was doing with a secretary who worked in the office.

This secretary really did not want to be a secretary; she wanted to be a guidance counselor but did not have the necessary credentials. She came from a very dysfunctional family herself, and was very nurturing to some difficult students in the school who came from similar sorts of backgrounds. The office, as a result, was frequently filled with students, and because the secretary seemed incapable of saying no and setting limits, it was also often chaotic.

This problem was a longstanding one. Another secretary had left before my arrival on the scene because she could not tolerate the chaos in the office. Faculty members informed me that in their opinion the wrong secretary had gone away. Faculty continued to complain about the chaos in the office during my tenure, and the person hired to replace the secretary who had departed was beginning to talk about moving on, despite her affection for her co-worker. Since the new secretary was a consummate professional, I was quite concerned about the prospect of losing her. I also found that, despite my rather high tolerance for chaos, the office was a bit too chaotic even for my taste.

So I met with the secretary frequently and used my best Argyris Model II techniques: I indicated that I appreciated her nurturing of students, but that there was also a legitimate need to keep the office quiet and orderly so that the work could get done, co-workers would not become frustrated, teachers would have confidence that the office would take care of matters professionally, a positive image would be projected to parents and other visitors, and so that I could talk on the telephone without going behind closed doors. I also proposed a host of solutions for this problem and invited her to do the same. One of the solutions I proposed, for instance, was to move her desk to the guidance area where we in fact wanted a magnet to attract troubled students. I had talked with the guidance counselors, who indicated they would welcome the secretary in their area, provided she learned to set limits so that the chaos that was in the outer office was not simply transferred to their domain.

Every time I spoke to the secretary about the chaotic office problem and every time I proposed a solution, however, she indicated that there was really no reason to work on the matter because she was going to resign fairly soon. I then proceeded to plead with her to stay and to tell her how much I valued her and how much I valued the nurturing she offered troubled students.

This ritual went on for over a month. Dysfunctional family theory and the notion of enabling found in that theory finally caused me to reexamine what I was doing. I began to realize that I was, in fact, encouraging a certain kind of behavior which, in the end, was not functional for anybody. At one point, therefore, when the secretary delivered her line about leaving, I resisted saying my next line in the script we had jointly created, and stated, instead, that I would need a specific resignation date. Either we were going to work on the office chaos problem, I indicated, or the secretary should give me a letter of resignation. I am fairly certain that, without a knowledge of the dysfunctional family literature and without the construct of enabling that this literature provides, I would have continued a pattern that was functional for neither the school nor the secretary. In short, in this example and the previous one, it did not matter that the sort of universal truth social scientists seek had not been conclusively demonstrated. The theories in question fit the particular context I was working in, and consequently were exceedingly useful to me, even though I continue to view them as suspect from the perspective of social science.

Before proceeding, let me summarize what I have said in this section. I have indicated that my experience provides both good news and bad news for those of us involved in administration preparation programs. On the credit side, I employed many of the theories we teach in our programs in the process of doing my job. These theories—Argyris's work and the work on school culture, in particular—I found to be highly functional for a variety of reasons.

I also indicated, however, that I did not employ knowledge of specific research studies, and that, with the exception of the legal aspects of special education, I did not need much in the way of specialized technical knowledge, and further, that understanding generated from a liberal education and even from journalism was as important as understanding generated from special training in educational administration. Finally, I suggested that theory not considered particularly good by social scientists' criteria may, in fact, be quite functional if used wisely in a particular situation.

Knowing That, Knowing How. . . and Knowing What

In this section I want to extend the final point I made above by arguing the adverse: Even the best of social science theory may not be very good if it is applied inadequately. Let me start by referencing and extending a fairly well established philosophical distinction. The philosopher Gilbert Ryle has talked about two types of knowledge: "knowing that," which involves theoretical knowledge, and "knowing how," which involves skills and the ability to perform particular kinds of actions. While playing the principal role, I found I also needed a third kind of knowledge, which for want of another name I will call *knowing what*. This third type of knowledge involves understanding when it is appropriate to apply a particular theory or skill.

My one major blunder in my tenure as principal, in fact, occurred because I employed the wrong set of skills for a particular set of circumstances: A few hours after my encounter with the coach, which I described above, and my brief but highly successful transformation into a directive, no-nonsense, top-down leader, I had a telephone conversation with a person in the district's data-processing office. Many of my teachers had expressed frustration because they had not been provided with the kinds of services that they had been promised. At their behest, I called the computer people. When the person with whom I was speaking would not even entertain the idea that there were problems in the data-processing office and after she contradicted herself, I once again turned myself into a directive, no-nonsense, top-down leader, the sort of leader who had been so successful with my basketball coach just hours before.

To say that this strategy was unsuccessful in this new situation would be to grossly understate the situation. Indeed, I think it is safe to say that the Mr. Macho strategy I chose was probably the most inappropriate strategy I could have employed in this situation. By the end of my telephone conversation, I had a data-processing employee in tears, her boss irate, and the issue I called about in the first place totally obscured.

I believe there is virtually no component of the administrative preparation program in which I work—or any other program with which I am familiar—that would have helped me avoid this situation, that would have helped me, in other words, predict that a strategy so successful only hours before would be so unsuccessful in this new situation. In our administrative preparation programs—and in administrative programs in general—we provide lots of theory (knowing that). We may even provide occasional opportunities to practice and develop skills (knowing how). To my knowledge, however, these programs spend virtually no time developing the kind of awareness that allows people to match up appropriate skills and theory with particular circumstances. The "knowing what" knowledge base remains a black hole in most administrative preparation efforts.

Visceral Knowledge

There is one additional sort of knowledge which came into play constantly during my tenure as a principal. The philosopher Isaiah Berlin describes the sort of knowledge I am talking about as follows:

> When the Jews are enjoined in the Bible to protect strangers' "For ye know the soul of a stranger, seeing ye were strangers in the land of Egypt" (Exodus 23:9), this knowledge is neither deductive, nor inductive, nor founded on direct inspection, but akin to the "I know" of "I know what it is to be hungry and poor," or "I know how political bodies function," or "I know what is to be a Brahmin." This is neither (to use Professor Gilbert Ryle's useful classification) "knowing that" which the sciences provide, nor the "knowing how" which is the possession of a disposition or skill, nor the experience of direct perception, acquaintance, memory, but the type of knowledge that an administrator or politician must possess of the men with whom he deals. (45)

The sort of knowledge Berlin is talking about was essential to my accomplishing what I discovered to be my primary task while playing the principal role: mediating disputes. To successfully mediate disputes—whether they were between teacher and teacher, between student and teacher, between teacher and parent, between student and student—I needed a knowledge that involved more than understanding the truth or falsehood of propositions, more than mastering specific technique and even more than understanding when theory and technique should be applied. I needed a kind of knowledge that was as much affective as it was cognitive, one that involved empathy as well as analysis. I needed, in short, a sort of visceral literacy that could enable me to enter imaginatively into the lives of others and share vicariously at least some of their problems. I needed to do this in order to understand what the problems really were, in order to communicate honestly—not just through words but through the aesthetics of voice and gesture— that I understood the problem, and in order to help contending parties see their adversaries' needs and desires as at least somewhat legitimate. In most instances, each of these conditions were necessary prerequisites to finding a solution acceptable to all.

I could cite numerous examples of situations in which the sort of knowledge I have been talking about came into play; here I will discuss two occasions. One occasion involved a dispute between an English teacher and a teacher of gifted students. These two teachers shared a group of students and alternated teaching them from quarter to quarter. During one quarter the students were with the gifted and talented teacher for a small seminar experience in English; during the next quarter they were back in their regular English classroom. When the students returned to their English classroom after working one quarter with the gifted and talented teacher, the English class was engaged in a study of a novel. The regular classroom teacher expected them to take the test on the novel even though that meant they had to catch up on what went on before their return. The gifted and talented teacher sided with students who felt the expectation that they be tested on work covered when they were not in the classroom was unfair.

At first, it appeared that this conflict would be easy to resolve. In fact, I had already met with the students in question and we had developed a solution to the problem. Because the students had agreed to the solution willingly and without coercion on my part, and because the solution gave the English teacher everything she wanted (The students agreed to take the English teacher's objective test if they were also permitted to write a paper on the book for extra credit if they received a bad grade on the test), I assumed both teachers would also find the solution satisfactory. Both did, but neither was quite satisfied. As we talked, it became apparent that the particular problem we were addressing was only a symptom of a more general problem—or to be more precise, two somewhat different general problems, as each teacher framed the issues in fundamentally different ways. Each wanted the general difficulties to be addressed at least as much—and I suspect more—than the specific issue I was trying to solve.

To know this and to understand what the more general problems looked like—and felt like—I had to enter vicariously the lives of each of these two teachers in this particular school. I had to come to understand the frustration of the regular classroom teacher who was, in a sense, set up: No matter how good a teacher she was, she had to teach thirty students at a time rather than ten, and, therefore found it difficult, probably impossible, to be as good as the gifted and talented teacher, at least in the eyes of her students. When the regular teacher's colleague became the students' ally in a battle with her, salt was rubbed even deeper into a festering wound.

I also had to understand the frustrations of the gifted and talented teacher, who saw this latest requirement as just the latest in a series of petty and unreasonable acts committed by the regular English teacher and her teammates to undermine the gifted and talented program. I also needed to have some sense of what it felt like to be a so-called "special" teacher in a school where regular teachers were organized into teams that provided emotional and political support.

To summarize: At least as much as (and I suspect more than) a solution to the specific problem that had arisen, each teacher seemed to want someone—in this instance, me—to understand and appreciate the situation into which they had been placed. A real solution to this situation, in other words, would have required either a structural change or an appreciation on the part of each teacher of her colleague's plight.

Another example of a similar dispute involved a white physical education teacher who had confiscated several gym uniforms because they were in lockers without locks (a violation of her clearly stated rules) and a black parent who claimed the teacher was picking on her daughter because of her daughter's race. In this situation, I needed to understand something impossible for me ever to completely understand: what it is like to be a black person living in a white person's world. It was only after I countered (ever so gently, ever so sympathetically) the teacher's declamation that she was not a racist by noting that, in our racist society, we may all be affected by racism even if we do not want to be, or even if we are unaware of it, that the parent began to relax and entertain other explanations for the teacher's actions.

Similarly, I needed to be sensitive to the experiences of the physical education teacher. I needed to know what it was like to be accused of racism when you honestly felt race had not been a factor in your actions and to know what it was like to feel defenseless in such a situation. At a more general level, I needed to understand—and I needed to help the parent understand—what it was like to teach literally hundreds of students, in the course of a day, in a subject like physical education. We needed to appreciate the necessity in such a situation for rules and standard operating procedures, just as the physical education teacher and I needed to understand the frustration of a parent when the rules and standard operating procedures led to the loss of a daughter's costly gym equipment.

These examples are typical of the sorts of problems I encountered in the course of a typical day. I do not believe, however, that most administrative preparation programs help to prepare future administrators for such situations. The mediation processes I engaged in, for example, bore at best only a slight family resemblance to the type of mediation process talked about in most classes on collective bargaining. My mediation situations were much more informal; the issues in these situations was much more personalized, emotional and idiosyncratic; and, consequently, the need to understand the perspectives of the participants viscerally, rather than simply on an intellectual level was essential.

A large part of the administrator's preparation in this area must, of course, come from life experience, but I believe I was fortunate to have two types of formal training, which were helpful in managing the mediation process and developing the sort of affect-laden understanding I have suggested as an essential component of being an effective mediator. One bit of formal training came from my experiences with using anthropological research methods. Anthropology's emic/etic dialectic, that is, its tendency to encourage researchers to be simultaneously both an insider and an outsider, a participant and an observer, a friend and a stranger, is roughly equivalent to the stance required of a successful mediator, in the sense that I am using the term.

I also, while waiting to be drafted into military service, worked briefly as an actor. Training and experience in the dramatic arts, I believe, helped develop a sensitivity to and comfort with affect. Being simultaneously engrossed in the action on the stage and aware of the audience and its reaction also gave me an opportunity to try out the sort of in-the-situation/out-of-the situation dialectical stance which is required for successful mediation.

There are no analogs in most administrative preparation programs to either my experience in the theatre or the experience I gained with anthropological research. I believe both of these experiences, however, contributed immensely to my playing the role of principal successfully.

Implications

As I look back on my experiences in the field and ask what they might contribute to the current debate about a knowledge base for educational administration, I am struck by several things. First, I am struck by the heuristic function of knowledge in the field and the serendipity associated with knowledge use. During my time in the field, I needed very little in the way of specialized technical knowledge to do my job and never thought of a single research study, even though reading and doing research studies makes up a large portion of my professional life. I did employ social science theory, but the social science theory I employed while on the job came from a wide array of sources, not just from work that had been or is likely to be corralled by the educational administration field. Furthermore, so-called "bad" social science theory proved incredibly useful and the best social science theory proved useless (or worse) if applied inappropriately. One final point with respect to serendipity: Insights from journalism and images from the arts were often as helpful as insights from social science.

The reference to the contributions of the arts in the previous paragraph leads to a second insight I have gleaned from my experience about the sort of knowledge school administrators need. This insight relates to the importance of affect, intuition, and empathy. My success as a school principal depended on my ability to read the feelings of others and to manage and encode my own feelings in appropriate ways. If we want to talk about the sorts of knowledge and skills that allow administrators to do such things, however, we must expand the definition of knowledge well beyond the one employed by most social scientists, even those working at the epistemological cutting edge. For example, the work included in Primis, the computerized document base produced by The University Council of Educational Administration's (UCEA) knowledge base project, certainly represents some epistemological and methodological diversity, but it is all still pretty heady stuff. After reflecting on my experience in the fields I find myself much more sympathetic to philosophers' talk of "embodied knowledge"— namely, the notion that such things as meaning, imagination, and even reason have quite literally a bodily basis (see, for example, Johnson 1987)—even as I worry about how we can put embodied knowledge on paper, much less in a computerized document base. A partial answer to this question may be found in literature and the arts. I know that I am now more receptive to the case some of our colleagues have tried to make for using fiction in administrative preparation programs (see, for example, Brieschke 1993) than I was before I returned to the field. I certainly hope that if UCEA continues to expand the Primis document base—as it currently is planning to do—consideration will be given to including works of fiction, even though such works may not customarily be thought of as a source of professional knowledge. I suspect it may also be useful not to limit our conception of documents to printed material.

At a more fundamental level, my experience back in the field has caused me to raise questions about the desirability of efforts such as the ten-year knowledge base articulation effort UCEA has undertaken, as well as the appropriateness of the knowledge base metaphor itself. Let me comment on this second, more theoretical question first.

From my practitioner perspective, knowledge was not primarily a prescribed, static commodity; it was not a predetermined bottom line; it was not best imaged as a base. A more appropriate metaphor would be one conjuring up constant motion and focussing our attention more on process rather than product. Prefashioned concepts and images get employed in the process, of course, but the sources of these concepts and images are incredibly diverse. Furthermore, the concepts and images must always be used heuristically; that is, they must constantly be reshaped to accommodate the idiosyncracies of particular people, places, and events.

This critique of the knowledge base metaphor translates at a more applied level to concerns and questions about the utility of recent attempts to "map the knowledge base for educational administration" (UCEA 1992). The problem, as I see it, is not primarily with the work that has been done thus far. Indeed, the Primis document base should make some very good empirical and theoretical work readily accessible to large numbers of people. As long as Primis does not become a de facto cannon for the field—in effect, as long as Primis does not preclude the sort of serendipity with respect to knowledge use that I experienced upon returning to the field—the Primis document base represents a useful (albeit, I suspect, a relatively modest) contribution to the field.

I do have concern with regard to the second stage of the Primis project. Here the aspirations seem to be considerably grander. Among the goals Patrick Forsyth (1993), UCEA's executive director, lists for the second stage of the UCEA knowledge base project are the following:

- to review the completeness of the seven domain structure, making adjustments and additions where necessary

- to analyze each knowledge domain for adequacy

- to articulate the knowledge of each domain (p. 3)

My concern here is not that UCEA will accomplish its stated goal of mapping the knowledge base for educational administration. My experience with the serendipity of knowledge use suggests that such a task can never really be accomplished. Furthermore, even if an official cannon for the field is established, I am confident that practicing administrators will continue to do what they have always done and what I, myself, did when I took on an administrative role: Ignore knowledge taught in administrative preparation programs when it is not useful and use knowledge not taught in formal preparation programs when it is functional to do so.

My real concern with the agenda UCEA has set for the academic wing of the field is that it will obscure important questions that need to be asked about preparing school administrators and distract us from doing important work that desperately needs to be done. Let me use two metaphors to make my point. The first metaphor: I fear that those who heed the National Policy Board's recommendation to articulate a knowledge base for the field may be fishing in the wrong stream. The second metaphor is a bit more melodramatic, but, after my sojourn in the field, I fear the melodrama may be appropriate: We may be fiddling while our schools burn.

For me, our seminal question should be a pedagogical rather than an epistemic one. We should not be asking: What is our knowledge *base*? The question, though intellectually interesting, is ultimately unanswerable and, hence, a distraction. Instead our primary question should be: What sorts of experiences should our students have; what experience will best prepare them for the complex, idiosyncratic, affect-laden world they will encounter when they attempt to do administrative work in educational settings?

My personal answer to this question since returning from the field is to make my classes as life-like as possible. I define a life-like experience as any experience that (1) puts discussions of theory into the context of reflections on practice; (2) allows for reflecting on the "knowing what" question; and/or (3) brings the affective dimension of experience into the educational process. Operationally for me, at least, this translates into an increased use of case material (Shulman 1992), role playing and sociodrama (Sternberg and Garcia 1989), problem based learning (Bridges 1992), and products from literary and artistic fields. I am not satisfied with my answers to date, particularly the way I am using them, but I am fairly certain my question is right. I hope the major professional association within the field will begin to address pedagogical questions with the same energy and enthusiasm it has exhibited in its attempt to map the field's knowledge base.

Conclusion

There may be important political and sociological reasons for the field of educational administration's efforts to articulate a knowledge base. (A specialized, identifiable knowledge base is, after all, frequently considered to be a prerequisite for a field obtaining professional status.) A discussion of this issue is beyond the scope of this discussion. Here the focus is more limited: I have used my experiences with knowledge use while serving as an acting principal to raise questions about the relative *educational* value of knowledge base articulation efforts for our field.

My experience suggests that knowledge use in the field is characterized by serendipity, and that traditional and even cutting-edge social scientists' conceptions of knowledge may not be adequate to capture the sorts of understandings and insights that practitioners employ in the course of doing their work. This latter point suggests the need to consider expanding the kind of work included in the document bases that teachers of administrators draw from when planning learning experiences for their students. The discussion of serendipity raises more fundamental questions about the utility of attempts to map the knowledge base for our field. Given the complexity and idiosyncracy of educational phenomena and the resulting unpredictability associated with knowledge use, we should at least consider whether time might be better spent asking different sorts of questions and engaging in very different sorts of tasks.

References

Argyris, C. and Schön, D. 1985. Theory into Practice: Increasing professional effectiveness. San Francisco: Jossey-Bass.

Bridges, E. M. 1992. *Problem based learning for administrators.* ERIC Clearinghouse of Educational Management, University of Oregon.

Brieschke, P. A. 1993. Interpreting ourselves: administrators in modern fiction. *Theory into Practice* 32(4):229–35.

Bruner, J. 1979. On knowing: essays for the left hand. Cambridge, Mass.: Belknap Press of Harvard University Press.

Bruner, J. 1986. Actual minds, possible worlds. Cambridge, Mass: Harvard University Press.

Connelly, F. M., and Clandinin, F. M. 1990. Stories of Experience and Narrative Inquiry 19(5):2–14.

Deal, T., and Kennedy, A. 1982. Corporate culture: The rites and rituals of corporate life. Reading, Mass.: Addison-Wesley.

Donmoyer, R. 1994. The concept of a knowledge base. In F. Murray, ed. Knowledge base for teacher education. New York: Jossey Bass.

Forsyth, P. 1993. *Educational Administration: The UCEA document base*. New York: McGraw Hill.

Johnson, M. 1987. *The body is the mind: The bodily basis of meaning, imagination, and reason*. Chicago: University of Chicago Press.

McPherson, G. 1972. Small town teacher. Cambridge, Mass: Harvard University Press.

Murray, F. 1994. *Knowledge base for teacher education*. New York: Jossey Bass.

Peshkin, A. 1988. In search of subjectivity—one's own. *Educational Researcher* 17(7) 17–22.

Reynolds, M. 1989. *Knowledge base for the beginning teacher.* New York: Pergamon Press.

Shulman, J., ed. 1992. *Case methods in teacher education*. New York: Teachers College Press.

Sternberg, P., and Garcia, A. 1989. *Sociodrama: "who's in your shoes."* New York: Praeger.

UCEA. 1992. Essential knowledge for school leaders: a proposal to map the knowledge base of educational administration. Unpublished proposal.

Wolcott, H. *The Teacher as Enemy*. 1974. In G. Spindler, ed. *Education and Cultural Process: toward an anthropology of education*. New York: Holt, Rinehart and Winston.

Craft Knowledge and Institutional Constraints

Rodney Muth

Janine Frank, the new assistant principal at Peak High School, looked tiredly at the pile of papers she still had to go through. She looked, too, at the clock; it said 6:45 p.m.—time to go home, after more than twelve hours spent at school. Besides, the papers could wait, and her husband and two teenagers were probaby wondering if she'd ever join them for dinner.

During her twenty-minute drive home, she thought back on her day, remembering her intensive discussion with the principal after school was dismissed. They had talked over her detailed oral and written recommendations about how to improve the drop-out problem at Peak, which she had made that morning to the School Community Council as the site leader of the school-university partnership. Thank heavens, she thought, for the training she'd gotten in her Master's program. If it hadn't been for her year-long apprenticeship under the wings of Mrs. Vision, the principal at High View High, and Ken Connect, her supervising professor at Uplift University, as well as the field- and problem-based seminars she'd had there, she might not have had the confidence to attempt the task.

Clearly, she thought with pride, my applied studies at Uplift prepared me to be an open and active learner, able to tackle unfamiliar situations, to get background information and think broadly about the context of specific problems, to diagnose problems and collect necessary data appropriately, and to apply the data to clarifying and resolving the problems. And I held my own with my university colleagues! If nothing else, she thought, today's presentation proved Professor Connect's maxim: "Experience is the best teacher."

While this brief scenario may seem idealistic, it reflects what all of us who teach school administration would like to have happen.

That is, we'd all like our graduates to enter the field confident in their ability to anticipate or react to problems effectively; confident that they are conversant with important issues and problems; confident that they know how to ask good questions about the context of problems as well as the problems themselves; confident that they know how to get and use information and data to address issues; and confident that they can work with diverse groups to identify problems, find solutions, and accomplish tasks. We'd probably all like to lay claim to graduates who can use what they know, combining their classroom-based content learnings with field-based applications. Such ideal graduates from an administrator preparation program would value knowledge and research about educational phenomena and could apply both knowledge and research to solving difficult problems of practice. These reflective practitioner-scholars would be the clear link between theory and practice that many of us have sought.

Constraints

Unfortunately, the places in which many of us ply our trade do not lend themselves easily to creating the enviromnents—either in the university or in the field—that might facilitate our proudly identifying such graduates. The problems we face in creating programs that are more sensitive to the issues addressed in the preceding chapters of this book are not just those of ideologues vying for supremacy. Indeed, many of the problems that we face—and some of which we can remedy—are based in the institutional lives that we live, lives that reinforce traditional approaches and discourage innovation, change, or risk. Just a few of these barriers are enough to inhibit or undermine most innovative efforts. And too many barriers virtually eliminate possibilities for reform.

Institutional Support

The lack of institutional support for innovation is demonstrated in various ways, most of which are structural. These impediments to reform are historical and controlling. Many are bureaucratic, administrative expectations, to which faculty accede by virtue of tradition, desire for academic status, or ignorance.

COURSE CREDITS

Time spent on scholarship and service is difficult to define, regularize, routinize, and quantify—which bureaucrats naturally need to do. Thus, because universities need consistent and simple ways to define professional time and productivity, they account for the professional work done by faculty in terms of courses taught. Released time, buy-outs, and other changes in responsibility are generally related only to the number of courses or credits taught. Course credits are the currency of academe. (Ask anyone in a university the last time a dean agreed to release a faculty member from scholarly expectations, rather than from course work, to perform more service.)

Today's trend is to package credits in three-unit groups, a norm reinforced by standardized expectations for load, accrediting practices, state certification systems, and policies on classroom contact hours per credit. Counting credits in these ways says irrefutably to both faculty and students that what does count is the time put in (quantity), not the results (quality). The system also reinforces the notion that learning only takes place when professors lecture in classrooms and students dutifully take notes. And, of course, such campus-based, clock-bound structures also make accountability easier.

MONEY

While the rhetoric of graduate education, particularly doctoral education, focuses on terms such as "the community of scholars," "mentorship," and "learning from the masters," institutional support for such opportunities has diminished significantly or vanished almost entirely. Assistantships, for example, which once funded full-time study, no longer exist in the quantity or quality most of us writing for this volume remember from our own graduate days. It is rarely possible nowadays for mid-career adults with families and employment responsibilities to subordinate such obligations to full-time scholarship, to a so-called "life of the mind," however brief. The rising costs of higher education make it difficult to support even a few full-time students, even at a pittance. Today, the tables are turned. Instead of expanding funds for graduate study, universities relentlessly seek resources by maximizing student credit hours—and therefore income—through high numbers, short programs, and after-work time schedules. Besides making it difficult for faculty to offer high-quality experiences in three-credit packages, these arrangements make it difficult for part-time students to produce the same quality of effort that they could if they were full-time students. Quality takes a back seat to expediency.

TRADITIONAL TEACHING METHODS

Traditional teaching expectations also constrain practice- and problem-oriented approaches to the training of educational administrators. Faculty have been socialized by their own experience, too often reinforced by their own need to dominate less powerful students. Nontraditional teaching approaches also take more time and preparation, as does reading papers and field notes, not to mention supplying feedback about writing and thinking abilities and providing opportunities for improvements in these areas.

Typical teaching evaluation methods, namely student satisfaction surveys, also do not support innovation or risk-taking. Most students expect teachers to give them information and test them for it, just as they have been taught throughout their formal education, and most evaluation instruments are designed to assess this approach. If a professor deviates and requires students to become engaged in their own learning, to undertake field studies or critical analyses of research or of current thought or practice, and to do more than listen, take notes, and regurgitate information, then evaluation scores can suffer. If scores are low, particularly if they are continuously low, they can spell trouble at review time. Thus, junior faculty tend to be conservative in how and what they teach, becoming habituated to and reinforced in such practices as they move toward tenure and promotion.

CRITERIA FOR RETENTION, TENURE, AND PROMOTION (RTP)

Universities usually define expectations for retention, tenure, and promotion in three areas: scholarship (40%), teaching (40%), and service (20%). Working closely with school people to address problems of practice (typically viewed as service) is of limited value in this hierarchy.

Even though many schools and colleges of education work to redefine criteria within these three areas to allow for alternative models of scholarship, teaching, or service (and for their interconnections), they struggle against tradition and against anti-professional school biases. Unlike the fields of medicine and law, for example, where the creation and dissemination of practice-improvement knowledge are honored, liberal arts reward systems tend to denigrate field activities. Even rhetoricians and composition professors traditionally have been second-class citizens in English faculties, where teaching students how to analyze literature has been valued over the practical skill of teaching them how write.

Another consequence of most RTP systems is that they discourage risk-taking and collaboration or other activities not perceived to have immediate payoff in publishable output for refereed journals. In educational administration programs, as in the fields of medicine, law, or English composition, impact on practice should be the goal. Reward structures, however, are like budgets; they set the policies by which we operate. It would not be rational to do otherwise.

FIELD WORK

Field work is an obvious complement to classroom-based learning, but field work carries with it multiple inhibitors. First, it often requires more effort just to get to a field location. Second, a field site rarely offers the so-called "comforts of home" (easy access to a library, a bookstore, AV equipment, telephones, computers, and the like). It usually lacks university colleagues, the peace of a closed door, or students who arrive only after their work day is over, though most field personnel take such deprivations or distractions for granted. Third, field work is perceived as difficult to relate to one's retention, tenure, or promotion, because the university's model of scholarship remains steeped in ivory tower traditions that look askance at more professional models of knowledge production and dissemination. The academic model continues to value refereed publications as the dominant exchange for retention. Its interpretation in many schools and colleges of education also places a premium on solitary, data-based, statistical products. For education, and educational administration professors particularly, this expectation too often leads to trivial research pursuits. And all the while, field personnel remain dismayed at the inapplicability of much of what universities call "research."

TIME

Field work also takes time. And, when various activities compete for precious resources, those with the most determining power usually win. Besides campus-based teaching activities with all of the preparation and follow-up they require, campus governance, curriculum maintenance or reform, institutional reviews, external accreditation processes, and the like consume major amounts of time and important energies. Their significance is affirmed every time an untenured faculty member is told to limit her or his service activities to protect time for teaching and scholarship—while being told that some service is necessary to ensure collegiality and later support. For most newer faculty, the message is usually quite clear: spend time on research that can be done quickly (not field or qualitative research), because the quantity of scholarly production is what counts.

For established professors of educational administration, institutional demands on time include late-night classes for part-time students who cannot get away from their full-time, day-time employment. Yet these late classes are coupled with institutional nine-to-five operations (including work done by secretaries, administrators, and support services). Governance and other maintenance requirements include morning meetings, thus producing long days, interrupted research activities, and little time for field work.

RESEARCH VERSUS SERVICE AND FIELD ACTIVITIES

In reality, most educational administration programs train practitioners who return to the field. A few programs may focus on training professors or researchers, but many of their graduates also return to the field. Some of these field practitioners eventually may become professors, but often not until the end of their field careers.

As we know too well, it is not impact on practice but scholarly productivity that measures worth in higher education. Yet, for professors of educational administration—and for most professors in schools and colleges of education—it is field service, working on problems of practice, that our field colleagues most cherish. The conflict is resolved, of course, in survival terms: those who do extensive field service or field research learn quickly that such efforts bring few rewards, are lightly regarded, and can lead to unfavorable retention decisions by their primary institutions. Or, those who do invest themselves in field service or field research learn to publish from it—no small trick, given the orientation of refereed journals and the criteria for association presentations—or get paid as consultants to compensate for lack of university advancement.

How research is defined also affects how one's work is perceived and rewarded. If it is assumed, for example, that a course or two in statistics, usually taught in so-called "data-free" classrooms, is sufficient to inoculate students with enough methodological understanding to make them effective researchers, then it is also likely that statistically based research by faculty will be valued by those making retention decisions—and that other inquiry products will not be valued. Such views prevail, despite the need for significant research on real problems that have meaning for the students, faculty, and field, and use methods and techniques appropriate to the problem at hand. Without such meaning, the research injection will never produce quality results. And continued focus on trivial research to complete the program or get tenure will not solve the difficult problems of improving practice.

URBAN INSTITUTIONS

Collaborative activities are also less likely to occur in urban institutions where faculty or sites are not in proximity to one another. Faculty, usually widely dispersed throughout an urban area, generally tend not to get together outside of the university. Unlike their small-college counterparts, who often live close to one another and frequently socialize, urban faculty tend to be more isolated, establishing non-university friendship circles. Further, faculty generally must compete for scarce resources inside the university, which include merit pay and short- and long-term retention. Departmental structures reinforce isolation and discourage interdisciplinary activity because so-called "turf" battles over credit hours, faculty lines, and other resources often make it undesirable to associate with other faculty members.

While the availability of sites for research and service in urban areas is much greater than in non-urban areas, proximity also plays a role. Simple convenience can often determine whether a faculty member will take on the tasks associated with an urban research or service site. Faculty who actually live in an urban area may be more likely to engage with urban schools, while faculty living in outlying, suburban areas may be more inclined to work with schools located in those areas. Since faculty often cannot afford to live in urban housing close to their campuses, the tendency is to live in suburbs and commute. The inconvenience of distance makes it easy to rationalize limiting time on campus or in urban schools.

Field Relations

Field sites, and the personnel who staff them, also are structured not to facilitate cooperative problem solving. The bureaucratic nature of schools—time schedules, rules, and the like—works to the detriment of school-university partnerships. For example, to work with teachers requires pulling them from their classroom or otherwise disrupting their teaching activities, meeting during their lunch or preparation periods, or meeting before or after school. Meeting after school is often difficult, as university faculty in schools of education teach afternoon and evening classes. Meeting before school is often inconvenient since it makes for long days for both university and school faculty. Meeting during the day, while easier on a university schedule, is more problematic for the school teacher who is free only for short periods of time. Administrators in schools can be more flexible, but they, too, are hindered by the flow of the school day.

Further, the cultures of the two institutions differ greatly with universities generally valuing knowledge creation and inquiry processes and schools valuing established knowledge and pedagogy. Although the so-called "teachers-as-inquirers" process is now widely discussed, most teachers have not been trained to be inquirers and their work lives and settings are not designed to support or reward such behaviors. Further, just as universities reward individualized research and scholarly activity to the detriment of cooperative, collaborative efforts, the schools reward classroom teaching, not inquiry or collaboration with university partners, and thus inhibit cooperative activities.

The Nature of Faculty Work

How faculty do what they do is another impediment to achieving reform in the training of educational administrators and the reform of schooling practices. First, it is simply easier to teach in classrooms than it is to work or teach in the field. Instruction in classrooms follows time-honored tradition, permits universities explicit means of accounting for professional activities, and is less difficult than conducting classes at inconvenient or poorly equipped field sites. Additionally, classroom-based teaching tends to be more lecture- than problem-oriented because it seems to be easier to dominate through knowledge than it is to apply knowledge to the difficult problems of practice. Even though classroom teaching is challenging and requires well-grounded and configured lecture notes and, maybe, an entertaining style, field work is often more difficult and demands flexibility, the capacity for dealing with uncertainty, and the willingness to include students as equals in the learning enterprise. Field activities involve real-time applications of knowledge to practice, something practitioners must do daily.

Second, while some programs are moving toward more problem-based curricula, such curricula still tend to be classroom-based.

That is, simulations, case studies, micro-problems, video- or computer-based activities still only represent reality in the comfortable confines of campus classrooms. Action-oriented project design and implementation is much harder to achieve and much more difficult to control than simulations. Thus, such field-based learning in cooperative groups generally is rare.

The time required for field-based learning is also much less controllable than that for campus-based learning, where credits and clock hours provide structure. In the field, while credits and clock hours may set the framework, reality almost always overtakes ideality. Field problems, and the people who care about them, simply do not fit into neat time blocks. Solving field problems is distinguished more by lack of structure and by the problem's requirements than by the clock.

Third, good field work, particularly service, is characterized by team work—groups of people working together, sharing ideas and strategies, assuming responsibility for parts of larger tasks, and lending expertise where needed. On the other hand, faculty work typically involves one individual instructing several others. It is harder, most recognize, to team-teach than it is to teach alone. Besides allocating additional time for conferences to establish course content and responsibility, to plan sessions, to debrief, and to react to papers and other assignments, faculty must share their authority in order to work with other faculty. They must also be able to take occasional criticism from a colleague, be willing to teach in the company of a partner, and have their standards and grading practices scrutinized by a peer. For many, such vulnerability is too threatening.

Fourth, most faculty, particularly in educational administration, are not broadly trained in research methods, and field inquiry requires a broad base of research expertise, because problems generate methods, not the reverse. Thus, field problems require a comprehensive research background or the ability to recognize the nature of problems and find needed research capability in fairly short order. Too often, problems are molded to fit existing expertise, thus either trivializing the problem or missing the mark altogether. In fact, the primary data-gathering technique, especially in educational administration, tends to be the survey, when more anthropologically grounded methods probably should be used instead. Further, the psychological-positivistic model tends to dominate training in research in most schools or colleges of education. In educational administration, however, problems of organization, structure, decision making, policy, and so forth are often neither psychologically based nor profitably subject to experimental designs or parametric analyses. Rather, narrative descriptions, intensive interviewing and content analysis, participant observation, longitudinal designs, and cultural analyses may be more appropriate approaches.

Fifth, site-based activities frequently are time intensive, requiring significant investments that often have little immediate payoff. And the time demands of the methods appropriate to assess school-based difficulties can create problems of scholarly productivity, particularly for newer faculty. Except for zealous users of non-positivist methods, the pressures of the "publish or perish" regime lead away from time-intensive efforts toward so-called "quick-and-dirty" research activities that assist institutional glorification, not necessarily school improvement.

Sixth, for similar reasons, facilitating learning about decision-making and research techniques through data-based exercises tends to be less prevalent than simply learning about the techniques themselves, the formulae, if you will. Typically, classroom-based chalk-board and paper-and-pencil exercises relate almost not at all to real-world problem identification, assessment, and resolution. This problem has not decreased significantly even with the advent of computers, which make the use of data sets for analysis, interpretation, and application exercises more practical. Suggesting that faculty also take the next step and work with students to define variables and collect real data as part of the process of learning the use of research tools is, according to some, tantamount to suggesting that faculty double their workload.

Power Relations

Power relations in higher education also work against constructive alternatives to the status quo. Junior faculty are usually just that: junior in status, perceived ability, in all of the things that count; they are, in a word, powerless. To earn equality, they must prove themselves by managing a series of hurdles over seven-plus years. These hurdles often are even more difficult to surmount for minorities, who must overcome additional stereotypes. Thus, it is no wonder that professors view students in similar lights, making them even more junior than newer faculty. The possibilities for collaboration, then, are limited to those few faculty who express and act upon interests in collegiality and co-equality.

Complicating matters is the issue of gender. Who has not heard of the "old boys" network? "Young boys," and particularly women, are systematically excluded from the network, as are male and female students. The travesty of this system is heightened for practitioners who want to gain more knowledge or credentials. To do so, they must submit to the indignities of this status system when they are already competent, well-paid adults who bring with them considerable expertise, expertise that is often at direct odds with the expertise of campus-bound faculty.

The difference in university-student culture and the culture of practice for students in educational administration programs creates additional problems. Graduate students in educational administration who operate in an oral environment on a day-to-day basis must submit to expression primarily through writing. They must also sit passively, absorbing dispensed knowledge, when their operational world demands active engagement in problems and issues. Finally, in contrast to the teamwork (or at least a sense of the corporate whole and the place of ones' work within it) valued in their practice settings, individualism and isolation are the norm in university classrooms, just as they are for faculty success.

Instrumentalism

Students, too, contribute to the inefficacy of learning in educational administration programs. Many view their graduate education as purely instrumental, having little to do with intellect or moral values and everything to do with obtaining the so-called "union card" that secures their financial future or lets them escape from the perceived (and too often real) dead end of classroom teaching. State certification requirements, which drive most preservice training programs, only add to this view. University programs often translate state certification requirements into fairly lock-step, traditionally conceived, technically oriented courses that rarely challenge assumptions, force students to clarify their values and become sensitive to those of others, or test theory against practice.

Further, because most preservice and other programs in educational administration are filled with part-time students, it is the rare student today who can afford to attend to her or his enlightenment full-time. They expect—and are expected—to take an instrumental approach to getting their degree. This attitude is reinforced by campus-based courses offered in late afternoon and evening, when the rest of the campus is closed for the day and few student services are available. Late afternoon classes, following busy workdays, prevent most students from doing more than jumping hurdles, cramming for exams, hurriedly writing papers, and immediately discarding the knowledge used to get the grade needed to maintain their self-image or their graduate status. This forgotten knowledge is too often irretrievable when situations arise in practice that might benefit from its application. Think of the number of students who do not pick up papers or final exams at the end of a course. By this action alone, feedback and intellectual growth do not seem to be highly valued—or expected.

Some Ways to Reduce or Eliminate These Constraints

Regardless of these barriers, many of us have worked or are working to change what we do and how we do it, and notable successes exist. Unfortunately, progress has been too slow on too many fronts. Even so, some of the ways to reduce or eliminate these constraints may be relatively simple, although we often make complex excuses for why we do not try them. Usually, reforms fail because they are not in the self-interest of those who could make them work. Inevitably, individual commitment to reform must be supported, reinforced, and rewarded by institutional commitment to reform.

The following brief and tentative agenda for reform addresses only a few of the barriers or constraints identified. It is up to each and all of us, working together dialectically, within and across programs, to face the challenges and recognize that only we can change the institutional barriers that impede progress.

Institutional Support

The most effective means for changing how educational administration and other education faculty approach their tasks is to change criteria for retention, tenure, and promotion. The answer is not to do away with the standards themselves. The traditional expectations—scholarship, teaching, and service—are what makes universities distinctive. All three do, in fact, facilitate contributions to knowledge about, understanding of, and improvements in field practices. Rather, the criteria—the bases for assessing the expectations or standards—need to reflect what must be done to focus more intensively on improving practice. Issues of how faculty spend their time, what role field work plays in their regimen, and how collaboration is supported can be addressed by closely aligning RTP criteria with preferred outcomes in these areas. That is, teaching, research, and service must be seen as an integrated whole, in which field service activities—teaching and research for improved practice—play a prominent role. When the criteria used to reward faculty effort match the school or college mission and when both match the agenda for reform, faculty will be far more likely to pursue the stated mission.

Even though individual autonomy is honored in academe, the decision to change criteria is not an individual one. As it now stands, most schools and colleges of education simply acquiesce to traditional academic criteria, often called the "arts and sciences" model. Instead, they need to build and sustain practice-oriented models more appropriate to a professional school and the delivery of services—including research—that improve practice. Essentially, institutional value has to be placed on, and norms of expectation developed for, practice improvement as a respected and rewarded outcome of teaching, research, and service.

Just as unit-based decisions on retention, tenure, and promotion are made according to standards adopted by schools and colleges, so can schools and colleges decide to reward faculty for their work. Schools and colleges must determine what activities serve the best interests of their primary constituencies—children, schools, and communities as well as their students—and then devise the appropriate criteria to encourage, support, and reward faculty for such activities. No formulae exist, and every faculty must undertake the arduous task of redefining their collective interests through the process of redefining individual interests.

And the window of opportunity to make necessary changes is open wide now. Given the continuing ferment in education and the struggles that confront educators—teachers, professors, school administrators, activist parents, and governors alike—many higher educational institutions are searching for ways to improve their relations with elementary and secondary education and the rest of the educational establishment.

As the criteria change, so too can many of the other institutional factors that constrain more professional approaches to educating administrative practitioners. An integrated approach to teaching, research, and service in the field can decrease the deleterious effects of field work, for example, by making it an essential part of each professor's regimen. Hiring and other intake decisions can then be geared to this expectation, perhaps resulting in new faculty whose skills are better aligned with such a mission.

Connected to redefinitions of RTP are changes in how we teach. While problem-based orientations are gaining credibility and use, in-class simulations of real-world problems are simply insufficient substitutes for real-life, hands-on, field-based activities that require students and professors alike to grapple with the application of knowledge to the difficult problems of practice. Much of what is now taught in traditional educational administration programs could better be learned in the field in practice settings, under the joint tutelage of university- and field-based professors. Thus, cooperative agreements are needed to ensure that field labs are available for problem-oriented activities and that students can be available during school hours to work with field practitioners on the problems they need to solve. While field people are learning from us, we can learn from them.

This strategy will, of course, require that some learning experiences be exported to field sites and may require that instructional packages be reconfigured into application units, as opposed to the content units dear to state departments, accrediting bodies, and university accountants. Rethinking curricula and how it is delivered might lead to developing what we might call "learning packets" for self-directed study on important topics that do not deserve full course credit, to moving to the field instructional activities that are more appropriately learned in hands-on applications, and to fostering real-life problem-solving activities that make a difference in educational outcomes. As working in the field becomes part of the daily regimen, perceptions of the detrimental effects of field activities can be reduced and the time they require seen as a contribution to one's research and advancement. Moving course-related activities to the field can also help integrate teaching, research, and service. They become virtually one and the same, with all three collaborators (students, practitioners, and faculty) learning from one another as they work to solve problems of practice.

Such changes also may excite long overdue—and involved—discussions about faculty load. How universities account for faculty time might change with learning outcomes, programs completed, and impact on practice becoming the new currency. Even now, course credits are insufficient measures of faculty work. The integration of teaching, research, and service in application units aimed at practice improvement provides a more complex but more defensible basis for calculating faculty loads. The university and the faculty need to devise better, more portfolio-like measures of work and work products.

Money issues, often the ones most easily invoked to explain why changes cannot occur, become somewhat moot in this scenario.

Collaborating with schools to improve practice suggests that schools would take a much more active and equal role in identifying personnel who might be sponsored as teacher trainees or receive advanced training. Programs would not be able to take all comers because job slots would not exist for them and school districts would not be able to afford investing in their career development. Thus, combined approaches to selecting and training school administrators would have at least two dramatic effects: what we might term the immediate "down-sizing" of the numbers of students in most collaborative, field-based programs, and the availability of more full-, three-quarter-, or half-time students. Cooperative arrangements like these between districts and universities might become the norm as state departments and higher educational governing bodies examine the costs involved in preparing anyone who passes minimal entry requirements for programs leading to certification or licensure. Such an approach requires all of us to challenge the traditional credit-by-credit, cash-cow mentality with the benefits to the community of better-trained school administrators, better-led schools, and the long-run economic and social benefits of better-educated children.

Urban institutions in particular can benefit from consortial arrangements with area districts, and the numbers of minorities and women served by such programs should increase significantly. New credibility can be gained by those metropolitan universities that roll up their institutional sleeves, get into the trenches along with those who fight every day to educate urban children, and show by action, not rhetoric, that they are willing to effect the hard changes necessary to improve the life chances of future generations of inner-city children.

Field Relations

The gulf between school or college of education outcome values and those of elementary and secondary institutions keeps each at arm's length from the other. Neither trusts the other because their purposes are perceived as conflicting ones. Focusing on problems of practice, however, could be central to both. Improved relations with people in elementary and secondary schools are likely when RTP criteria are reconceptualized to integrate research, teaching, and service; when field practitioners are included in the selection and training of students; when schools become laboratories that facilitate examining problems of practice; when cooperative problem solving becomes the principal means by which to learn methodologies; and when university expectations and learning cultures are more carefully matched to the real needs of field people and sites. As university people get serious by changing what is rewarded and demonstrating their commitment to practice improvement, school people will take them seriously.

The Nature of Faculty Work

With broader movement toward field-based learning, teaching with field practitioners will become natural, as will using field problems as the primary focus of attention for students, university faculty, and practitioners. University classroom simulations, useful to a point, will take a back seat to on-site project design and implementation. Under this model, more, and more intensive, time would be spent by university faculty with students and their field counterparts jointly diagnosing problems, determining knowledge needed to address the problem, and trying on ways to solve the problem. Credits and clock hours in this scenario would become less effective both for arranging learning experiences and for managing them. As indicated earlier, measures of the integration of teaching, research, and service may try university accountants, but better methods need to be found to ensure close cooperation among learners, to help them master what they need to learn where it needs to be learned.

Power Relations

Processes of collegial inquiry can eventually break down traditional status and power differences. As common ground is discovered in the process of solving difficult problems of practice, university professors, students, and field practitioners can be strengthened by their interdependence, and power will decline as an issue. The problems of practice can become the dominant focus.

Instrumentalism

Connecting learning to solving problems and making eventual state licensing heavily dependent upon demonstrating practical, knowledge-based, practice-improvement skills could decrease further the mismatch between current university expectations and student needs. Knowledge applied to problems is retained better for later retrieval and use. Students, sponsored and supported by their districts, can spend more time learning what they need to know to be effective practitioners.

Many of us have long been engaged in pursuing ways to reform what we do, learning as we go, seeking more ways to teach, to use research to improve practice, and to work more closely with the field. For too long, however, we have not done much to change the conditions or methods of our work. The problems we face are both the product of our institutional histories and our individual preferences. The time is ripe for demonstrable, essential change. So far, even the mightiest rhetoric of the most august commissions has had little impact.

Organizational Counterproductivism in Educational Administration

Michael Imber

I recently took a poll of educational administrators and trainees, in which I asked them what they know about running schools and leading education that the average person does not know. To those who professed not to understand the question, I asked that they think about how they would respond to claims that educational administration is no more than common sense, that training is unconnected to the work that administrators actually do, and that schools would be just as effective if they hired their leaders from among the general public rather than those with training and experience in education and administration. My goal in asking these questions was to begin to get an empirical handle on the knowledge base of educational administration or, to put it more simply, to find out what, if anything, educational administrators actually know.

While some of my subjects, even after considerable prodding, were unable to respond or could offer only vague generalities, such as "I know how to run a school," most did claim to possess special knowledge that qualified them for the administrative jobs they held or desired. Many of them—perhaps at least partly in deference to my position as a professor of educational administration specializing in education law—suggested that they knew the things that had been taught in their courses. As one subject put it, "I know ed. law, finance, personnel, curriculum, all the courses." When asked to be more specific about what he knew in law that helped him do his job, he responded, "Student Rights," and on further prodding, "I know that you can't expel a student without a hearing." Similarly, respondents often offered facts or lists of facts that they believed bore directly on successful performance of administrative tasks. These usually related to legal or other concrete constraints on administrator prerogatives and much less frequently to organizational or pedagogical theory or to psychology, philosophy or other "foundations" of education.

However, some respondents did offer theories or at least generalizations that they claimed play a significant role in guiding their practice. Some of these generalizations came from research ("The more time spent studying a subject, the more a student will tend to learn it"; "Tracking doesn't work"), while others were the product of experience or intuition ("The best thing I can do as a principal is to hire good teachers and let them teach"). Some of the intuitive theories seemed to contradict research findings ("Students learn more in small classes"). As the examples illustrate, some of the generalizations were pedagogical while others (far fewer) related to schools as organizations. Finally, some respondents offered intensely practical theories of administration: "The most important thing I do is to keep the parents and school board happy."

Academic Discipline vs. Field of Practice

Conspicuously absent from the responses to my poll was any mention of the kind of theory often emphasized in organizational theory and general administration courses and in the literature of educational administration. Noone spoke of the difficulties involved in trying to change bureaucracies or schools. Noone said, "I believe in contingency theory, so my approach is to. . ." or, "Poststructural feminist theory has taught me that. . ." or, "Behaviorism is the basis of my practice," or even, "My approach to administration is theoretically eclectic." Nor did any implicit theoretical foundation for practice emerge from any of the conversations beyond the mostly experientially-based generalizations discussed above.

The pattern of response to my inquiries suggests a wide gap between educational administration as an academic discipline and educational administration as a field of practice. At the very least, there seems to be a great deal of difference between what professors teach and write about and what practitioners say they know and do. The situation is analogous to a group of working economists failing to mention theories of markets or pricing or concepts like supply and demand in discussions of their work, or to physicists viewing their jobs as unconnected to relativity, quantum theory, or classical mechanics.

The seeming irrelevance of theory to the practical work of educational administrators calls into question the status of both theorists and practitioners. If those whose job is to apply the teachings of an academic discipline find little connection between the theoretical core of their training and their actual work, does the theory lose its legitimacy? (Is it a dance party if people come but no one dances?) On the other hand, does not professional status require application of systematically derived knowledge, the possession of which separates professionals from the laity. (If those on the dance floor pay no attention to the music or the prescribed steps, are they still dancing?)

Curiously, however, almost all the administrators I talked to claimed that their training had been very useful to them. In support of this view, they most often referred once again to specific facts that they needed in order to deal with their job-related tasks. Perhaps it is the nature of applied fields that their knowledge bases consist of sets of principles and facts that relate to the performance of specific tasks by practitioners. Some of these facts may be derived from and serve to confirm central theories within the academic discipline that supports the field, but the theories themselves may be too far removed from practice to have any direct effect. In medicine, for example, doctors typically have knowledge of the structure and function of the human body and its parts and of the etiology, pathology, and treatment of disease, but they may be less aware of the theoretical bases that set allopathic medicine apart from homeopathic or chiropractic medicine.

Three Categories of Knowledge in Educational Administration

The knowledge that my respondents claimed to possess falls into three somewhat overlapping categories. (Any profession's knowledge could probably be similarly divided.) The first category, which I call *theoretical knowledge*, consists of specialized theory-based knowledge that relates to the accomplishment of the fundamental goals of education (or of the relevant profession). Theories and principles that make it possible for administrators to plan and execute programmatic changes that result in increased student learning or otherwise enhance educational outcomes fall into this category. These theories and principles are the primary subject matter of many courses in administrative and organizational theory, supervision, leadership, and, to a lesser extent, planned change, personnel, and instructional leadership.

However, as mentioned, with the exception of a few generalizations, mostly in the area of pedagogy and mostly based on experience ("Kids learn at different rates"), this type of knowledge was rarely claimed by the administrators with whom I spoke. The impressive body of literature documenting the unfocused nature and dismal record of educational reform efforts, whether large-scale or small, supports the contention that educational administrators generally possess little relevant theoretical knowledge. Even the occasional administrator or consultant who can claim knowledge of, say, structuralism (or poststructularism) seems unable to utilize that knowledge to exercise control over schools or to make kids learn more.

The second category of knowledge that educational administrators may claim to possess is *technical knowledge*. Technical knowledge consists of information that relates to the performance of the various specific tasks involved in running a school or school system, such as the maintenance of school facilities, the creation of schedules, the minimization of litigation risks, and the procurement of books and supplies. Technical knowledge is most often expressed as facts (School prayer is illegal), collections of facts (How to make a budget), and principles (The Constitution is the highest law.) The application of technical knowledge may promote the realization of educational goals, generally in an incremental way, and thus contribute to successful school administration.

Most of the knowledge that my respondents claimed to possess falls into this category, as does much of what is taught in most administrative training programs, especially in courses, such as educational law, finance, facilities management, and personnel. Here we seem to have consistency between at least some of what administrators have been taught and what they claim to know. An emphasis on technical knowledge is also consistent with the hypothesis offered above, that the knowledge base of applied fields generally consists of sets of facts and principles that are directly applicable to the perfnmance of the tasks of the profession.

Perhaps, then, it is the case that the specialized knowledge of educational administration consists primarily of technical knowledge rather than theoretical knowledge. Perhaps what sets qualified school administrators apart from lay people is that, like doctors, administrators know and are able to make use of large amounts of information that lay people do not possess. In other words, as a result of their training and experience, administrators may have attained a sort of professional cultural literacy that makes it possible for them to effectively lead schools.

If this is the case, it ought to be possible to list many facts that school administrators or specific categories of school administrators could be expected to possess and employ in their practice. This list would constitute the bulk of the knowledge base of the field. (One could create such a list for most medical specialties—e.g. diagnostic criteria for various diseases, standard dosages of drugs—or for skilled trades such as electrician.) In my specific area of teaching, education law, there is indeed a long list of facts and principles that I believe should be known by all school administrators. The question, then, is this: Do administrators know these facts?

Karla Liebham, a student of mine, recently surveyed a group of practicing high school principals with regard to one such set of facts—their knowledge and understanding of the Equal Access Act. One third of those surveyed admitted no knowledge of the Act. Of those who claimed to have heard of it, more than half incorrectly believed that it had to do with providing disabled people access to the school building. Only about one in five principals could come close to accurately stating the requirements of the law, even though it is directly applicable to all their schools. Previous studies of this type, as well as my own interviews and conversations with practicing administrators suggest a similar lack of knowledge of even the most basic principles of education law. I suspect that the same findings would obtain with regard to the other areas of technical knowledge that educational administrators claim to possess and preparation programs claim to teach. In fact, I think it would be very difficult to list any facts or principles needed to successfully lead a school that most school administrators possess, but that the general public does not.

Career knowledge is the third kind of knowledge that administrators sometimes claim to possess. Unlike theoretical and technical knowledge, career knowledge has nothing to do with successful performance of the tasks of school administration or realization of the goals of education. Rather, career knowledge is knowledge that enhances the quality of an administrator's work life. It is the knowledge one needs to be hired and retained as a school administrator and the knowledge that leads to greater comfort, security, satisfaction, or likelihood of advancement on the job. Career knowledge includes knowing how to prepare a resumé, how to perform at an interview (including perhaps appearing to have theoretical and factual knowledge whether one does or not), how to fit into a bureaucracy, to dress, to make small talk, and generally to relate to parents, bosses, school boards, students, and the various other constituencies that can affect an administrator's career. Much of career knowledge has to do with public relations. (I am not claiming that knowledge and ability in human relations is irrelevant to attaining the goals of schooling, only that some human relations skills may be used to advance an individual's career in ways that are irrelevant or even contrary to the goals of schooling.) A number of my respondents claimed this type of knowledge, especially with regard to their ability to keep parents happy. The very fact that they are employed in the field indicates that all school administrators possess at least some career knowledge. Training programs do not usually emphasize career knowledge with anything like the enthusiasm they show for theoretical and technical knowledge, although most probably touch on it (perhaps some more than they would like to admit), especially in courses taught by practicing administrator-adjunct professors.

What Educational Administrators Really Know

What, then, is the operational knowledge base of educational administration as a field of practice? In other words, what knowledge do administrators actually employ in their work? First, theoretical knowledge seems to have almost no effect on what educational administrators do. I base this conclusion both on my survey and on the fact that neither the theoretical nor the practical literature of the field seems to make any claim to the contrary. Even the staunchest theoreticians do not claim that administrators use theory to shape their practice, let alone to achieve the organizational results they seek. At most, their claim is that the theories they profess serve to explain, after the fact, the actions of administrators and the organizational outcomes of those actions. Even if we accept this claim, theory has no effect on what administrators do; it only enhances our understanding of why they acted as they did. Thus, unlike the knowledge base of educational administration as it is taught in universities, the knowledge base of educational administration as a field of practice contains little or no theoretical knowledge.

Second, educational administrators vary greatly with regard to the technical knowledge they possess. Unlike doctors or, I suspect, practitioners of a wide range of professions and skilled trades, educational administrators are unable to list a significant number of technical facts, principles, or skills, that all practitioners of the field, but not outsiders, can be expected to know. Indeed, it is difficult to list even a single fact or principle that all educational administrators are required to know. Most of the specialized knowledge that administrators claim to possess is general, intuitive, and learned through experience on the job.

To be sure, some educational administrators are familiar with a large number of facts and principles concerning pedagogy, instructional leadership, and educational law, finance, personnel, and building management, but many of these knowledgeable administrators do not regularly employ their specialized knowledge when performing their jobs. The administrators I spoke with were rarely able to identify specific aspects of their practice that were based on whatever specialized knowledge they claimed to possess. Some made general claims, for instance that their work with students was based on their knowledge of child development, but even these administrators could not say how they might act differently if they did not know about development.

Nor does utilizing whatever factual knowledge they do possess seem to be a high priority for school administrators. Fewer than half the principals who responded to the Equal Access Act survey had policies that were consistent with the Act, whether they were familiar with it or not. Those who were familiar with the Act seemed to view it more as an intrusion than as a guide to practice. Only about five percent of all schools surveyed had altered their policies in response to the Act, in each case as a result of controversy or threat of litigation. Thus, the large majority of administrators simply continued to do as they wished or as directed by their central administrators and school board, with no particular concern for complying with the law. Compliance occurred only by coincidence or when necessary to avoid trouble.

Third, all educational administrators, like all practitioners of every profession, possess career knowledge. By definition, they must not only possess but also utilize a certain amount of career knowledge to obtain and retain their jobs. Moreover, most administrators, again like most practitioners of every profession, also possess and utilize additional career knowledge that contributes to the quality of their work life. Even when they are part of an organization, all people will work to promote their own ends.

This is not in itself problematic as long as the utilization of career knowledge does not impede good practice. Ideally, any profession's practitioners' career knowledge should include the knowledge that rewards will come from possessing as much theoretical and technical knowledge as exists within the field and utilizing this knowledge to the greatest extent possible. In other words, for a profession to function well, its practitioners must know that the same actions will promote both the goals of the organization and their careers, in other words, that they will be rewarded if they do a good job. Presumably, this is the case for doctors and electricians, whose practices will thrive if they achieve a high rate of success with their clients.

This is often not the case for educational administrators, however, for whom the course of action implied by career knowledge often contradicts the course implied by technical knowledge. Administrators often find themselves in positions where to do what their training or the literature of the field or the best interest of their students says is right and proper would actually be detrimental to their enjoyment of their careers. For example, of the many courses of action available to a principal dealing with an incompetent teacher, attempted remediation, followed, if successful, by close monitoring and if unsuccessful, by dismissal, may be the most educationally sound. But every step of this process can be time-consuming and painful and has the potential to create friction between the administrator and teachers, the union, parents and even the school board. In many situations, alternative courses of action that are educationally indefensible, such as transferring the teacher or doing nothing at all, are far less likely to diminish the quality of the administrator's work life.

This explains why so few of the principals in the Equal Access Act survey keep up with developments in education law and why so few were concerned with complying with the Act unless forced to do so. Many realized long ago that neither their employers nor the public cares if they are technically knowledgeable and that to insist on doing what is educationally, morally, or legally right often leads to personal trouble for them. Administrators are bureaucrats who must preserve their own place within the organization. And for most educational administrators, survival requires that career knowledge be put first.

The firing of Joseph Fernandez as chancellor of the New York City schools illusrates this point. Many of Fernandez's most vocal detractors, including several of the school board members who voted to fire him, said that they believed he was a good educator, that he always tried to do what was best for kids, and that the schools were going in the right direction under his leadership. On the other hand, even his supporters admitted that his firing was probably inevitable because he was not politically adept. According to local and national media that covered the story, Fernandez's political problems stemmed from his lack of tact and deference in dealing with parents, special interest groups, political leaders, and the board. New York Mayor David Dinkins summed up the situation as follows: "Regrettably, . . . sound educational policy took a back seat to parochial politics." Regrettable perhaps, but not surprising or unusual.

By contrast, Philadelphia's superintendent, Constance Clayton, has received much notice and praise for the political skill that kept her in office for more than ten years. A recent *New York Times* article noted that unlike Fernandez, who received much criticism and lost support when he spearheaded a condom distribution program, Clayton was able to avoid any negative consequences from a similar program in her schools by having the school board initiate the program. Never mind that in both cities the board is ultimately responsible for policy and that both administrators' roles are the same; namely, to make recommendations to the board and to implement the programs they approve. Nor did the article say one word about whether either program was successful from an educational, social, or medical standpoint or justified from a moral one. The only thing that really mattered was that Fernandez's program was detrimental to his career but Clayton's was not.

Educational Administration as an Academic Discipline

If this analysis is correct, the question arises as to why professors of educational administration continue to teach and write about theories that have little or no potential to affect the work that educational administrators actually do. Part of the answer is that professors behave as they do in response to their own career knowledge and to the demands of the organizations for which they work. First, most educational administration professors, at least at research universities, have a dual function: examination and explanation (research) and preparation of practitioners. Because theory often seems valuable as an explanatory tool, they may assume that it will serve equally well in practice. In any case, theory provides pedagogical matter that is weighty, impressive, and interesting to teach. It also serves the interest of students by imbuing their training with a complexity and mystery that justifies their future status as professionals. (This last point helps to explain why administrators tend to avow the benefits of their training while ignoring much of what they were taught.)

Second, an emphasis on theory enhances the legitimacy and status of educational administration as a university discipline, and thus the legitimacy and status of professors of educational administration within the university. At most research universities, educational administration must engage in a continual process of self-justification. One way to succeed in this process is to appear to be as similar to the high-status disciplines, especially the hard sciences, as possible. A theoretical knowledge base is a key element in maintaining this appearance, however irrelevant the knowledge base may be to practitioners of the field.

This is not to suggest that educational administration training programs are irrelevant, or that they should be shut down. Educational administration is an extremely complex task, one that cannot possibly be performed effectively without a great deal of technical knowledge. Insofar as administrator training programs stress the knowledge that can aid in the realization of educational outcomes, they fulfill a crucial function. Unfortunately, the current system of educational organization and governance makes it impossible for many administrators to apply much of their technical knowledge of the field. In effect, they can have successful careers without doing a good job. This explains why many administrators may undervalue the possession of technical knowledge, but it does not justify their abandoning this knowledge.

Nor am I suggesting that universities should adjust the curriculum of educational administration training programs to teach future administrators to follow in the footsteps of current administrators. The idea that the knowledge base for administration must come from practice is fallacious if interpreted to equate actual practice with desirable practice. Training in any field should impart the knowledge necessary for best practice, and in educational administration best practice requires possession of a great deal of technical knowledge.

A Professor's Conclusion

Educational administration operates with two very different knowledge bases, neither of which serves the profession very well. Professors propose a theoretically-rooted knowledge base, one in keeping with the value system of and their need for status within the university. While potentially useful for explaining and understanding, theories of administration have little value for controlling such complex organizations as schools or for creating educational outcomes.

For their part, some educational administrators possess a great deal of technical knowledge, while others have little or none. Much of this technical knowledge, if skillfully applied, can be useful in leading a school toward the attainment of its goals. But, whatever the state of their knowledge, all educational administrators are bureaucrats subject to political control, who must subordinate whatever technical knowledge they possess to career knowledge. Some administrators find themselves in situations where having and applying a great deal of technical knowledge is valued and rewarded, but the majority do not. For most administrators, career success depends on a knowledge base that is often irrelevant and sometimes contrary to the promotion of educational goals.

Since I am a professor, I suppose I should validate the ideas I am proposing by anointing them as a theory and labelling them with an *ism*. I therefore offer the term *organizational counterproductivism* to describe a situation in which members of a profession can enhance their own careers or the quality of their work lives by acting in ways that detract from the goals of the profession or the organization for which they work. Educational administration, both as an academic discipline and as a field of practice, is a prime example of organizational counterproductivism. It will remain so as an academic discipline as long as theory remains the sine qua non of academic legitimacy. It will remain so as a field of practice as long as education is politically controlled and bureaucratically organized.

Narrative Knowledge and Educational Administration: The Stories that Guide Our Practice

Gary L. Anderson and Bonnie Page

Before the theory movement emerged in educational administration, it was not uncommon for courses in the field to consist of the transmission of practitioner knowledge through narrative. Because of the paucity of educational administration theory, courses often consisted of the so-called "war stories" that principals and superintendents (mostly male) brought into the classroom from the "trenches." In fact, like teacher training, most administrative training (at least, that which went beyond handing over the keys to the school) was based on an apprenticeship model, in which older practitioners shared stories of practice with younger initiates.

It is important to note that these practitioner narratives constituted the knowledge base of the field and continue to do so today. Holland (1992) recounts that, "While plenty of stories get told by practitioners, they function as part of an oral craft tradition, heard only by those within earshot and fading in the air that briefly holds them" (200).

The theory movement represented an attempt to replace this knowledge base with an academic one that consisted mainly of academic narratives of organization and human motivation drawn from industrial psychology and functionalist sociology. As a field, we have paid a great price for such a dramatic shift away from practitioner knowledge. Time and again, when practitioners are asked how they learned what they know, university coursework falls near the bottom of the list (Lortie 1975; Wolcott 1976). The educational administration professoriate, however, continues to cling to an applied theory framework derived from arts and sciences. The self-flagellation that has taken place in our field for the last thirty years over our lack of theoretical maturity continues in Pohland's (1992) recent lament in the *UCEA Review*, where he states that educational administration is a "preparadigmatic field" rather than a "mature discipline". Meanwhile, the current UCEA knowlege domains reassert for the nineties the privileging of technical knowledge and a continued quest for an academic knowledge base that has given scant attention to the stories that practitioners themselves tell.

Although we believe that the UCEA knowledge domains are inadequate, if not inappropriate, the purpose of this chapter is not naively to enthrone practitioner narratives and return the knowledge base of the field to the pretheoretical knowledge of educational practitioners. First, we now know, as Argyris and Schon (1974) have so well illustrated, there is no such thing as nontheoretical practice. All practitioners have so-called "theories-in-use" which they may or may not be able to articulate. And second, an uncritical privileging of practitioner knowledge may, if Goodlad (1984), Sarason (1982), and others are right, serve to support an undesirable status quo rather than to change it. We believe that educational administrators and those who prepare them need to understand better the practitioner narratives that currently drive educational practice and the academic narratives that the educational administration professoriate promote (often unwittingly) to replace them.

Narrative and Metanarrative in Educational Administration

All of us live within a constellation of narratives, stories we are told and tell each other, which help us make sense of our lives. Educational practitioners also live within a set of narratives that serve as invisible frames for the ways they think about their practice and the actions they take. As Cherryholmes (1988) points out, narratives are often nested within larger or "meta" narratives. These metanarratives produce recurrent themes that characterize educational discourse and practices. "The substructures of many [themes] that are dominant emphasize order, accountability, structure, systematization, rationalization, expertise, specialization, linear development, and control" (9).

For example, the individual administrator's attention to standardized testing, classroom control, and linear curricula is part of a larger metanarrative that began with the enlightenment, ran through our fascination with positivism and later culminated in industrial psychology and Taylorism, out of which our factory-model schooling system emerged. Therefore, the kinds of stories we tell ourselves about schooling and the administration of schools often have their origins in older and larger stories about human nature and social organization. Some metanarratives, like the Eurocentric story of Columbus's, "discovery," the American "melting pot" story, or the Horatio Alger story about social mobility are stories deeply ingrained in the American psyche and so linked to the interests of dominant social groups that they have, in the minds of many, ceased to be stories at all, but rather are viewed as reality. This is what Sarason (1982) had in mind when he talked about the "regularities" of schooling, or those social arrangements that in the minds of so many are viewed as reality rather than as products of the stories we've been told and tell ourselves about schooling.

Only when educational practices are inconsistent with our metanarratives do we tend to change them. For example, many schools are eliminating tracking practices, in large part because academic tracking is inconsistent with the story of schools providing an equal opportunity to compete for society's goods. According to this narrative, schools must allocate students in a fair and neutral manner. As in the case of de-tracking, school reforms often represent a shoring up of a narrative that has lost coherence, rather than a shift to a new narrative. If, in fact, a new narrative is adopted about how dominant interests in society use schooling to maintain their status, then we might argue that once tracking is eliminated, these groups will find new ways to reproduce themselves.

Conflicting narratives often compete for legitimation. There is the story of heroic teachers and principals who create schools that are safe havens amidst communities of so-called "undeserving poor and minority parents," replete with "welfare queens" who buy cable TV instead of breakfast for their children. The competing narrative is one of schools as hostile places where poor and minority parents and children are victims, shut out of the white, middle-class culture of power that teachers and princlpals create and reinforce within the schools and classrooms. It should not be difficult to see how educational practices in a given school depend on which of these narratives is dominant among its teachers and administrators.

Surfacing and Problematizing
Our Knowledge Base

The notion of narrative we are elaborating here combines the out-of-awareness aspect of Argyris and Schon's (1974) "theories-in-use," the sociopolitical emphasis of Kamen's (1977) conception of "legitimating myths," and Cherryholmes (1988) use of "metanarrative." If the narratives and metanarrative that constitute our knowledge base have become invisible frames that legitimate our educational practices and discourses, then it follows that a major thrust of administrator preparation should serve to bring these narratives and metanarratives to the surface for analysis. In spite of recent attention within educational administration to case studies and reflective practice, little attempt has been made to problematize the metanarratives that serve as invisible frames for practitioner reflection.

These largely invisible and unanalyzed metanarratives seep into our administrative preparation programs and drive our school reform efforts. They tend to exist in the reified realm of the commonsensical and taken-for-granted. For this reason, any discussion of a prescriptive knowledge base for educational administration must take place within the context of the narrative knowledge base from which policy-makers, school administrators and administrative preparation programs currently operate. Administrator preparation programs and educational reform efforts whose purpose is to change the status quo will have little effect until these powerful metanarratives are made explicit and held up for analysis.

The Metanarrative of Accountability:
An Example

Accountability will be taken as an example of a metanarrative that has legitimated many educational practices during recent decades. Accountability is one of the oldest human stories. Since Adam and Eve, we have been giving account of ourselves to authority. Accountability is a frame, intractable as it is invisible, which has so permeated our culture that it is a constant, a metanarrative. Early on, the social pyramid came to represent top-down accountability. Today, hierarchies in every strata of our society play out the economy that the individual most accountable in an organization has the most status and the most wealth. That person may not be the most effective in the organization but represents the place, as Harry Truman put it, "where the buck stops." Power and athority accompany the chain of accounting up the line, accumulating at the highest levels in the sanction to make decisions over the lives, freedoms and economies of others.

If we back track from the present to understand why this so-called "accounting" changed from a relating of one's experience to the form that has generated monolithic bureaucracies, it is easy to identify the role of the printing press. It allowed for the objectification of information; the human voicing of reality was no longer a necessity. Reality could be described, measured, counted and catalogued. It could be kept in binders, books and banks far beyond the personal time of the actors in any social event.

The metanarrative of accountability has not yet paid much credence to an N of one, even though much of the literature recounts the dramatic failure of research dissemination efforts and the inability of generalizable, propositional knowledge to effect changes in educational practice (Lindlom and Cohen 1979). There is some evidence of a push against a system of hierarchical accountabilty and a return to lived experience as important knowledge. The establishment of human account as the core of social accountability apears to hold great promise for restructuring the previous accountability frame. "Our own existence," wrote the philosopher Paul Ricoer (cited in Hopkins, 1994), "cannot be separated from the account we can give of ourselves. It is in telling our own stories that we give ourselves an identity" (16). This shift is evident in innovations like portfolio assessments, cooperative learning, and increased community voice and empowerment in educational decision-making.

At the same time, another important ideological shift in accountability has occured during the last decade, one which has gone almost unperceived by educational administrators. The new instrument of accountability in education has become the free market. The metaphors of business have seeped into our field from the surrounding culture, with virtually no challenge nor analysis from educationists. Just as the metaphors of industrial psychology drove our field in the past, so now the metaphors of the marketplace have crept imperceptibly into our vocabulary. Suddenly students are *customers*; school administrators seek *ownership* and *buy-ins* for their reforms; and moral and ideological commitments are replaced by *bottom lines*. This new metanarrative incorporates many aspects of the former one. A standardized national test will allow all schools, classrooms, and teachers to be compared to each other, or in the new business lingo, "held accountable by market forces." Real estate agents can now flash up a local school's reading scores on their computers. Commercial billboards selling candy have appeared in the hallways of our public schools. In thousands of American schools, teachers are under contract to show television commercials to our children in the public space of their classroom during instructional time. A school principal was quoted in a local paper as saying, "What's the big deal; they see them at home every day."

The failure to problematize the new metanarrative of accountability may destroy the very distinctions that Dewey (1944) made between educative, noneducative, and *mis*educative experiences. Embedded in this new metanarrative are stories about human nature, in which humans are essentially competitive and competition wins out over cultural identity or ideological and moral commitment.

Many see the new accountability narrative as one promoted by corportate interests, which see the privatization of public schools as a massive new market waiting to be tapped. Chubb and Moe (1990) attempt to justify the abandonment of all public education on the grounds that choice in the educational marketplace will produce both corporate profits and educational excellence. Consider the following:

> Whittle's commercials for Snickers, Burger King, and other products on Channel One, shown in 10,000 schools, are required viewing for almost 8 million students daily—more than a third of all teenagers in the nation's schools. *U.S. News and World Report* notes that Whittle is tapping "the potential for widespread commercial penetration" of a student market in which more than $80 billion worth of products are sold yearly. At $157,000 for a 30-second ad— double the advertising rate of prime-time network news— Whittle grosses $630,000 from the four ads run each day bringing him gross annual revenues of more than $100 million. (Kozol 1992, 17)

Our purpose here is not to replace a dominant narrative about how business and free markets can save American education from the clutches of bureaucracy and mediocrity with a counter narrative of corporate greed penetrating public schools and brainwashing students with a pro-business, neoliberal ideology. The purpose rather is to make our invisible frames more visible so that we can submit them to scrutiny. Perhaps the accountability metanarrative that places human accounts over those of both standardization and the marketplace would be a more appealing one.

The accountability narrative is merely one of hundreds of stories that guide our practice. Even apparently neutral areas of our field such as law, finance, and organizational theory consist of narratives about right and wrong, equity, and the nature of organizing. How certain narratives have become dominant, and the transformations they undergo over time, should be part of the knowledge base of those who manage our schools. Only then can we fully understand that what UCEA is calling a knowledge base is, in fact, a series of domininant narratives and metanarratives. In other words, the UCEA knowledge base, as it is manifested in programs throughout the country, uncritically promotes the legitimating myths that reproduce our schools and our society from one generation to the next.

Toward a New Approach to Our Knowledge Base: Decentering Technical Knowledge

In this chapter, we have stressed the narrativity of practitioner knowledge and argued that these practitioner narratives, and the metanarratives that drive them, constitute the current knowledge base of our field. The concept of narrativity, however, provides us with a way to fully reconceptualize the preparation of educational administrators (and other educational practitioners as well) by paying attention to the ways in which narrativity is basic to all of the domains of knowledge from which administrators draw. Elsewhere, the authors have extrapolated from the narratives of school principals the various domains of knowledge that are utilized in decision-making.[1] We will briefly review these here and show how narrativity is basic to each.

We will begin with technical knowledge because it is the domain at the center of most administrative preparation programs. Academic knowedge is technical in the sense that it is propositional knowledge purporting to provide the research and theoretical justification for so-called "technical" decisions. Because we have already shown how this type of technical knowledge is embedded in metanarrative, we will concentrate here on *technical knowledge* as the nuts and bolts of educational administration. Such technical knowledge includes the more practical tasks of administration, such as knowing how to get the boiler fixed when it breaks down, how to do scheduling, how to use a data base, how to do a budget, and so forth. Administrator preparation programs make much of this type of knowledge, but, in fact, this too is narrative knowledge. Narratives about how to approach the maintenance office with a problem, how to do budgets, and how to fill out forms are shared daily among educational practitioners themselves. Nor is this knowledge free of metanarratives; One's approach to so-called technical tasks, for instance, is often a highly political story. After all, how school administrators choose to heat their buildings (gas heat over solar heat, for example) is part of a larger metanarrative about corporate interests versus environmental concerns.

Local knowledge includes the narratives that are idiosyncratic to a local school or community setting. Principals are gatherers of local narratives told by community members and school staff, and take in as well the cultural norms and social rules that those narratives reflect. Included within this domain is knowledge of local politics and local cultures and subcultures.

Craft knowledge consists of the repertoire of examples, images, understandings, and actions that practitioners build up over time. This is the domain of knowlededge that is the focus of most work on reflective practice by Schon (1983) and his numerous followers in educational administration. What these theorists fail to realize is that craft knowledge is not as neutral as many would like to suggest. Schon is fond of using the example of learning to ride a bicycle to illustrate the out-of-awareness accumulation of craft knowledge. However, the technical skill of riding a bicycle is hardly the same as the moral and ethical craft of teaching children and managing meaning in schools.[2] Craft knowledge also consists of submerged narratives and metanarratives that are embedded in practices and passed along from generation to generation.

Personal knowlege is what the Getzels and Guba model, on which we all cut our teeth, called "need disposition," in characteristically ideographic language. In fact, the notion that school administrators are human beings with life histories, genders, social class affiliations, ethnic and racial identities, sexual orientations and ideological committments, has been totally ignored within our knowledge base. For example, the experience of having raised an adolescent child is an important source of narrative knowledge for a high school principal. It's hard to imagine where narratives that administrators bring from their lives fit into our current UCEA conception of a knowledge base in educational administration.

Finally, there is a *tacit* dimension to each knowledge domain. It is usually referred to as "intuition" or as a "gut feeling" but it, too, is tied to narrative. These are the narratives that are out of awareness and therefore, not clearly articulated. This is the domain from which the metanarratives we confuse with common sense so powerfully guide the decisions we make. It is from this tacit dimension that we must foster *critical knowledge*. Critical knowledge is less a domain of new knowledge than it is the process of surfacing metanarratives for analysis.

Several models of critical reflection exist. Argyris's more recent work on double-loop learning and action science, influenced by the German critical theorist Jurgens Habermas, holds great promise (Argyris et al. 1986; Robinson 1989). Liston and Zelchner's (1991) social reconstructionist approach to teacher education, which incorporates critical reflection, journaling, and practitioner inquiry, has worked out conceptually and in practice many of the problems that a narrative approach would encounter in the preparation of administrators. The sociological paradigms of Burrell and Morgan (1979) have been used extensively in a number of fields to help illustrate how many practices are bound by paradigms, and by implication, how new perspectives can be brought to bear on the problems of practice. (Mercer in press; Adams 1988). Shakeshaft (1989) has brought to the surface and deconstructed the male metanarratives embedded in our field's theories of leadership and management. Finally, the potential for critical inquiry based on Paulo Freire's (1970) work around the "generative themes" embedded in practitioner narratives have gone virtually untapped in the field of educational administration.

Conclusion

We are not suggesting here that programs add more courses in educational foundations or social and cultural influences on schooling. The add-an approach of UCEA misses the point. Structural solutions will not address the knowedge-base problem. The additions of more courses, more hours of internship, and, our favorite marginalization strategy, the infusion of multiculturalism (or some other knowledge that is viewed as marginal) throughout the curriculum may be helpful, but ultimately serve as strategies to salvage the functionalist nature of our administrative preparation programs. Discussions should not be concerned so much with how we *structure* our programs or content for a knowledge base, but rather with how we choose the *processes* we use to engage with practitioners around the knowledge base that they already possess. Only by taking the narrativity of experience seriously can we produce dialogue and critical reflection in our programs, and model the process necessary to promote empowered practitioners and democratic educational institutions.

Notes

1. There have been several attempts (Petrie 1989; Shulman 1987) to describe the practitioner's epistemology of practice by attempting to classify the kinds of knowledge practitioners draw on. Most of these studies have been done on teachers. The domains of practitioner knowledge discussed in this section were extrapolated from a study of principals. For a more thorough discussion of these domains, see Anderson and Page 1989.

2. For a more in-depth critique of work in the field of educational administration that is derivitive of Schon, see Anderson, 1989.

References

Adams, D. 1988. Extending the educational planning discourse: Conceptual and paradigmatic explorations. *Comparative Education Review* 32(4):400–415.

Anderson, G. L., and Page, B. 1989. *Practitioner knowledge and the uses of narrative.* Paper presented at the 3rd annual meeting of the University Council for Educational Administration. Phoenix, Ariz.

Anderson, G. L. 1989. *Dare Administrators build a new social order? From reflection-in-action to critical reflection.* Paper presented at the 3rd annual meeting of the University Council for Educational Administration. Phoenix, Ariz.

Argyris, C., and Schon, D. 1974. *Theory in practice.* San Francisco: Jossey-Bass.

Argyris, C., Putnam, R., and Smith, D. M. 1986. *Action science.* San Francisco: Jossey-Bass.

Burrell, G., and Morgan, G. 1979. *Sociological paradigms and organizational analysis.* Portsmouth, N.H.: Heinemann.

Cherryholmes, C. 1988. *Power and criticism: Poststructural investigations in education.* New York: Teachers College Press.

Chubb, J. E., and Moe, T. M. 1990. *Politics, markets, and America's schools.* Washington D.C.: The Brookings Institution.

Dewey, J. 1944. *Democracy and education.* New York: The Free Press.

Freire, P. 1970. *Pedagogy of the oppressed.* New York: Continuum.

Goodlad, J. I. 1984. *A place called school.* New York: McGraw-Hill.

Holland, P. 1992. Recovering the story: Understanding practice through interpretation of educational narratives. In N. Haggerson and A. Bowman, eds. *Informing educational policy and practice through interpretive inquiry,* 199–215. Lancaster, Pa.: Technomic Pub.

Hopkins, R. (1994). *Narrative schooling: Experience and the transformation of American education.* New York: Teachers College Press.

Kamens, D. H. 1977. Legitimating myths and educational organization: The relationship between organizational ideology and formal structure. *American Sociological Review* 42:208–19.

Kozol, J. 1992. Whittle's raid on public education. In R. Lowe and B. Miner, eds. *False choices: Why school vouchers threaten our children's future.* Milwaukee: Rethinking Schools, Ltd.

Lindlom, C., and Cohen, D. 1979. *Usable knowledge: social science and social problem solving.* New Haven: Yale University Press.

Liston, D. and Zeichner, K. 1991. *Teacher education and the social conditions of schooling.* New York: Routledge.

Lortie, D. 1975. *Schoolteacher.* Chicago: University of Chicago Press.

Mercer, J. (in press). The impact of changing paradigms of disability on mental retardation in the year 2000. In L. Rowitz, ed. *Mental retardation in the year 2000,* 15–38. New York: Springer-Verlagg.

Petrie, H. 1989. Teacher knowledge and teacher practice: A new view. Paper presented at the annual meeting of the American Educational Research Association. San Francisco.

Pohland, P. 1992. Paradigm and prospect: Educational administration and reform. *UCEA Review* 33(2):4–5.

Robinson, V. 1989. The nature and conduct of a critical dialogue. *New Zealand Journal of Educational Studies* 24(2):175–86.

Sarason, S. B. 1982. *The culture of the school and the problem of change.* 2nd ed. Boston: Allyn & Bacon.

Schon, D. 1983. *The reflective practitioner.* New York: Basic books.

Shakeshaft, C. 1989. *Women in educational administration.* Newbury Park, CA: Sage.

Shulman, L. 1987. Knowledge and teaching: Foundations of the new reform. *Harvard Educational Review* 57(1):1–22.

Wolcott, H. 1976. Maintaining the system: The socialization of a principal. In J. Roberts and S. Akinsanya eds. *Schooling in the cultural context*, 448–79. New York: David McKay Co.

PART II

*Hearing Traditionally
Excluded Voices:
Race, Ethnicity, and
Gender in
Educational Administration*

A Cup Half Full: A Gender Critique of the Knowledge Base in Educational Administration

Charol Shakeshaft

The knowledge base in educational administration has been critiqued on many fronts, some of them addressed in plans to restructure the field of educational administration. The plans, no matter how well conceived, all seem to come from a similar perspective: they propose to regroup rather than rethink the knowledge base. The proposals for what administrators should know take already existing theory and realign it into new categories. Few, if any, of these proposals question the adequacy of these theories and practices.

I will argue that most theory and practice in organizational and administrative thought is based upon studies and behaviors of white males and that it is adequate for understanding human behavior only to the extent that women and people of color interpret the world and respond like white males. I will further argue that in many important ways, women and people of color do not experience the world in the ways that white males do, and that these differences result in some very real departures for both the understanding and the managing of organizations. I will conclude that the knowledge base in educational administration—and organizational theory—is inadequate in every category as a conceptual foundation for understanding and informing practice in organizations.

Androcentric Nature of Organizational Theory

For many reasons, some understandable and others less clear, research on organizations has largely looked at the male experience. It is not new to say that women have been excluded from the production of knowledge. Science and science-making tend to reinforce and perpetuate dominant social values and conceptions of reality. The funding of research, the objects of study, and the use of research have to date been dominated by white males. Not unexpectedly, they have forged forms of thought within an all-male world and, perhaps without realizing it, have mistaken it for a universal reality. As a consequence, these outcomes have become the standards and norms by which all experience is measured and valued, with women as but one of the nondominant groups that have been unrepresented.

Acknowledging the limitations that a singular perspective has in understanding social reality, scholars in the social science disciplines that inform educational administration have been critical of male-based theory and research. For over a decade, researchers in these fields have questioned the validity of the theoretical constructs undergirding their perspectives. These researchers have uncovered theoretical foundations, conceptualizations, and methodological practices that have resulted in impoverished theories (Daniels 1975; Eichler 1980; Gilligan 1982; Miller 1977; Parker and Parker 1979; Parlee 1979; Sherif 1979; Slocum 1980; Smith 1979; Smith-Rosenberg 1983; Spender 1981). These scholars have shown that theories and concepts emerging solely from a male consciousness may be irrelevant to the female experience and inadequate for explaining female behavior.

In order to understand the dominance of the white male world view in research and knowledge, scholars first needed a way to name, and thus know, male-defined scholarship. Differing labels have been given to such work (some call it patriarchal, others sexist), but the term that seems most descriptive and the one I use is *androcentrism,* the practice of viewing the world and shaping reality through a male lens.

Essential to understanding the limitations of an androcentric world view is the acknowledgement that all research reflects a set of beliefs or values. The harm comes not so much from the world view, but rather from a claim that it is the only lens through which one can understand human behavior. Studying male behavior, and more particularly the behaviors of white males, is not in and of itself a problem. It becomes a problem when the results of studying male behavior are assumed to be appropriate means for understanding all behavior. Of paramount importance in trusting and using research are the abilities to recognize perspective and explain the methods and findings in ways that make it unmistakably clear to the consumer just what the perspective is.

To label a piece of research, a theory, concept, or model as androcentric is merely to identify the framework within which the thinking and work occurred. Such labelling attempts to establish for the consumer a set of parameters to be used in accepting, internalizing, and applying the results of such research, and becomes as well a way of addressing what is missing, what has been overlooked, what has not been stated. Labelling heightens the awareness of both producer and consumer and reveals the limitations and restrictions of a one-sided system of knowledge. Its purpose is to assist in the re-envisioning of our world.

If all the players in organizations were white males, androcentric research and theory would not be problematic. Nor would it mislead our understanding of the behavior of people who are not white males if there were no differences between the ways men and women, majorities and minorities behave in groups. However, since we now know that gender and race differences in behavior and perspective do exist (Garfinkel 1988; Gilligan 1982; Shakeshaft 1987), it becomes important to examine theory and research for androcentrism as well as to expand theory and research to include the perspectives of nondominant groups.

Let me begin by making some distinctions. Sex is a biological description, one that divides most of humankind into two types of people, namely, females and males. I say most of humankind, because even a variable such as sex, which we believe is easily distinguished, turns out to have some ambiguity that depends upon the evidence we use to determine who is male and who is female. Gender, on the other hand, is a cultural term. It describes the characteristics that we ascribe to people because of their sex, the ways we believe they behave, or the characteristics we believe they have based upon our cultural expectations of what is considered male and female. As far as I can determine from my work and the work of others, one's biological identification as male or female has very little to do with how people behave and the work they do in schools. However, one's gender identification has a tremendous influence on behavior, perceptions, and effectiveness.

Interestingly, gender has somehow become identified, and in some cases synonymous, with women. That's unfortunate, since it has led to some confusion about both the direction and the importance of research that examines the influence of gender on organizational dynamics. Research on men is still seen as mainstream and central, while research on women and/or gender issues (both male and female) is often considered a special topic and not central to the understanding of organizational behavior.

It is not surprising, then, that research in educational administration is weak both in research on women in organizations and research on the impact of gender on behavior. Traditional research for theory and practice has neglected both the female experience and the influence of gender on actions and outcomes; it is both androcentric and barren of gender (Shakeshaft and Hanson 1986).

Analyses of the theories dominating the fields of educational administration and organizational behavior indicate that they are based upon a white-male behavior and world view. For instance, examination of some of the most cited theories in educational administration and management texts—Social Systems Models, Two-Factor Leadership Behavior Models, Organizational Climate Research, Situational Leadership Research, and Motivational Research—indicates not only that these theories are only based upon studies of white men, but that they don't hold up when applied to women and people of color (Shakeshaft 1987; Shakeshaft and Nowell 1984).

The following sections will explore some of the areas in which the behavior of women differs from that of men and the gender interactions that must be considered if we are to build a knowledge base that explains more than we can currently account for about human behavior in organizations. While the research discussed in these sections was conducted in schools, the work of others in private-sector enterprises indicate that the findings would be similar in those settings (Ferguson 1984).

Gender as an Explanatory Variable in Theories and Practice in Supervision

Although the area of supervision abounds with theories and scripts, little has been written on the impact of gender on successful supervision. This issue seems particularly salient, given the sex structuring of schools that results in an organization in which males most often supervise females. It takes on added importance if we examine the sexually stereotyped expectations of behavior and status, and go on to imagine what implications they might have when the norm is reversed and a female supervises a male.

Thus, gender and gender expectations may partially determine how supervisors interact with those whom they supervise. For instance, research tells us that the sex of participants affects what is communicated and how it is communicated (Borisoff and Merrill 1985). The same words spoken by a male supervisor have different meanings for male and female teachers. Conversely, an interaction occurring between a female principal and a male teacher is not the same as one occurring between a female principal and a female teacher.

We know that men and women communicate differently and that they listen for different information (Borisoff and Merrill 1985). It may be the case that in a supervisory conference in which a principal is discussing an instructional issue with the teacher, the woman participant is listening for the feeling and the man for the facts. It may also be the case, given what we know of the values males and females carry into their jobs in schools, that the woman focuses on an instructional issue or a matter concerning the child, while the man chooses to discuss an administrative problem.

Further, research tells us that there may be discomfort in communicating with a member of the other sex. Certainly, we know that male teachers exhibit more hostility in dealing with female administrators than do female teachers. We also know that women administrators have to work harder to get male teachers to "hear" them. (Lee 1991)

Perceptions of competence may also influence supervisory styles and effectiveness. We know that women are initially evaluated less favorably than equally competent men (Shakeshaft 1987), and that males evaluate females more harshly than females evaluate females (Lee 1991). These perceptions may affect supervisory interactions, both when the woman is being supervised and when she is the supervisor.

Nowhere does the impact of gender on supervision become more evident than in the area of feedback. Men receive both more feedback, and more types of feedback, than do women. Women are more likely to get non-evaluative feedback or neutral responses. Men receive both more positive and more negative responses.

A 1987 study (Shakeshaft) found that male administrators are less likely to give direct feedback to females but more likely to give it to males. For instance, when a male subordinate makes a mistake or doesn't live up to the expectations of his boss, his supervisor tends to level with him, "telling it like it is". When a female errs, she often isn't even informed of her mistake. Instead, the mistake is corrected by others without her knowledge. The results are twofold. For the male, learning takes place instantly. He gets criticism and the chance to change his behavior. He learns to deal with negative opinions of his work and has the option of improving it.

Females often never hear anything negative, as they are given neutral or slightly positive cues even if their performance is less than ideal. This results in a woman's misconception of her abilities or at least the level of her performance. If she isn't directly told that her work is not meeting expectations, she has neither the opportunity to improve nor the opportunity to reassess her abilities.

These differential feedback patterns are not unique to the adult work setting. The work of Sadker and Sadker (1986) describe similar patterns throughout K–12 schooling, where boys receive more feedback and a wider range of feedback. Observing these early differences not only helps us to understand why we behave as we do when we become adult workers, but also helps us to understand women's reactions to criticism in the rare instances when they get it first-hand (women always receive criticism; the issue is whether or not they get to hear it).

In interviews with women administrators (Shakeshaft 1987), the women were found to take criticism hard. They tended to think it was an assessment of their very essence. The first time they received criticism or the first time they failed, women administrators coded it as a sign that they were inferior and that they never should have tried to become an administrator in the first place. This is hardly surprising for two reasons. First, females in this society are less valued than men. Thus, women, from birth, throughout their school years, and into adult life, receive subtle and not so subtle messages about their worth. These messages offer some reasons to explain why women have been found to have lower self-images and less self-esteem than men. Second, if females, as girls, received very little direct criticism, then as women they have not been given the opportunities to learn not to take critical comments personally. This lack of experience lends itself to an understanding of why supervisors of women tend to shy away from giving them this critical feedback.

In interviews with male superintendents and principals asking them why they didn't confront women with their misgivings and dissatisfactions, one of the major reasons that was given was the fear of women's tears (Shakeshaft 1987). Most of the men were uncomfortable with the prospect of tears. When questioned about what they expected from men to whom they gave negative feedback, most anticipated anger. While none of the administrators in this study liked confronting anyone with negative feedback, the prospect of an angry response was easier to face than the prospect of tears. Male superintendents and principals said they didn't like to deal with angry subordinates, but that they had the skills to do so. They were much less comfortable with crying, and because of this discomfort, most of the men failed to give women important corrective feedback that would have allowed the women to improve their performance as educators.

This fear of tears led us to examine who cries and how often. What we found was that there is not a lot of crying in public schools, and that although women cry in front of supervisors slightly more than men, the difference in frequency is very small. However, women are reported to cry equally often in front of females and males, while males only cried in front of women. Thus, we learn that it is the fear of tears—rather than overwhelming evidence of actual crying—that paralyzes male administrators. We also learn that both men and women cry, so it isn't solely a female problem. Finally, we learn to understand that although it is not solely a female problem, and although nobody cries very much, the fear of tears or the gender expectations about what women do keep women from getting honest feedback about their performance and impairs the effectiveness of the supervisory styles of male administrators.

The importance of this discussion about supervisory styles and feedback is that gender perceptions influence behavior and interfere with effectiveness. Because of our beliefs about who men are and who women are, many administrative actions are censored or changed, depending upon the person with whom we are interacting. The issues are difficult for both men and women. Women must be aware of the feedback loop and try to determine whether or not they are getting helpful evaluative information. Men, on the other hand, often perceive themselves as caught in a "damned if you do, damned if you don't" position. If a man treats a woman as he does a man, he may be accused of being harsh or unfair. If he doesn't treat a woman in the same manner, he may be accused of not giving her helpful or corrective feedback. We need to examine our expectations about male and female behavior and confront the issue so that both men and women are as effective as they can be in a supervisory relationship.

The studies of behavior discussed above led to an examination of whether or not the written evaluations of job performance show similar differences. Specifically, an investigation of whether or not there were differences in the evaluations of teachers written by male and female principals was undertaken, using my earlier work

(1987) as a guide for exploration. My previous research had indicated that:

1. Relationships with others are more central to all actions for women than they are for male administrators.
2. Teaching and learning is more often the major focus for women than it is for male administrators.
3. Building community is more often an essential part of the woman administrator's style than it is for the man.

In this study (Shakeshaft, Nowell, and Perry 1991), a content analysis of the written evaluations of 108 female teachers by 8 principals (5 males and 3 females) attempted to determine whether or not male and female principals highlighted different things. All of the principals worked in the same school district and all had received the same amount of training in the Hunter technique. The evaluations were coded without knowledge of the sex of the principal; interrater reliability was 77%.

We did find some differences in the things that women and men focused on. Women were more likely than men to encourage the empowerment of their teachers, establish instructional priorities, be attentive to the social and emotional development of the students, focus on student relationships, be attentive to the feelings of teachers, include more so-called "facts" in the evaluation, look for the teachers' personal effects on the lives of children, place emphasis on the technical skills of teaching, make comments on the content and quality of the educational program to provide information gathered from other sources, involve the teacher in decision-making, issue directives for improvement, provide immediate feedback on performance, and emphasize curricular programs. Men, on the other hand, were more likely than women to emphasize organizational structure and to avoid conflict.

These findings support the literature that says women may approach the supervisory process by valuing different characteristics and concentrating on a different set of criteria than do men. This study suggests that even when they are trained similarly in methods of supervisory interaction, males and females may still bring with them expectations and behaviors based upon gender. While this study is in no way definitive, it does provide us with some additional support for our need to understand gender in all aspects of school administration, especially supervision.

We would argue that gender makes a difference in how we behave as supervisors. Sometimes these behaviors are just different and interesting. However, at other times, gendered behaviors may signal treatment that is not only different but more favorable to one sex than to another. When the latter is the case, we need to reexamine practice.

Sexuality and Administrative Behavior

While administrators often joke about sex, they seldom examine how their attitudes and beliefs about their own sexuality guide their administrative behavior. While both males and females are uncomfortable with sexual issues, male discomfort serves as a larger impediment to effective administration than does female discomfort, for three reasons. First, there are more male administrators at every level in schools than there are female administrators. Second, females have had to learn to understand a white-male world to succeed in it, and therefore, are more likely to have already dealt with issues of sexuality. Third, women and men have been socialized differently around the issues of sexuality, and women's socialization is less likely than men's to be the kind that impairs effective administrative functioning.

Sexual issues shape many management strategies. For instance, hiring practices, organizational climate, and team building practices are all affected by fears, discomfort, or displays of sexuality. The following discussion briefly examines how sexuality interacts with some typical management behaviors and, more specifically, how male discomfort with the sexual self impedes effective management. Issues of gender pervade the analysis of the role sexuality plays in management issues. Without rigid gender roles, sexuality issues would not be so potent. It is because of the gender expectation of a woman's sexual purpose that sexuality becomes an issue.

Hiring Practices

An example of how beliefs about sexuality affect administrative behavior can be found in an examination of who male administrators hire and why. In a study of the hiring practices of male superintendents (Shakeshaft 1989), we asked these superintendents if they would hire an attractive female. Almost all of the superintendents in our study said, "Sure, I'd hire an attractive woman." When we asked for what job they would hire such a woman, almost all had her slotted for an elementary principalship. When we followed up and asked if these superintendents would hire this imaginary woman as an assistant superintendent, in a role that involved working closely with the superintendent, very few of the superintendents said they would do so. The issue for them was the combination of the intensity of the working relationship and the attractiveness of the woman. Most admitted that they felt uncomfortable in a close working relationship with an attractive woman.

Some, however, not only did not feel uncomfortable, but said they had, indeed, hired a woman to work closely with them, usually as assistant superintendent. We then interviewed both groups of superintendents about their beliefs or experiences with hiring women, in an attempt to get an understanding of some of the issues that might surface when men think about working closely with women.

The first reason superintendents gave for not hiring a woman to work closely with them was their concern that school board members would see something unseemly in the relationship and that this perception would threaten the superintendents' effectiveness with their boards. We interviewed those superintendents who had hired a woman and asked them if they had received negative feedback from board members. While a few reported suggestive comments or sexual jokes from board members, they all said that they in no way felt that working with a woman had hurt their reputations or threatened their effectiveness in the eyes of the board.

The second reason the superintendents gave for not hiring attractive women was their worry that it would cause marital friction and few wanted the additional stress of what they called "trouble on the homefront" added to their already stressful lives. Interviews with those superintendents who had hired women indicated they didn't find this a problem. None of these superintendents reported experiencing the jealousy or friction that their colleagues anticipated. However, the fear of jealousy wasn't confined to superintendents who didn't hire women. The women assistant superintendents worried about the possibility and reported that they made a special effort to build a relationship with the wife of their "boss." These women assistant superintendents described ways in which they tried to ensure that the wives of the men to whom they reported would not worry about romantic relationships between their husbands and the women assistant superintendents.

The third reason that the superintendents gave for not hiring a woman with whom to work closely is that most of the male superintendents said they wouldn't feel comfortable working closely with an attractive woman because these men weren't sure they wouldn't be sexually attracted to her. And if they were, it seemed to them like a no-win situation. If the superintendent were attracted to his female subordinate and she didn't return the feelings, the superintendent felt he ran the risk of being charged with sexual harrassment. On the other hand, if she were similarly attracted, the superintendent's first two fears, school board disapproval and marital discord, might become reality. Thus, fear of their own lack of sexual control led these superintendents to a position that it was better not to work closely with women. The superintendents who had hired women didn't deny that they might become sexually attracted to the women who worked with them, but what set them apart from their colleagues who would not hire a woman was that these superintendents didn't believe that feeling attracted to a woman meant they had to act on the feeling. In other words, they didn't equate attraction with action.

Thus, in this study, most male superintendents did not want to work closely with women because they saw women as a threat. Because of the superintendents' gender expectations that women are made for sex and that women, thus, constitute a sexual danger to the superintendents, most men in our study said they would not hire a woman. This example demonstrates how male discomfort with sexuality, as well as social definitions of what it is to be a man, prevent women from holding positions in school administration.

Team Building

The sexual issues discussed in hiring practices are also found in the creation of work groups. Even if a woman is hired into a position, a man's discomfort with his own sexuality may cause him to not include her in a team situation. From the woman's perspective, the issue of sexuality is also a problem. Women administrators report being cautious and suspicious of attention from male superordinates and unclear about what the underlying message is. Whether or not there is a spoken or unspoken sexual message, women process the possibility and think about their responses and actions in light of that possibility. Administrative action is influenced by gender expectations, which are based upon the stereotype that when men and women are together the outcome is sexual.

Again, this isn't surprising. Sex integration rarely occurs in American school systems. Starting in about the second grade, boys and girls move apart and segregate themselves along sex lines (Best 1983). Little is done to change this pattern of segregation by sex, and observations of classrooms and playgrounds find ample evidence of boys-against-girls spelling bees or athletic contests.

When males and females do come together again during late adolescence, it is for sexual or romantic reasons. Men and women have very little training or practice in working together as people rather than as representatives of different sexes. It's not surprising, then, that sexuality (and particularly heterosexuality) gets in the way of easy working relationships between women and men. The presence of these patterns, in the absence of a curriculum that helps students explore their own sexuality, insures that when these students become adults they, too, will have difficulty working with members of the other sex. This is how a curriculum that does not include discussions of sexual issues is a threat to a well-functioning workforce.

Organizational Climate

Male socialization has contributed to behavior that creates an organizational climate not welcoming to women. Sexual jokes, references to female anatomy or appearance, and sexual innuendo are behaviors that women say make them uncomfortable and create a climate that is experienced by women as hostile.

A not uncommon example of ways in which male administrators allowed male teachers to create a hostile environment, using sexuality as a tool, can be found in the following example from a school district on Long Island:

> The male teachers pasted a nude centerfold over a poster announcing Women's History Week. The message was not only that Women's History Week is unimportant, but also that it is acceptable and humorous to equate Women's History Week with the viewing of women as sex objects. [When women teachers complained to the administration they] were told that they lacked a sense of humor if they didn't laugh. (Shakeshaft 1986)

This is just one of the many instances women report of a hostile environment that uses sexuality to make women uncomfortable.

Women are often coded by men as sexual objects, whether or not they have chosen to present themselves in this way. Research by Abbey (1982; Abbey and Melby 1986; Abbey et al. 1987) indicates that men interpret women's behavior as sexual, even if women mean the behavior to be friendly. These miscodings on the part of men (along with hostility toward women on the part of some men) may then lead to unwanted and threatening sexual advances toward women teachers and administrators. Interviews with women administrators indicate that most can report at least one incident of unwanted sexual advancement by male colleagues and board members (Shakeshaft, unpublished data). These women describe having to be careful about how they present themselves—both physically and verbally—in order to make sure that unwanted sexual advances by men don't occur. And when those advances do occur, the women report that they are frightened for their jobs and their physical safety. Thus, the school world for women employees is one that has elements of sexual fear and threat—in other words, it is a world they perceive as unsafe and hostile.

This issue of sexuality comes first to our attention because it helps to explain some of the reasons why men are reluctant to hire women into jobs that will cause them to work closely together. However, further exploration of sexuality highlights the importance of the cultural meanings we give to people because of their sex and the implications these meanings have for administrative behavior. We need to understand how the issue of sexuality overlays the behavior of men and women in organizations and explore how it both helps and hurts the players involved. We need to understand also that this is a gender issue. It is our gender expectations that make sexuality a barrier to effective management, rather than just a normal part of every day life.

Gender and the Determination of Appropriate and Ethical Administrative Behavior

Studies of what males and females believe to be appropriate and ethical behavior indicate that those behaviors may be coded differently by males and females. In other words, what women think is ethical and appropriate administrative behavior may not be what men think is ethical and appropriate. An example illustrating these differences can be found in studies that attempted to determine whether or not men and women superintendents conceptualize their administrative teams differently and whether or not these superintendents and their team members value different traits in team members (Garfinkel 1988; Shakeshaft 1989). Garfinkel found that both men and women value competence and trust, but that they give each a different priority. For women superintendents, competence is the first thing they look for in a team member; trust is lower on the list. Men superintendents, on the other hand, identify trust as their number one criteria for team membership, and view competence as less important. To complicate matters, especially for team members, men and women have differing definitions of trust. Men, both superintendents and team members, are more likely to describe trust as the "ability and comfort to say what they wished to say, confident that the persons they were sharing their thoughts or opinions with would not ridicule or repeat these thoughts elsewhere" (Garfinkel 1988, 311). Women superintendents defined trust as "an expectancy held by an individual, that the word, promise or written statement of another individual or group can be relied on" (311).

These differing conceptions of trust call for different indicators of proof, and illustrate as well some basic distinctions men and women draw with regard to talk (Shakeshaft n.d.). For men to see a person as trustworthy, that person must not divulge information or discuss actions or conversations with others. Men said they assumed that if they told a subordinate something, the subordinate would not tell others unless he or she had been instructed to do so. Men were very clear that a trustworthy subordinate wouldn't talk and that this was such an accepted code of behavior that the men interviewed didn't think it necessary to remind subordinates "not to tell."

Women saw things very differently. Not only did women not code "telling something" as disloyal, they said they expected subordinates to tell unless specifically instructed otherwise. They expected people to discuss conversations, actions, and feelings with others. Women went even further; they said it would be "wrong" of them to expect people not to discuss issues that related to their work. These women administrators said that talk was important and that for them to restrict talk, without an extraordinarily compelling reason, would be inappropriate and unfair.

Here we see two very different expectations. Men believed that subordinates should and would not discuss issues unless so instructed and that to do so was not only a disloyal act, but the mark of an inexperienced and inept administrator. Women believed that subordinates would talk and had the right to talk about issues they had discussed, and the women superordinates believed that to instruct subordinates otherwise was wrong and immoral.

Women did code some behavior as untrustworthy. What women saw as untrustworthy was someone failing to do what they said they would do, when they said they would do it. Men didn't identify a person as untrustworthy if he or she didn't deliver on time. Rather, they saw that as a time-management or competency issue.

Thus, women supervisors would talk about a person's lack of loyalty, or say they couldn't trust that person if he or she hadn't done the work. Men described a subordinate as untrustworthy if he or she discussed issues with others without permission.

In addition to the differing perceptions of trust and loyalty held by superordinates, these studies found that subordinates also held polar views of how a loyal team member should act. Men team members, for instance, said that the way they would show loyalty was not to disagree with the "boss", except in a private conversation. Even if they didn't agree that the boss was right, men team members said that to be loyal they would need to support whatever the boss did. These male team members said that if they couldn't go along with the boss's agenda without major disagreement, the only honorable thing for them to do would be to find another job. Female team members conceptualized loyal and ethical behavior differently. Over and over, they said that a loyal team member was one who spoke up when he or she disagreed with the course of action the boss was taking. These women would say, "It is my responsibility as a professional to let my boss know when I disagree. It would be unethical and unprofessional of me to keep quiet if I didn't think my boss's idea was a good one. It would be immoral not to speak up." The team members' conflicting conceptualizations were carried through in the ways that the male and female superintendents coded loyal and ethical behavior. Thus, male superintendents described subordinates as disloyal for publically disagreeing, while female superintendents coded subordinates as disloyal for not speaking up.

The point of examining these differences is not to say one approach is right and one is wrong (the way theory and practice up to now have done), but rather to help us understand that males and females may be coming from very different places, and that unless we understand these differences, we aren't likely to work well together.

Summary

What can this discussion of research, as seen through women's eyes, tell us about the knowledge base in educational administration in general? I think that first of all, these cases illustrate the absence of essential practical information for administrators in the traditional literature. The traditional literature of educational administration not only leaves women without a clear understanding of issues important to them, but also deprives men from understanding how their cultural identity as males interacts with women's cultural identity as females and the effects this interaction has on organizational dynamics.

The study of gender and organizations also illuminates rather clearly the connection between theory and practice and, perhaps, prods us into rethinking what the subject matter in educational administration research ought to be. Looking at the world as females experience it and trying to document those perspectives will help to expand the knowledge base of practice in educational administration. Observational studies of women administrators will help us document how women work as administrators and how their gender helps or hinders their work. Interviews with women will help us understand the way they think and speak about their worlds.

Similarly, examining the role gender plays in the ways people behave in organizations will help us develop theories that encompass the many factors influencing behavior. Gender isn't only about women. We must also observe male behavior and listen to men speak about working with women. What are the issues for both men and women? Is sexuality a force? Do competitive approaches to work, particularly verbal competitiveness, have an equal impact on men and women? Do men trust women? Do women trust men?

These topics offer a practical and useful role for the study of women's worlds and gender interactions. Improving practice and expanding theory is no small accomplishment and there is certainly room to include both in the research on educational administration. It also argues against reorganizing the knowledge base into different boxes and for expanding the knowledge base to include the experiences of women.

References

Abbey, A. 1982. Sex differences in attribution for friendly behavior: Do males misperceive females' friendliness? *Journal of Personality and Social Psychology* 42 (5): 38.

Abbey, A., C. Cozzorelli, K. McLaughlin, and R. Harnish. 1987. The effects of clothing and dyad sex composition on perceptions of sexual intent: Do women and men evaluate these cues differently? *Journal of Applied Social Psychology* 17: 108–26.

Abbey, A., and C. Melby. 1986. The effects of nonverbal cues on gender differences in perceptions of sexual intent. *Sex Roles* 15 (5/6): 283–98.

Bell, C. 1989. Essay Review. *Educational Administration Quarterly.*

Best, R. 1983. *We've all got scars.* Bloomington: Indiana University Press.

Borisoff, D., and Merrill, L. 1985. *The power to communicate: Gender differences as barriers.* Prospect Heights, Ill.: Waveland Press.

Daniels, A. K. 1975. Feminist perspectives in sociological research. In M. Millman & R. M. Kanter, eds., *Another voice:* 340–80. New York: Anchor Press/Doubleday.

Eichler, M. 1980. *The double standard.* New York: St. Martin's.

Ferguson, K. E. 1984. *The feminist case against bureaucracy.* Philadelphia: Temple University Press.

Garfinkel, E. 1988. *Ways men and women in school administration conceptualize the administrative team.* Unpublished doctoral dissertation. Hofstra University, Hempstead, N. Y.

Gilligan, C. 1982. *In a different voice.* Cambridge, Mass.: Harvard University Press.

Gutek, B. A. 1989. Sexuality in the workplace: Key issues in social research and organizational practice. In J. Hearn, D. L. Sheppard, P. Tancred-Sheriff and G. Burrell, eds., *The Sexuality of Organizations.* Newbury Park, Calif.: Sage.

Klein, R. D. 1983. How to do what we want to do: Thoughts about feminist methodology. G. Bowles and R. D. Klein, eds., *Theories of women's studies:* 88–104. London: Routledge & Kegan Paul.

Lee, V. (in press). Teachers and principals: Gender-related perceptions of leadership and power in secondary schools. *Educational Administration Quarterly.*

Miller, J. B. 1976. *Toward a new psychology of women*. Boston: Beacon.

Parker, S., and Parker, H. 1979. The myth of male superiority: Rise and demise. *American Anthropologist 81*(2): 289–309.

Parlee, M. B. 1979. Psychology and women. *Signs 5*(1): 121–33.

Sadker, M., and Sadker, D. 1986. Sexism in the classroom: From grade school to graduate school. *Phi Delta Kappan*. March: 512–15.

Schuster, M., and Van Dyne, S. 1984. Placing women in the liberal arts: Stages of curriculum transformation. *Harvard Educational Review 54*(4): 413–428.

Shakeshaft, C. 1987. *Women in educational administration*. Newbury Park, Calif.: Sage.

———. 1989. The gender gap in research in educational administration. *Educational Administration Quarterly 25*(3).

———. (n.d.). Unpublished data.

———, and Hanson, M. 1986. Androcentric bias in the Educational Administration Quarterly. *Educational Administration Quarterly 22*(1): 68–92.

———, and Nowell, I. 1984. Research on theories, concepts, and models of organizational behavior: The influence of gender. *Issues in Education II*(3).

———, Nowell, I., and Perry, A. 1991. Gender and supervision. *Theory into Practice 30*(2): 134–139.

Sherif, C. W. 1979. Bias in psychology. In A. J. Sherman and E. T. Beck, eds., *The prism of sex*: 93–133. Madison: University of Wisconsin Press.

Slocum, S. 1980. Woman the gatherer: Male bias in anthropology. In S. Ruth, ed., *Issues in feminism*: 214–22. Boston: Houghton Mifflin.

Smith, D. E. 1979. A sociology for women. In J. A. Sherman and E. T. Beck, eds., *The prism of sex*: 135–87. Madison: The University of Wisconsin Press.

Smith-Rosenberg, C. 1983. The feminist reconstruction of history. *Academe 69*(5): 26–37.

Spender, D., ed. 1981. *Men's studies modified: The impact of feminism on the academic disciplines.* Oxford, England: Pergamon Press.

How Gender and Ethnicity Interact in the Practice of Educational Administration: The Case of Hispanic Female Superintendents

Flora Ida Ortiz and David Jude Ortiz

This chapter is designed to illustrate how gender and ethnicity interact to affect success in educational administration. Two cases in which Hispanic female superintendents are used as subjects illustrate how gender and ethnicity play out in concert with traditional knowledge-based training. The intent is to demonstrate that educational administration practice, as it is presently conducted, is directly lodged on the knowledge base formulated by and for white males. This knowledge base is deficient for Hispanic females, so it is critical that they adjust to it in order to be successful. To demonstrate this adjustment we have organized our chapter into two major sections that deal respectively with the source of knowledge and the application of knowledge. Each section is subdivided into those areas that are most critical and problemmatic for Hispanic females' success as superintendents.

Sources of Knowledge Bases

Graduate Work

The two cases of the Hispanic female superintendents demonstrate the gender difference in the acquisition of the educational administration knowledge base. Both women received their doctoral degrees from outstanding universities and studied with the leading scholars in the field.

That gender is a consideration for success for the two women is indicated in the topic of their dissertations. Dr. Singer's dissertation, "Characteristics for Promotion to Administrative Positions Above the Principalship as Perceived by California School Superintendents," reports that superintendents promote principals on the bases of certain characteristics. Items considered essential to promotion included the following: (1) the ability to delegate responsibility, (2) the ability to work well with and train subordinates, (3) the ability to cope with stress, (4) a sense of timing for decision-making, (5) excellent references, and (6) a sense of humor. Dr. Singer's findings did not show any differences in characteristics benefiting male candidates more than female candidates or vice versa.

In contrast, Dr. Zagala's dissertation, "The Recruitment and Selection of Female School Board Candidates for Rural Districts in California," showed that factors of influence and motivation were important in elections. However, major differences between male and female candidates were not revealed. The findings showed that the support of current or retiring board members enhanced female candidates' opportunities. Increased superintendent contact with female candidates increased the likelihood of success. Campaign issues attracted female candidates but also increased election loss. In sum, throughout the conduct of their research required in their dissertation, both women looked for gender differences in areas perceived to provide an understanding of their work world, possibly because this issue had not been addressed in their prior training.

Career Ladder

Having established a regional and statewide reputation as a school administrator who had worked her way up the ranks, Dr. Singer obtained the superintendency, which included all of the traditional support systems. As an associate superintendent for personnel for several years in a school district requiring extensive union negotiation, her successful resolution of both classified and certificated union conflicts was well known.

Dr. Zagala, on the other hand, was less experienced and younger. Support systems and networks for her job were not extensively developed. There is some evidence of sponsorship from a university professor and the board president during the time when she was hired. The university professor provided some advice regarding the structure of the central office, and the board president had known Dr. Zagala when they were both state school board members.

Community Needs

Both women were hired by school districts that differed in their composition, size, and condition. However, they were both hired because it was expected that their gender and ethnicity would be beneficial to the district. Both were unanimously supported when they were hired. Dr. Singer was hired by a school district that was in a state of desperate instability. It was also one of the largest school districts in the state and served one of the most diverse student populations in the country. The major issues faced by the district were finances, personnel morale, student performance, overcrowding, and aging school buildings. Dr. Singer was hired with the mandate to resolve the issues.

Dr. Zagala was hired by a district located in a multifarious community. Disparities in the socioeconomic and cultural backgrounds shaping this community were some of the more extreme of any area in the country. Further, tension existed in these communities, in that the long-established agricultural industry was being driven out by powerful tourist and housing industries. The local newspaper reported the search for a new superintendent in the following manner: "The Arena Unified School District is looking for a bilingual superintendent, someone able to mix comfortably at a service club meeting in a predominantly Anglo arena and a Cinco de Mayo celebration in Plaza Alegre. We want someone who not only lives in the district full time, but is involved in the community."

Even though Dr. Zagala was hired during a so-called "troublesome time" following the departure of a terminally ill superintendent and a year-and-a-half period in which the district was without a fulltime superintendent, she was not hired to "fix anything up." Instead, the community perceived the school district as stable; however, the increasing proportion (55%) of Hispanic children in the district called for some attention. The community and board agreed that one of the key requirements for the new superintendent would be bilingualism in Spanish. Also, unlike Dr. Singer's case, there was the expectation that Dr. Zagala would live in the community and become involved in local affairs.

The incoming superintendent was asked to develop an accountability system throughout the district, to develop techniques and strategies to address those populations identified as "getting short shrift," to deal with the school construction program, and to focus on the fiscal situation.

The Appointment Process

The appointment to the superintendency of both of these women was a symbolic one, with a greater onus on Dr. Zagala. Dr. Singer secured her position through the contract by requesting a completely new cabinet and insisting on a buy-out clause for herself and the cabinet members. Dr. Zagala's contract contained none of these conditions. These differing actions can be explained in one of two ways. Dr. Singer's experience and the condition of the school district enabled her to acquire the necessary contract for increased likelihood of success, whereas Dr. Zagala's lack of experience and the fact that the school district did not require "fixing" did not legitimate such a contract.

Gender and ethnicity become part of the educational adminis-tration's equation of success for Hispanic female superintendents when they are appointed for symbolic reasons. In the cases we are reporting, Dr. Zagala's appointment was more symbolically signi-ficant than was Dr. Singer's. Dr. Zagala's symbolic appointment as a bilingual superintendent raised expectations and mobilized the Hispanic community at the same time that it increased suspicion and apprehension in the non-Hispanic community.

The local newspaper reported the appointment by highlighting the salary. It also emphasized the fact that Dr. Zagala had served as both principal and superintendent of a tiny, unionized elementary school district of 400 students and was now moving to a unified school district of 15,000 students. She was described as the first woman and the first Hispanic to be hired in the twenty-six-year history of the district. The paper's description of her first public appearance was that she was unflappable and addressed the audience in both Spanish and English.

The superintendent viewed her appointment as one that required her to act as an executive and school leader. But as she said, "The board really cares about kids. I will draw on their energy. I am going to need it to make sure the kids get a maximum education." The expectations from the board were explicitly presented: "We were looking for one who would be a rising star. We specifically advertised as a desirable in our superintendent bilinguality in the Spanish language and willingness to live and be involved in local affairs." Dr. Zagala proceeded to act out the expectations. As the current school board president later stated, "Our move was too bold and forward."

The symbolic significance attached to the appointment of a Hispanic female is best illustrated by Dr. Zagala's experience. At the time of her appointment, the board president was a Hispanic male, Mr. Martinez. She was highly visible and famous as the first Hispanic female executive in that region. The presence of two Hispanics in the top ranks raised suspicions within the organization and the non-Hispanic community. Good faith in the superintendent was never fully granted. One of the newspaper releases opened with "No soy monedita de oro para caerles bien bien a todos. I am not a little golden coin which is going to settle well with everyone." This tension was foreshadowed by the consultant, who stated, "She should want to do what any good superintendent should do, focus on the kids and keep it there, not play politics. That's the biggest danger to any superintendent."

The symbolic appointment of both superintendents resulted in different consequences. The symbolism for Dr. Singer receded into the background, whereas Dr. Zagala's polarized the community and school district. The attempt to focus on children, instruction, and schooling was not successful because the initial condition of the school district was not severe and the primary intent for hiring her was symbolic, rather than to stabilize the district, as in Dr. Singer's case.

Application of Knowledge

Enacting the Leadership Role

For school superintendents, the first requirement for success is the establishment of an executive relationship with the president of the school board. Even though all of the board members supported and approved the appointment, Mr. Martinez, the school board president at that time, provided what Dr. Zagala refers to as "more direct communication and protection for my decision." She said, "We spent a lot of time together and we were criticized for it. I felt we did spend a lot of time together, but it was pretty valuable. The decisions were buffered more than they are now." Dr. Zagala referred to the district's practice of changing board presidents every year and stated that when the board presidency was turned over to a white male her support lessened. She described the change: "Under the current president, you are the administrator. You can do your thing, but then the decisions can be questioned or someone can raise a question or be asked why did you do that?"

The second requirement for success for school superintendents is to have a loyal and committed cabinet. Unlike Dr. Singer, Dr Zagala inherited the cabinet created by the former superintendent. The cabinet opposed Dr. Zagala's appointment, and the members' perception of her as a symbol enabled them to ignore her decisions and actions. Unable to obtain the cabinet's cooperation, Dr. Zagala requested help from a former university professor. His advice was to expand the cabinet to include the former members and newcomers in order to diffuse the hostility. The consequence of the expanded cabinet, however, was the further loss of individual control. With the exception of one Black female, the cabinet was composed entirely of white males and females, which served to isolate Dr. Zagala even further.

The tenuous relationship with both the school board and central office encouraged the non-Hispanic community to express their opposition. A "no faith" petition, full of complaints, was filed. Some of the complaints were that she spoke Spanish at a staff training session and was too assertive; in addition, it was rumored that an unethical situation involving the superintendent and school board member was taking place. The investigation into the allegations showed that Dr. Zagala had appointed one Hispanic and six non-Hispanics to administrative posts. She demanded and got an apology regarding the allegations of unethical conduct. These actions served to polarize both the school district and community.

Blea (1992) explains that when Hispanic women act in nontraditional ways they are often thought of as deviant; they are not normal, but somehow strange. When "she strays from cultural prescriptions, there is always a negative consequence" (9). In the case of Dr. Zagala, in addition to the complaints cited above, the local fashion magazine featured an article recommending she cut her hair. These are examples in which the "powerful impose upon the less powerful definitions of what is deviant" (Blea 1992, 9). Because Dr. Zagala indicated that as a Hispanic she had not "accepted all Anglo norms and values," and that she had her own values, she was "not as strongly controlled by the dominant society in the informal way that Anglos are controlled by their own society" (12). Her behavioral differences became occasions of discussion and opposition for both the community and school district.

Sergiovanni (1984) claims that "educational administration is a science of designing courses of action aimed at changing existing situations into preferred ones" (278). The appointment of Dr. Zagala was an effort to move in that direction. However, neither the school district nor the community were prepared to alter the existing situation beyond the change that had occurred as a result of her appointment. This means that Dr. Zagala was not hired to administer, but to serve as a symbol.

In the case of Dr. Singer, we note how the symbolic attribution was reduced as she assumed administrative responsibilities. First, Dr. Singer's appointment of her cabinet was designed to reduce the ethnic tension. She referred to her cabinet as a rainbow, one consisting of two outsiders and one insider. One member was Chinese female, the businessman was a white male and the personnel woman was black. The women were all mixed; each representing more than one ethnic group. The superintendent explained:

> No one can claim any of these individuals. They claim what they can, but they can't get it all. The Chinese woman has blue eyes. The Black woman's mother is American Indian. My mother is half Asian of some kind. We do not fit any stereotypical profile. We are, nevertheless, identifiable more with one group than with another. The Hispanics do come to me. But by the same token, my husband is Jewish, so they know I cannot possibly have total allegiance to the Hispanics. The Chinese woman's fiancé is white. We are not exclusive to a group personally. So that, I believe, serves to permit people to act more neutrally. While we are claimed by any one group there is not a way to depend absolutely on our inclination to lean toward that group. For example, the white male feels that whites expect him to speak for them. He cannot do that too freely while he is being watched by the three of us!

The appointment of this highly diverse cabinet served to highlight the representation of each group in the community. Dr. Singer's actions served to diffuse the ethnic identity issue for herself and her appointees, whereas Dr. Zagala's symbolic role overshadowed her intent.

Communicating Throughout the Organization

Communication problems arise many times due to organizational changes superintendents wish to make. Greenfield (1982) claims that "it is the individual who acts; organizations cannot act because they do not exist in the common definition of this term. Organizations are constructs. We live in separate realities. What is true for one person is not for another. The understanding of an organization depends on the understanding of individual intention—why individuals act as they do" (5). The literature in educational administration tends to separate personnel issues from communication issues. In the case of Hispanic female superintendents, personnel changes are challenged on the basis of communication. For Hispanic females, changes regarding school personnel are particularly sensitive. The following incidents illustrate the occurrences, interpretation, and consequences of the interrelationship between personnel changes and communication.

A board member opposing Dr. Singer's proposed new hire said, "We have layers and layers of administrative crud. Hiring any more offends me." The superintendent objected to the remark and at the end of the meeting asked the board to meet in closed session. The audience expected the superintendent to resign. The superintendent explained to the board members how a remark from one of them has an effect. She said, "The thing that is going around here about this administrative crud is creating rumors or jokes like, where are you? Are you a top layer or bottom? Are you a thin layer or a fat one? Are you a hard layer or a soft layer? It is not funny around here. The board has no right to talk that way."

The organizational structure that was created by this verbal exchange was one in which the superintendent immediately responded to the hostile remarks. The response was one of instruction to the board regarding the impact of one of its members' remarks. The board can tell the administrators what they want, but they have to allow them to figure out how to do it. This action taken by Dr. Singer served to avoid further conflict and to retain her executive direction.

In contrast, Dr. Zagala explained how she went about hiring principals and how that action was interpreted. She described the process. "I hired a Hispanic principal for a key position in the district and I think that for the good old boys in the system the expectation is that the next duck in line takes the swim and I did not choose the next duck in line. I chose who I thought would be the best person for that particular school. The person applied and went through the process as did all others. It wasn't that I said, 'I want that candidate and ignored the process.'" But her action was not perceived as legitimate. The principals complained and reported their grievances to the board. One principal's opinion was the following: "Her mistakes are lodged in her lack of experience. I call them scars that you have to develop as you work your way up. You develop scar tissue as you make mistakes and go up the ladder. In comparing her to the other superintendents I have worked for and worked under, the mistakes she makes appear to be those from an individual who isn't properly prepared at the various lower levels."

Two different explanations can be provided for the above situation. Both explanations may well be related to communication difficulties, but they may also be associated with the fact that the superintendent is female and Hispanic. First, the impetus to complain and report grievances to the board regarding their superintendent's actions was more likely to originate when the superintendent was perceived as vulnerable and weakly supported by the school board and community. School board members would be attentive to complaints and grievances lodged against her.

Second, the appointment of a Hispanic principal was considered deviant behavior. The Hispanic appointee was not in the so-called "sponsorship" net, and the basis of the claim that Dr. Zagala was not properly prepared is that she failed to adhere to the traditional practice by which school administrators made appointments. Educational administration literature (Griffiths 1965; Valverde 1974; McCarthy 1981; Ortiz 1982) shows that promotion and access to administrative posts is a sponsored process. The term "good old boys" refers to this practice. Hispanic individuals are less likely to be part of such a system and access to administration would require intervention. Dr. Zagala's decision was based on trying to place the best person for that particular school, whereas, among the principals, it was expected that the personnel decision would be based on who has been sponsored and prepared for the next vacancy in the district, and that Dr. Zagala would know that norm.

Dr. Zagala knew about the norm, but her sense of organizational responsibility was dominant. She explained her dilemma: "And I knew that it was going to eventually come back to bite me. But I have always kept the board informed. I informed them this was going to come back. I said, 'Somebody isn't going to like this. They wanted this person, but I hired this other one.'"

The principals' complaints and grievances were attended to by the board. Dr. Zagala explained how this process took place.

The ideal thing would be that when the question comes up, "Did you know that Dr. Zagala hired someone that. . .?" the board should say, "Yes, the gentleman was selected through a process and we support the superintendent. We need someone bilingual there." Instead, the board member remarks, "Gee, let's look into it." It is the remark, "Let's look into it," that gives a detractor an automatic opportunity of a window of saying, "Something is wrong."

Where is the deviancy lodged? The district does not presently have a proportion of Hispanic principals equal to the proportion of Hispanics in the population at large. Thus, the appointment could not be viewed in terms of having too many Hispanic principals, but it could be thought that this superintendent might replace present principals with Hispanic principals.

When the practice has been to hire principals through sponsorship, white males, perceiving themselves equally capable of being principals, line up for the next vacancy. Dr. Zagala's neglect of the sponsorship procedural order challenged white men's opportunities. The resulting tension created among the principals was over the fact that who would be promoted was uncertain, because the superintendent's action placed the sponsorship practice in jeopardy. In short, the traditional structure of school administration was altered by the presence of the Hispanic female superintendent.

Dr. Zagala's precise and formal communication style was an attempt to avoid further misunderstandings. She explained how she made decisions.

> If I make a decision, I'll write it up in the Friday letter. This is to ensure that three months later one of the principals or someone else may not like the decision and behind the scenes call a board member and say, "I don't like that decision." If it is a very difficult decision that might carry a lot of resistance or public outcry, I will touch bases with the president. He or she will call the board members or we will write about it, or say, "Okay, are we ready?" And then we will go with the decision. Major decisions are packaged. Emergency decisions are the only ones which are not. For example, shall we close the schools or not? I don't have time to call for those kinds of decisions. After the decision is made, I will call the board members and tell them. Most of the decisions we make are not emergency. They are are more or less routine.

The former president of the board confirmed the process and added, "What I do is that I keep every Friday letter because I know somewhere along the line there is an issue she wrote us about and regardless of whether she agrees or disagrees, she will have that down in the letter. And that way we, the board members, can't say, 'No, we were not aware.' This letter shows we are aware."

Men and women listen for different information. Shakeshaft (1992) claims males are less likely to give direct feedback to females. In the case of Hispanic females, the feedback is sequential. The first response is a lack of acknowledgement, then there is a warning, and finally, there is preparation for relieving the person of the position. Dr. Zagala explains how the process occurred.

> From my perspective, ideally the situation would be being hired with something specific in mind and being supported throughout the process. It is probably the ideal way. I think what happens, not only in Arena, but in many organizations, is being hired with the understanding of the specific purpose but people go about their business and forget about the reason why somebody was brought in and then you do something. In the meantime, you cannot change values, and there are still people who know, but are saying, "What the hell are we doing with a Hispanic superintendent here? She doesn't know what she's talking about." People look for any slipping of decisions or error and I think that is where there has to be consistency.

One of the principals explained how communication plays a part in being successful: "I suppose it is the feeling of communication. To be a person that they feel they can communicate with and that when they get a no it is justifiable. I don't think principals think there is that sense of sincerity of communication."

Another principal explained why communication with this superintendent is an issue.

> She is from Mexico originally. . .I think that puts her at a disadvantage because you don't understand the innuendos. I mean, she picks them up quickly but still, if you have someone to ask the question or don't know what question to ask, that does block communication. It is hard to distinguish if that is blocking communication or if it is just a personal understanding. But the result is the same. Her Hispanic background and the fact that she speaks another language certainly helps the Hispanic here.

A review of the elements that served to delegitimize Dr. Zagala's executive actions highlights the interplay between ethnicity and gender. Hiring a Hispanic principal was viewed as a mistake. The formalizing of channels of communication was resented. The lack of communication was lodged on her bilingualism, her country of origin, her inexperience, and finally, on her perceived incompetence.

In contrast, Dr. Singer arranged a variety of means to communicate with principals, to work with them, and to involve them with the central office. She engaged in "executing a large number of little things" (March 1984, 22). The intent was to create a working group among the principals and to attach the principals to the central office. These "little things" included written communication, acknowledgements of a principal's efforts, central office reports, and scheduled meetings of various sorts (Groom, 1983). Principals were encouraged to work together to improve their schools. They were encouraged to utilize the central office's services and they were expected to run their schools consistent with Dr. Singer's vision. The central office staff, directed by the cabinet members, facilitated these working relationships. Dr. Singer explained:

> School site management is imperative, but principal's efforts must be consistent with my vision of school district productivity. I do not want a favorite school. I do not want abandoned or slighted schools in this district. If uniformity across the district is going to take place, I am the person who has to ensure that. Thus, I have to develop an intensive relationship with principals. A system of communication is necessary.

The consequences of Dr. Singer's strategy were that principals cooperated with each other and with the central office, and did not seek advice or support from the school board.

One might ask why Dr. Zagala was not successful in communicating with the school administrators. Dr. Zagala described how when she was first hired, "One of the board members told me, 'You have to be like the previous superintendent. He was very jovial, very social with his managers [principals].' So, I started being very social and we talked. They said jokes. I said jokes. We had a good time. In the meantime, they were documenting everything. They came back to the board saying that I had said this, that I had said that . . . So, I dropped the curtain on me."

"Dropping the curtain" meant, for Dr. Zagala, following procedural order and becoming formal. Her social behavior, a reaction to controversy and attacks based on suspicions, turned to a reduction in communciation and interpersonal interaction that might be open to a number of interpretations. A principal put it this way, "It is not so much what, it is how it is being done. It is not what is being said, it is how it is being said. It is almost being done in a way that seems that all of us who were here weren't working hard enough or fast enough, and therefore we are part of the problem. It is like putting blame on us."

Because she was unable to communicate successfully with the principals and did not receive support for the appointment of a Hispanic principal and for other actions, Dr. Zagala resigned from her position less than two years after her appointment. Anyon's (1983) expression sums up Dr. Zagala's legacy to Arena Unified School District: "While accommodation and resistance as modes of daily activity. . . provide ways of negotiating individually felt social conflict or oppression, this individual activity of everyday life remains just that; individual, fragmented, and isolated from group effort" (295).

The differences between the two superintendents, Dr. Singer and Dr. Zagala, accentuate the interplay between gender and ethnicity. Dr. Singer carried out an executive mandate with a rainbow cabinet. Dr. Zagala, who was bilingual in Spanish, willing to live in the community and become involved in local affairs, had her decisions perceived as inseparable from her ethnicity and gender. Dr. Singer acknowledged the issue of representation within the community without preferring any group. She made personnel decisions among principals by engaging in activities designed to communicate and include. She maintained her role with the board by immediately confronting a conflicting situation that jeopardized that relationship.

Dr. Zagala could not shed the symbolic attachments to her role. Her actions toward fulfilling the directive to improve the Hispanic population's condition was surrounded by controversy. Although the executive actions that Dr. Zagala performed are common ones, they became more open to controversy because they could be conveniently attributed to her gender and ethnicity.

Conclusions

This study of two Hispanic female superintendents serves to highlight the distinction of knowledge bases necessary for success in school administration. The success of Hispanic female superintendents is largely dependent on how the symbolic and practical aspects of the appointment are balanced. There are several important issues. First, the symbolic appointment will be accompanied by skepticism with regard to the superintendent's abilities and a suspicion that she will act to favor members of her own group. We need, therefore, to understand the bases on which personnel are brought into the organization. Particularly in the intitial stages of her administration, the superintendent's position will likely be invalidated due to a lack of support from the board and cabinet. Specifically, the vulnerability that accompanies the appointment of a superintendent will be promoted through her entering into a weak contract that has been offered by the school board. Further, the legitimation process necessary for the superintendent to be hired will be undermined by the inheritance of an unsupportive cabinet. An understanding of the superintendent's work group is instructive.

Second, as the superintendent's administration progresses and changes are made in the organization, the Hispanic female's need for support from the board will increase. When an outsider such as a Hispanic female makes those changes, the groups affected will be at odds with the decision and the person making the decision. The creation of adversarial parties within and without the organization will depend upon the percieved vulnerability of the superintendent. In particular, personnel issues will arise because Hispanic female superintendents are likely to ignore traditional networks and sponsorship systems. When the new hiree represents the superintendent's group, problems will be aggravated. The school board cannot abandon its candidate when the candidate fulfills the mandate. The knowledge base in this instance must cover the dilemma created when the justification for appointment is a symbolic gesture, rather than a quest for organizational leadership. Again, ultimately, the superintendent's position is likely to be invalidated due to lack of support from the board and central office.

The process by which all of this takes place is through the construction of different interpretations of the superintendent's actions. The first assumption regarding a Hispanic female super-intendent's leadership is that difficulties are a result of communica-tion problems. The command of another language provides an explanation for misunderstandings of English. Adversary groups move in to claim reverse racism. Finally the adversary groups link the subsequent organizational instability to incompetent and/or immobilized leadership.

In contrast, a reputation and support system developed while acquiring extensive and traditional experience serves to establish credibility and validity within the district. The suspicion that the superintendent will favor members of her group is then minimized.

The buy-out clause in the superintendent's contract locks the position and promotes an interdependence between the superintendent and board. Cooperation and a shared understanding between the board-superintendent roles and relationships develop through open and direct communication. By hiring for the executive cabinet a small number of diverse individuals who are well-recognized as competent and unified in the pursuit of organizational ends, the superintendent transmits a symbolic statement that restrains controversy. An intense interpersonal relationship between superintendent and principals creates close ties to the central office, through which uniformity, trust, and cooperation are maintained. Consequently, improvements are made in all the schools, and district personnel and the total community feel the impact of the superintendent's intentions. The superintendent's actions are thus validated and the superintendent is successful in retaining her job.

In conclusion, determining how Hispanic female superintendents succeed as educational administrators highlights issues of gender and ethnicity. Hispanic females must be keenly aware of the political forces and actors in order to avoid and diffuse situations that deter or prevent them from acting. Moreover, the Hispanic female superintendent must conceptualize her role and actions in fulfilling organizational ends with particular emphasis on uniformity and equity.

References

Anyon, J. 1983. Workers, labor and economic history, and textbook content. In M. W. Apple and L. Weis, eds., *Ideology and practice in schooling:* 37–60. Philadelphia: Temple University Press.

Blea, I. I. 1992. *La Chicana and the intersection of race, class, and gender.* New York: Praeger.

Greenfield, T. B. 1982. Against group mind: An anarchistic theory of organization. *McGill Journal of Education* 17 (1):3–11.

Griffiths, D. E., S. Goldman, and W. J. McFarland. 1965. Teacher mobility in New York City. *Educational Administration Quarterly* 1:15–31.

Gronn, P. 1983. Accomplishing the doing of school administration: Talk as the work. *Administrative Science Quarterly* 20 (2):65–92.

March, J. G. 1984. How we talk and how we act: Administrative Theory and Administrative life. In T. J. Sergiovanni and J. E. Corbally, eds., *Leadership and Organizational Culture: Perspectives on administrative theory and practice.* Urbana and Chicago: University of Illinois Press: 18–51.

McCarthy, M., and A. Zent. 1981. School administrators: 1980 profile. *Planning and Changing* 12(93):144–61.

Ortiz, F. I. 1982. *Career patterns in education: Women, men, and minorities in public school administration.* New York: Praeger.

Sergiovanni, T. J. 1984. Developing a relevant theory of administration. In *Leadership and organizational culture: Perspectives on administrative theory and practice*:275–92.

Shakeshaft, C. 1992. "Deconstructing the erected hierarchy: Sex and power in organizations." Speech presented at the 1992 Annual Meeting of the American Educational Research Association, San Francisco.

Valverde, L. A. 1974. *Succession socialization: Its influences on school administration candidates and its implication to the exclusion of minorities from administration,* Washington, DC: National Institute of Education Project 3-0813.

Gender, Race, Ethnicity and the Quest for a Knowledge Base in Educational Administration

Vivian Ikpa

As colleges and universities continue to ride the waves of educational reform, the debate concerning the preparation of educational administrators continues to rage. This debate gained national attention in 1987, when the University Council on Educational Administration (UCEA) focused attention upon preparation programs for students of educational administration. These concerns were elaborated in the 1987 report of the *National Commission on Excellence in Educational Administration*. The dominant issue reflected a concern for how colleges and universities prepare students of educational administration. Of primary concern was the extent to which preparation programs emphasized theoretical approaches at the expense of practical experiences.

Policy changes relevant to the preparation of students of educational administration are becoming pervasive. These policy changes are being shaped by state legislators. As Heck (1991) noted, state legislators have addressed the call for reform by supporting changes in the models utilized by colleges and universities in the preparation of school administrators. Many reformers, researchers and scholars contend that there is a specific set of competencies that can be identified in successful administrators: therefore, institutions can develop an appropriate relevant knowledge base. Many have come to realize that there is no common vision among reformers concerning what educational administrators need to know and what they need to do.

The impetus for the current reform movement in educational administration was generated by the issues raised by *Tomorrow's Teachers* (1986) and *Teachers For The 21st Century* (1986). These two reports were critical of how schools are structured and governed.

The reports were especially concerned about the ways in which institutions of higher education prepare individuals for leadership positions. In 1993, the waves of reform continue to force institutions to search for an appropriate knowledge base in the preparation of individuals for leadership and administrative positions.

This quest for a new knowledge base has led educators to reconceputalize existing paradigms. This chapter will argue that in their quest for an appropriate knowledge base, reformers have failed to consider the impact of gender, ethnicity and race. The search for an appropriate knowledge base in educational administration must first acknowledge the unique leadership characteristics and experiences of minorities and women. Scholars and researchers must come to the realization that the dominant philosophy of logical positivism enveloping the departments of educational leadership cannot incorporate diversities relevant to gender, race and ethnicity. The entrenched biases in dominant paradigms must be addressed in an effort to develop a inclusive knowledge base.

Additionally, this chapter suggests that individual assumptions and beliefs from the perspective of the white male are usually reflected in the discussions, debates and models of the educational administration knowledge base. This "race-gender exclusive" model should no longer represent the norm. Educational administration departments must rethink the ideological tenets that drive current paradigms. Any discussion of a knowledge base must be philosophically grounded in inclusiveness. That is, knowledge base paradigms must reflect societal diversity.

The Logical Positivism Paradigm

Today, the dominant paradigm governing the field of educational administration is aligned with the philosophy of logical positivism. Accordingly, educational administrators have looked to the literature produced by educational researchers to make rational decisions. As Smith and Blase (1991) noted, the majority of this research has been conducted within the framework of the empiricist theory of knowledge. Empiricism suggests that as researchers identify how educational processes operate, one gains both intellectual knowledge and practical mastery. That is, the study of educational administration will result in the discovery of generalizations and theories. Once generalizations are discovered, we can predict the consequences of alternate policies (Smith and Blase 1991).

The major problem with empiricism is that in education, no laws or generalizations relevant to educational administration have been established. As Holmes (1986) stated, generalizations relevant to such paradigms are primarily "Truisms, admonitions, aphorisms and tautologies." The philosophy of positivism has not produced law-related generalizations: therefore, our abilitiy to predict the consequences of our policies is limited (Smith and Blase 1991). Given these contentions, one may conclude that the field of educational administration cannot rely upon the empiricist paradigm to yield an appropriate knowledge base.

Cooper and Boyd (1987) reviewed the previous fifty years of preparation programs for educational administrators. They concluded that the training programs were a "state-controlled, university-based, credit-driven, certification-bound model"(3). This model reflected "the philosophical base of the One Best Model . . . which is a belief in empiricism, predictability and scientific certainty, taught by professors steeped in this approach" (4).

As Foster (1982) contends, the primary problem with positivism is that it is essentially a conservative position that has removed reflective and dialectical thought and allows the perpetuation of an extant social order. One cannot reduce human rationality to empirical, predictable, scientific certainty. Given these flaws, Foster (1988) considered an alternate perspective in the training of administrators:

> Clinical theory further, unabashedly endorses such values as liberation and equity, and sees the role of the social sciences not just in defining more appropriate control systems for running organizations but, more importantly, in self-reflective activity designed to recognize systems of domination, and in so doing, to increase the possibility for a truly democratic regime. (72)

As Bernstein (1976) stated, "Critical theory aspires to bring the subjects themselves to full consciousness of the contradictions implicit in their material existence, to penetrate the ideological mystifications and forms of false consciousness that distort the meaning of existing social conditions" (182). Perhaps, a shift toward the critical theory paradigm will facilitate the development of an appropriate knowledge base for educational administrators. If departments of educational administration are to assume leadership roles in reforming public education, the knowledge base must be placed in a sociophilosophical and critical context. Institutions must prepare individuals who are trained to interpret educational experiences from the perspectives of diverse groups.

The Missing Links: Women and Minorities

The underrepresentation of women and minorities in leadership positions continues to be pervasive in public schools and institutions of higher education. The National Committee on Excellence in Educational Administration (NCEEA) reported that the number of women superintendents increased from 1.7 percent in 1970 to 3 percent in 1987. During this same period, the UCEA (1987) noted that the percentage of female principals nationwide declined. Analysis of data from New York's State Department of Education indicated that between 1981 and 1986, women principals at the elementary level increased from 20.1 percent to 28.9 percentage. During this same period of time, the percentage of women principals working at the junior high level increased from 6.7 to 13.6 percent and 6.4 to 11.5 percent at the high school level (State Education Department, 1982; 1987).

In a 1988 survey conducted by the Executive Educator, 3 percent of superintendents, 10 percent of high school principals, and 13 percent of middle school principals were members of minority groups. Given the increasing minority population in our schools, it is obvious that the number of minorities in administrative positions must be increased. The low numbers of women and minorities in leadership positions convey a tacit message that implies that women and minorities are incapable of assuming administrative positions. The disprportionate number of white males in administrative roles suggests a closed system, which is not open to diverse skills, perspectives, and belief systems of minorities and women. If such diversities are excluded, the quest for a knowledge base in the preparation of students in educational administration becomes counterproductive. The missing links (minorities and women) must become a part of the system.

Race, Gender and the Knowledge Base

According to Owens (1991), all scientific inquiry reflects some basic assumptions and fundamental beliefs that are held by the inquirer. These fundamental beliefs include assumptions about the nature of human relationships, as well as the nature of reality (Schien 1985). In their quest for an appropriate knowledge base, reformers have failed to consider the impact of fundamental beliefs of women and minorities upon the conceptualization of educational administration paradigms. As Owens (1991) elaborates:

A hazard for any scholar lies in the fact that many of these basic assumptions are so taken for granted by the scholar, so implicitly held, and so thoroughly internalized as to be virtually invisible to the individual who holds them. They are shared among colleagues, friends and others in one's group or in one's culture. (88)

One may posit that the development of a knowledge base is based upon the assumptions and fundamental beliefs of those individuals in policymaking leadership positions. These individuals are likely to be white males. Shakeshaft (1987b) suggests that development of any knowledge-based model in educational leadership will describe society and the world as perceived through a "male prism" or a "male's lens."

The underlying assumption is that the experiences of males and females are the same and thus research on males is appropriate for generalizing to the female experience. In developing theories of administration, researchers didn't look at the context in general and therefore, were unable to document how the world was different for women. When female experiences were different, they were ignored or diminished (150).

Shakeshaft (1987) also posited an "androcentric" perspective that is defined as the practice of viewing the world and shaping reality through a male lens. Shakeshaft contends that androcentrism represents the elevation of the masculine to the level of the universal and the ideal and thereby honors men and male principles above women. This perception creates the belief in male superiority and a masculine value system in which women's values, experiences, and behaviors are viewed as inferior (94–95).

Shakeshaft contends as well that the work culture and experiences of males and females in educational organizations are quite different. She presents five characteristics of the female culture in educational oganizations:

1. "Women spend more time with people, communicate more, care more about individual differences, are concerned more with teachers and marginal students, and motivate more.... staffs of women administrators rate women higher, are more productive, and have higher morale. Students in schools with women principals also have higher morale and are more involved in student affairs.... parents are more favorable toward schools and districts run by women...

2. Women exhibit a more democratic, participatory style, involve themselves more with staff and students, ask for and get higher participation,. . .and maintain more closely knit organizations. They have higher job satisfaction and are more engaged in their work than male administrators. . .

3. Since women are more likely to behave the same way in public as they do in private, men often label their behavior inappropriate. . .

4. The female administrator is always vunerable to attack in the male culture of educational administration. Whether or not the assault actually occurs is less important than the knowledge that it is always possible. Women perceive their token status. . .

5. Women administrators exhibit greater knowledge of teaching methods and techniques, are more likely to help new teachers and supervise all teachers directly, and create a climate more conducive to learning, that is orderly, safer, and quieter. Academic achievement is higher in districts in which women are administrators. . .(197–198)

The work cultures of women and minorities are quite different (Edson 1988; Schmuck 1981; Shakeshaft 1987); therefore, these differences create at least two distinct cultures (Schaef 1981). These findings suggest that women and minorities must negotiate between their cultural contexts and the dominant white male culture. Before one can begin to rethink the knowledge base in educational administration, the distinctly different work cultures of white males, white females, nonwhite males, and nonwhite females must be considered. The experiences of these groups in a culture dominated by white males should not be ignored.

Can a Knowledge Base Be Developed?

Most scholars agree that educational administration is a legitimate field of inquiry. Thomson (1992) contends that education administration has at least four sources of knowledge:

1. What everyone knows: These are the generally accepted tenets and ideals of the profession, derived from the experiences of practioners and observers of educational administration practice.

2. What practice demonstrates: these are the strategies that have proven to produce certain effects.

3. What authorities say: these are observations, often expressed as generalizations or principles, made by those whose status, owing to experience and quality of their scholarly study, is given special credence.

4. What research confirms: These are findings that have been confirmed by evidence, arrived at through known procedures, and subjected to critical review and further testing. (18)

It is apparent that the connections among these four sources are weak at best. Unfortunately, "what everyone knows" has not been reflected in the tenets of the profession. The observers and practitioners continue to be guided by a model that reflects the ideals of a culture dominated by white males. The ideology does not reflect tenets of diversity. The practices continue to ignore what minority and women authorities say and what research has confirmed. As Thomson (1992) noted, with rapidly changing conditions, the knowledge base will never be complete or adequate.

Summary

The work environments for women and minorities have frequently been perceived as hostile and nonsupportive entities. Historically, leadership positions in educational organizations have been dominated by white males. Traditionally, these individuals have made decisions about who joins their organizations. Such decisions serve as agents of reproduction. This status quo model has failed to include women and minorities in positions of leadership and in discussions about the knowledge base in educational administration. Until these perspectives are included, any proposed knowledge base in educational administration is of little value.

References

Bernstein, R. 1976. The *Restructuring of Social and Political Theory*. New York: Harcourt Brace and Jovanovich.

Cooper, B., and W. Boyd, 1987. The Evolution of Training for School Administrators. In J. Murphy and P. Hallinger, eds., *Approaches to Administrative Training in Education*, Albany, NY: State University of New York Press, 3–27.

Edson, S. 1988. *Pushing The Limits: The Female Administrative Aspirant.* Albany: State University of New York Press.

Foster, W. P. 1984. Toward a Critical Theory of Educational Administration. In Sergiovanni, T., ed., *Leadership and Organizational Culture.* Urbana, Il.: University of Illinois Press, 240–59.

————. 1988. Educational Administration: A Critical Appraisal. In *Leaders for America's Schools.* NCEE: 68–81.

Holmes, M. 1986. Traditionalism and Educational Administration. Paper presented at the annual meeting of the American Educational Research Association, San Francisco, Calif.

Jacobson, S., and J. Conway. 1990. *Educational Leadership In An Age of Reform.* New York: Longman.

Owens, R. 1991. *Organizational Behavior In Education.* Englewood Cliffs, N.J.: Prentice Hall.

Schein, E. 1985. *Organizational Culture and Leadership.* San Francisco: Jossey Bass.

Schmuck, P. 1981. *Educational Policy and Management: Sex Differentials.* New York: Academic Press.

Shakeshaft, C. 1987. *Women In Educational Administration.* Newbury Park, Calif.: Sage Publications.

State Education Department. 1982; 1987. *Public School Professional Personnel Report.* New York State: 81–82, 86–87.

Smith, J. K., and J. Blase. 1991. From Empiricism to Hermeneutics: Educational Leadership as a Practical and Moral Activity. *Journal of Educational Administration.* 29(1) 1.

Thomson, S. 1992. *School Leadership.* Newbury Park, Calif.: Corwin Press.

University Council for Educational Administration 1987. *Leaders For America's Schools: The Report of NCEEA.* Tempe AZ.

Lessons of Leadership: A Critique of the Knowledge Base in Educational Administration

Jayminn Sulir Sanford, Ed.D.

The National Policy Board's recommendations for revising the curriculum in administrative preparation programs highlight seven areas of practice comprising the knowledge base in educational administration. Predictably, the areas broadly sweep the surfaces of long-accepted and comfortable categories of practice. This enables some well-intentioned educators to take a place in the treadmill of reform without making a genuine commitment to change. The propensity to interpret policy through lenses of the familiar is encouraged by the composition of seven subcommittees charged with articulating each area, and ensured in the language used by The Policy Board to outline the recommendations.

With the phrase "transmitting knowledge that is grounded in the problems of practice," The Policy Board first suggests that the process of teaching and learning is one of transferring knowledge from professors to students. This approach to instruction is conducive to a shallow interpretation of the seven areas comprising the recommendation. Scholarship about learning, some of which was generated in response to the call for a knowledge base in teacher education, has altered perspectives about teaching and learning. The active construction of meaning, beginning with existing knowledge builds upon the insight of early educational discourse, which emphasizes community-building and shared inquiry (Dewey 1932).

More recently, learning theorists have described the nature of teaching and learning as the application of student-constructed and content-specific strategies for approaching new information; these strategies are motivated by modeling and coached by teachers in cooperation with peers. This construction of teaching and learning directly impacts upon many areas of administrative practice, including the ways in which teachers are supervised and children are evaluated. This new scholarship should be reflected not only in what we teach aspiring school administrators, but in how we teach them.

The phrasing of the recommendation implies also that professors may, like their students, need to learn new ways to approach instruction in these seven comfortable areas of practice, in order to engage in a different kind of discourse about elements of effective school leadership. Thus, more than transmission of knowledge, there is a need for knowledge and skills to be developed and fostered through a continuous mutual process of action, reflection and reaction that interprets and makes relevant the scholarship about teaching and learning.

Likewise, characterizing the areas comprising the knowledge base as "problems of practice" suggests an interpretation of the practice of educational administration as one of skillfully managing obstacles. This is a negative approach to analyzing elements of administrative practice. Rather, there seems a need for aspiring school leaders to conceptualize the components of administrative processes by recognizing overt and latent opportunities to maximize school success.

If areas of administrative practice are conceptualized as problems of practice, one of two learning constructs may result. Either aspiring administrators learn that in college classrooms they cannot be taught ways to educate children and are therefore left to their own devices, or worse, aspiring administrators learn that they are preparing to lead an inherently problematic organization, which makes it unrealistic for them to expect to effect change. A more positive approach would be to conceptualize areas of administrative practice in terms of the possibilities for success, given the structure and dynamics of schools and ways in which school organizations have been successfully adapted to maximize success.

Such opportunities exist for each of the seven areas comprising the recommendation. In a seminar last Fall, a student described an experience in a local elementary school that operationally reflects several areas of administrative practice. Children were involved in a school-wide Halloween parade in which original costumes would be judged by a team of parents, students and teachers. The winner was to receive a gift certificate to a local toy store. The day before the event a number of students were involved in a disciplinary incident that resulted in their not being allowed to participate in the parade. The parent of one of the students involved in the incident had spent a good deal of time making the costumes that her three children were to wear in the parade. This parent was known to be boisterous and demanding. When she approached the principal on the morning of the parade, everyone expected trouble. The parent insisted that the principal rescind the disciplinary action and permit her eldest child to participate with his siblings. The teachers involved felt strongly that the principal should not give in. They wanted administrative support for their decision not to allow any of the children involved in the incident to participate. These teachers considered the principal's handling of the parent's demand to be a personal insult and a bad example for all of the children. The children felt that it was unfair for some to be allowed to participate when others, who were now unprepared because they had been told not to bring their costumes, would still be punished.

This simple example is typical of the kinds of incidents that occur in schools on a daily basis. This situation taps into each of the seven areas outlined by The Policy Board in that:

1. In this situation the school reflected unfairness that exists in society. All of the costumes were to be judged using the same criteria, even though some were made by children and others were obviously made by adults, who by their experiences and resources were more aptly prepared.

2. There was the last-minute possibility that some students would be forgiven their infraction and allowed to participate, while others would not be able to participate, even if they were forgiven as well. These are the ways in which we teach and learn about life. Such incidents, common to all schools, teach children the unfortunate but honest lesson that life is sometimes unfair.

3. The structure and dynamics of the school as an organization focused all attention on the principal as the final voice in interpreting school policy and practice regarding both discipline and appropriate relationships with parents.

4. The moral and ethical dimension of administrative practice placed the principal in the position of having to make an uncomfortable choice. By supporting the teachers' discipline, the principal could alienate an interested and involved parent whose younger children would be students there for four and five more years. In allowing the children to participate, the principal could set a negative precedent for teachers and students with regard to school discipline, negatively affect the morale and sense of teacher

empowerment and lose respect as a leader. Either decision could lead to negative consequences.

The principal's ultimate decision to allow all of the children, even those without costumes, to participate in the parade reflected a moral decision to let the adults take the heat, in order to teach the children about fairness as painlessly as possible, given the circumstances.

In a college classroom, if this example were conceptualized as a reflection of areas that are problems of administrative practice, the focus may turn to issues of annoying and sometimes intimidating parents, glitches in a policy allowing children's creativity to be measured with adults' and punishment that is inappropriately effected twenty-four hours after the infraction. If, on the other hand, this example were conceptualized as both an overt and latent opportunity for administrative success, the ensuing discussion would be more focused on creative possibility. The teaching and learning process, in the latter case, would require greater insight, a broader level of understanding and sense of discovery, and a deeper level of thought. How might this parent's creative talent and availability for involvement be channeled into activities that support the mission of the school? What actions might the Principal take to encourage teachers to think differently about punishment? How might the school create a learning environment in which children are taught both to value fairness and understand the negative realities of life? What should policies regarding contests and the awarding of prizes include with regard to equal opportunity? What aspects of the organization support this principal's choice? How might the principal and the superintendent effect change in this environment?

Inherent in the opportunity for a minimal-impact interpretation of The National Policy Board's recommendations is an opportunity for the University Council for Educational Administration committees to articulate these time-tested areas of administrative practice in an inclusive, compelling and timely manner. For this to happen, the work of the committees must be reflective of the voices of those with the most at stake—students, parents and teachers—and be grounded in a sense of professional ethics and moral responsibility for the future of leadership in the nation's schools.

While The Policy Board recognizes the importance of "societal and cultural influences on schooling", the phrasing of this area of practice understates the relationship between society and schools. Society does more than influence schools. Schools are, in fact, mirror

images of society, reflecting both its ills and its splendor. Encouraging administrators to view schools in the latter context characterizes the relationship between schools and society more appropriately. The educational reform debate becomes less focused on
ways in which the culture of schools is in opposition to the cultures
of the communities they service. Rather than conceptualizing
schools as being in opposition to community and needing to defend
themselves against society, the focus of the discourse can shift to
ways in which components of community cultures have or may
become a part of school culture.

Literature about successful urban schools. for example, cites
the importance of involving community groups and parents in
ongoing meaningful activities related to curriculum and instruction as well as to policy development. These schools are successful
to the extent that the involvement of the community is not
considered a problem, but rather is sought out, structured and
welcomed (Blase 1991; Sizemore 1987; Edmonds 1979; Comer 1980;
Irvine 1988; Taylor 1988; Gladden 1988; and others).

"The American Dilemma", a term coined by Gunnar Myrdal,
refers to the inconsistencies that exist between institutional discrimination and racism and the nation's stated ideals of equality
and justice. Human rights activists have experienced success in
fighting discrimination to the extent that they have been able to
pinpoint inconsistencies between societal behavior and societal
ideals. From this model of societal reform emerges an opportunity
for school reform. If leaders of educational institutions view schools
as reflectors of both the ills and splendor of society, there emerges
both opportunity and method for addressing these inconsistencies.
For those involved in preparing aspiring school administrators as
well as their students, this necessitates focusing on the ways in
which schools reflect society and on maximizing leaders' opportunities to enable teachers, students and parents to engage in
democratic processes and address inconsistencies between what is
real and what is ideal.

Additionally, if leaders understand that schools mirror society
and reflect the many variables that comprise culture (race,
nationality, social class, economic class, religion, and gender among
other areas of exceptionality), those leaders can begin to understand
ways in which institutions may be managed more effectively. The
combination of variables that define the culture of each individual
within the school affects the thinking and behavior of teachers and
students. The teaching implications of combined cultural characteristics and the effect on learning styles and teaching styles has

been well documented. (Cavanaugh 1981; Davidman 1981; Dunn 1980; Ellis 1981; Fischer 1980; Gregoric 1979; Hale-Benson 1982; Hunt 1977; Kirby 1980; Languis 1981; and others). The administrator's role becomes one of understanding, interpreting and mediating the cultural characteristics of individuals and groups within the school to maximize teaching and learning.

Therefore, administrative preparation programs must move beyond inclusion of sociological studies of communities, in order to develop educational leaders who have the ability to analyze ways in which societal realities and ideals are transmitted in casual discourse and daily interaction between and among teachers and students.

The second area of practice, that of "teaching and learning processes and school improvement," is worded to imply that The Policy Board realizes the need for school improvement with regard to the processes of teaching and learning. However, in order to be effective in this area administrators must become aware of hidden aspects of the curriculum in schools. Attention must be focused on the school's hidden curriculum and its implicit norms and values.

> A school has both a manifest and a hidden curriculum. The manifest curriculum consists of such factors as guides, textbooks, bulletin boards, and lesson plans. These aspects of the school environment are important and must be reformed to create a school culture that promotes positive attitudes toward diverse cultural groups and helps students from these groups experience academic success. However, the school's hidden or latent curriculum is often more cogent than its manifest or overt curriculum. The latent curriculum has been defined as the one that no teacher explicitly teaches but that all students learn. It is that powerful part of the school culture that communicates to students the school's attitudes toward a range of issues and problems, including how the school views them as human beings. (Banks, 21)

This can be said of curriculum in administrative preparation programs as well. While it realizes that there is need for improvement in teaching and learning processes in schools, The Policy Board does not recommend that administrative preparation programs engage with that process. In this sense, The Policy Board is asking people to teach what they do not know and may not know how to understand.

In articulating this area of practice, the University Council for Educational Administration must delineate the need for administrative preparation programs to model an examination of both overt and latent curriculum. Rather than sprinkling existing syllabi with works of a few acceptable women and people of color, courses in administration preparation programs must, by example, present each topic in an inclusive way. Attention must be given to the uses of language, tone and emphasis, as well as to the inclusion of scholarship of people of color and of women.

After interviewing students who represented educational administration graduate programs in three regions of the United States, Parker and Shapiro (1992) concluded that aspiring administrators felt their institutions were not adequately meeting their need to learn about ways in which the complexities of diversity affect interaction between groups in schools and society. Drawing from patterns of responses emerging during the course of the research, Parker and Shapiro recommend seven strategies for addressing this perceived inadequacy, including;

> ...preparation of school leaders to be well versed in different cultures and salient issues of curriculum, instruction and evaluation so they can become advocates for those less powerful and so they can articulate the case against standardized measures of traditional achievement and discipline procedures which work against minorities...and a broad perspective on issues of difference which extends beyond race, class and gender, into other areas (for example, differently able, sexual preference, age) which might create potential staff problems and [require] advocacy by a school leader. (24)

Only after administrative preparation programs have themselves engaged in this process of pedagogical self-analysis is it reasonable to expect that they will be able to teach aspiring administrators to do the same.

The third area, termed "organizational theory," and the fifth, "leadership and management process and functions," address the need for school leaders to be aware of the structure of schools and dynamics of group organizational life as well as of their role as organizational leaders. It is not enough to teach facilities management and financial planning, supervision and management theory. An important element of group facilitation in organizational life is that the leader understand clearly the purpose of the group, the perceptions of their role as leader, and the dynamics of group interaction.

The role of the leader or facilitator is to ensure that members of the group can accomplish their stated goals. The purpose of this focus is to ensure that each group member experiences egalitarianism, shares responsibility for what happens, and enacts an agenda that serves the group's purpose (Center for Conflict Resolution 1978). In school settings, the group leader is the administrator, the members of the group are teachers, students and parents, and the group's purpose is to ensure student achievement. The administrator must accept the responsibility for enabling the group to accomplish this one central goal—student achievement. All else is secondary.

Research about urban schools clearly cites visionary leadership as one of the characteristics most responsible for academic achievement. Edmonds (1979) concludes that "administrative behaviors, policies, and practices in schools appeared to have a significant impact on school effectiveness" (16). In 1988, Irvine included among common characteristics of successful urban schools, the "clearly stated, measurable goals that are understood and accepted by their students, staff, teachers, parents and community. Although these goals and objectives can be found in such traditional publications as manuals, handbooks, and newsletters, the principal is the key to operationalizing these goals" (238). Other scholars of urban education have drawn similar conclusions about ways in which the principal's leadership in establishing expectations that set the tone for the school, and the principal's ability to motivate achievement, is directly linked to school success (Blase 1991; Comer 1980; Taylor 1988; Gladden 1988; and others).

The experience of success is one of the simplest sources of human motivation. Enabling students and teachers to experience success is a challenge that should be one of the foci of organizational theory in administrative preparation programs. In articulating these two areas of practice, The Policy Board must consider the role of success in the dynamics of organizational life and in the perception of the school leader's role as visionary.

The fourth area outlined by The Policy Board, "organizational studies and policy analysis", and the sixth, "policy studies and politics of education", should include careful examination of practice, policy and politics in schools in which teachers and students are experiencing success. Articulation of this area of administrative practice must include developing administrators' abilities to think critically about what they read and observe. While educational literature is replete with examples of successful schools in high socioeconomic and monocultural neighborhoods is popular, administrative preparation programs must engage in an ongoing search for literature about successful schools in communities reflecting the global majority. (Such is the scholarship of Comer 1980; Hilliard 1991; Hughes 1988; Irvine 1988; Nicholsonne 1988; Pink 1987; Sizemore 1987; Taylor 1988; and others.) In addition to requiring that students engage in organizational studies of the spectrum of the nation's schools, administration preparation programs must contribute to this scholarship in meaningful ways.

The gap between theory and research begins to close when faculty members become meaningfully engaged with existing schools. To the extent that faculty scholarship is based on research questions that emerge from school practice, subsequent theories relate to practice in a way that administrators and teachers can recognize and interpret. The Policy Board must address the need for administrative preparation programs to become facilitators of meaningful scholarship about successful schools.

In today's schools, the politics of education requires administrators to interact effectively with corporations and civic groups, as well as with school boards, district administration and health and social service professionals. Principals and schools are dependent upon the continued generosity of civic support and corporate gifts, in some cases for elements of schooling as fundamental as dropout prevention. The welcomed response of industry and corporations to the crisis in education has rendered schools beholden to their charity. If we are to be earnest about preparing people for the schools they will enter and lead, we need to include this dimension of administrative practice in The Policy Board's articulation of the study and analysis of policy and politics of education.

It can be argued that the final area of practice outlined by The Policy Board, that of "moral and ethical dimensions of schooling", is the most important aspect of school leadership. Encouraging aspiring school leaders to develop, within their personal philosophies of education, a working knowledge of the role that morals and ethics play in schooling is fundamental to an understanding of cultural influences, teaching and learning processes, organizational theory and methods of study and analysis, and to management processes and politics.

Motivation to engage in study of administrative process, indeed for aspiring to school leadership, exists alongside a moral and ethical experience of one's role in society. Educators who become administrators were first teachers. Many became teachers because of a moral and ethical pull toward the service work of guiding and molding the next generation of citizens. Some have since become disenchanted with the teaching experience and have subsequently entered administration programs in an effort to make schools better places to work and to learn. Others seek financial and social advances symbolizing success in a Protestant work-ethic interpretation of the so-called "American Dream". In either case, these students are attempting to improve upon what they view as societal or personal realities. In this way, the decision to make educational leadership one's life's work is predicated on the personal, moral and ethical understandings that a person has of his or her role in society.

Similarly, the separation of church and state has not separated personal moral and ethical beliefs from personal political persuasion. In analyzing the belief that schooling is, by its very nature, a political activity, Foster (1986) contends that school leadership is a moral science. Critical theorists discuss ways in which administrators, students, teachers and parents cause political change (Yeakey 1987; Freire 1985; Dantley 1990; Graman 1988; and others). Dantley, in describing schools as "arenas of struggle and preparation for societal reconstruction," explains that "schools are the bastions of democratic policies and practices. . . serv[ing] as the preparatory arenas for the makers of political and social change. . .causing students to become critically reflexive citizens" (595). He explains as well that "Led by critically aware Principals,. . . schools. . . become arenas where the fundamentals of pedagogy also serve as the technology for political struggle" (594). The critical awareness referred to here calls upon administrators to responsibly embrace their role as school leaders in a society that is changing by necessity and by demand.

Students of school leadership enter into educational administration programs with their own ideas about needed changes in schools, which are a product of their personal understanding of morals and ethics. Decisions about which elements of schooling must change, in what ways and by what devices, are spawned by moral and ethical beliefs about ways in which society must change. In articulating this area of practice, The Policy Board must recognize that aspiring school leaders are empowered by this critical awareness of the political impact of education. Regardless of personal political persuasion, this sense of empowerment is likely to be reflected in an administrator's sense of professional purpose, longevity and commitment to education.

The National Policy Board's recommendations for a knowledge base in educational administration must be articulated and interpreted in a way that reflects thoughtful consideration of leadership in today's schools. This means validating time-tested areas of practice by including critical scholarship that interprets and articulates each of the seven areas outlined in the recommendations. Students of educational leadership have first-hand experience in schools and educational systems. They already know much of what is wrong and why. Aspiring school leaders expect to be provided with the most timely and relevant interpretations of their individual and collective potential for maximizing school success. They will accept no less.

References

Banks, J. and Banks, C. 1989. *Multicultural Education: Issues and Perspectives*. Boston: Allyn Bacon.

Blase, J. (ed.). 1991. *The Politics of Life in Schools*. Newbury Park: Sage.

Cavanaugh, D. 1981. "Student Learning Styles: A Diagnostic/ Prescriptive Approach to Instruction." *Phi Delta Kappa*. Bloomington, Indiana: Phi Delta Kappa, 202–03.

Center For Conflict Resulution. 1978. *A Manual For Group Facilitators*. Madison: Center for Conflict Resolution.

Comer, J. 1980. *School Power*. New York: The Free Press.

Dantley, M. 1990. "The Ineffectiveness of Effective Schools Leadership: An Analysis of the Effective Schools Movement from a Critical Perspective." *Journal of Negro Education*, 59(4): 585–98.

Davidman, L. 1981. "Learning Style: The Myth, The Panacea, The Wisdom." *Phi Delta Kappa*. Bloomington, Indiana: Phi Delta Kappa, 641–45.

Dewey, J. 1938. *Education and Experience*. New York: Macmillan.

Dijk, T. 1987. *Communicating Racism: Ethnic Prejudice in Thought and Talk*. Newbury Park: Sage.

Dunn, R. 1980. "Learning Styles/Teaching Styles: Should They, Can They Be Matched?" *Educational Leadership* 37: 238–44.

Edmonds, R. 1979. "Effective Schools For The Urban Poor." *Educational Leadership* 37: 15–23.

Ellis, S. 1981. "Models of Teaching: A Solution to the Teaching/Learning Style Dilemma." *Educational Leadership* 37: 274–77.

Feldman, D. 1983. *Managing Individual and Group Behavior in Organizations.* New York: McGraw Hill.

Fischer, B. 1980. "Styles in Teaching and Learning" *Educational Leadership* 37: 245–54.

Foster, W. 1986. *Paradigms and Promises: New Approaches to Educational Administration.* New York: Prometheus Books.

Freire, P. 1985. *The Politics of Education: Culture, Power and Liberation.* South Hadley, Mass. Bergin and Garvey.

Gladden, E. and Gladden, J. 1988. "The Dunbar Chronicle: A Case Study" *Journal of Negro Education* 57 (3): 372–93.

Glickman, C. (ed.). 1991. *Supervision in Transition.* Washington, D.C.: Association for Supervision and Curriculum Development.

Graman, T. 1988. "Education for Humanization: Applying Paolo Freire's Pedagogy to Learning a Second Language." *Harvard Educational Review* 58 (4): 433–48.

Gregorie, A. 1979. "Learning and Teaching Styles: Potent Forces Behind Them." *Educational Leadership* 37: 234–36.

Hale-Benson, J. 1982. *Black Children: Their Roots Culture and Learning Styles.* Baltimore: Johns Hopkins University Press.

Hilliard, A. 1991. "Do We Have the Will to Educate All Children?" *Educational Leadership* 37: 31–36.

Hughes, C. 1988. "The Success Story of Lee Elementary School: Arise Program" *Journal of Negro Education* 57 (3): 267–81.

Hunt, D. 1977. "Learning/Teaching Styles." In *Conference on Multiculturalism in Education,* ed. Sheilagh Dubois. Toronto: OISE.

Irene, J. 1988. "Urban Schools That Work: A Summary of Relevant Factors." *Journal of Negro Education* 57 (3): 236–42.

Jones, R. (ed.). 1980. *Black Psychology.* New York: Harper & Row.

Kirby, P. 1980. *Cognitive Style, Learning Style and Transfer Skill Acquisition.* Ohio: National Center for Research in Vocational Education.

Languis, M. 1981. "Learning Styles: A Point of View For Involving Young Learners." A Paper presented at National Association for the Education of Young Children.

Myrdal, G. 1962. *An American Dilemma: The Negro Problem and Modern Democracy.* New York: Harper & Row.

National Alliance of Black School Educators Inc. 1984. *Saving The African American Child.* Washington, D.C.: National Alliance of Black School Educators.

New York State African American Institute. 1986. *Dropping Out of School in New York State: The Invisible People of Color.* State University of New York: NYS African American Institute.

Nicholsanne, M. 1988. "Strides Toward Excellence: The Hartford Heights Model" *Journal of Negro Education* 57 (3): 282–91.

Norris, C. and Lebsack, J. 1992. "A Pathway to Restructuring: Discussion of a University Pilot for Principalship Preparation." *Journal of School Leadership* 2 (1): 45–59.

Parker, L. and Shapiro, J. 1992. "Where is the Discussion of Diversity in Educational Administration Programs? Graduate Students' Voices Addressing an Omission in their Preparation." *Journal of School Leadership* 2 (1): 7–34.

Pink, W. 1987. "Continuing The Struggle to Improve Urban Schools: An Effective Schools Project Revisited." *Journal of Negro Education* 56 (2): 184–202.

Shaefer, W. 1990. *Education Without Compromise.* San Franscisco: Jossey-Bass.

Sizemore, B. C. 1987. "The Effective African American Elementary School." In *Schooling in Social Context*, ed. George Noblit. New Jersey: Abbex, 175–202.

Taylor, L. 1988. "Success Against the Odds: Effective Educational of Inner-City Youth in a New York City Public High School." *Journal Negro Education* 57 (3): 347–61.

Yeakey, C. 1987. "Critical Thought and Administrative Theory: Conceptual Approaches to Decision Making." *Planning and Changing* 18 (1): 23–32.

Fe/male Voices: Leadership and the Knowledge Base

Rosemary Papalewis

Whether leaders are male or female does not automatically determine their patterns of communication or modes of conduct. However, because the socialization processes and personal experiences of men and women often differ considerably, the way that they express themselves and relate to others often differs, too.

Traditional writings in educational administration have tended to disregard the existence of different types of leadership "voices" and behaviors. Instead, scholars have seemed to prefer to ascribe to all educational leaders—regardless of their sex—a uniform, typically "male" way of perceiving and relating.

Lynch (1990), for example, notes that female experience has traditionally been explained by comparing it against theories derived from male experience. When these theories have not worked, scholars have typically concluded that the women were "lacking," rather than considering the possibility that the theories were incomplete.

The tendency of scholars to minimize, if not ignore, women's experiences has resulted in a biased presentation about male/female differences. This, in turn, has not only disadvantaged women who want to be leaders but has often made administrative programs more of a hindrance than a help in their development, It also has robbed leaders in the field of an opportunity to learn from what women can teach us, especially in the areas of communication and relationships.

This chapter makes a case for educational administration literature to be more inclusive and reflect the broad range of male and female communication and relationship styles. The focus is first on literature about general female patterns of communicating and relating, and then on how these general patterns manifest themselves when women take on leadership positions.

Female Patterns of Communicating and Relating

An important vehicle for the transmission of sex role behavior is language, both in its depiction of females and males and in its use by females and males (Borisoff and Merrill 1985; Scott 1979). The relative power or status of an individual is also largely conveyed through language.

A review of the literature pertaining to gender patterns of communication (Kahn 1984; Papalewis and Brown 1989; Shakeshaft 1987; Tannen 1990) identified a number of differences between women and men. For example, females look at a speaker when he or she is talking, whereas males do not (Shakeshaft 1987), and females are more likely than males to give testimony and speak about personal issues (Kahn 1984). In addition, females stress interpersonal relationships more than males do (Baird and Bradley 1979), and females joke by making fun of themselves, whereas males joke by poking fun at others (Kotthoff 1984; Shakeshaft 1987).

Other work (Borisoff and Merrill 1985; Kramer 1974; Lakoff 1973; Papalewis 1989; Papalewis and Brown 1989; Scott 1979; Shakeshaft 1991; 1987) supports the existence of two distinct language patterns, one for males and one for females; for instance, female speech has been depicted by Scott (1979) as more likely to be friendly, gentle, enthusiastic, smooth, and directed toward trivial topics. In comparison, male speech has been described as more likely to be forceful, loud, dominating and straight to the point. Scott has suggested that stereotypic characteristics typically assigned to female language (for example, showing concern for the listener, engaging in self-disclosure, and smiling) are more socially desirable than those associated with male language. Nevertheless, he said, female speech is often perceived as comparatively ineffective. Moreover, women speakers are often regarded as comparatively unimportant. His conclusions are in line with a large body of research that attempts to show that female communication patterns are systematically devalued (Broverman, Broverman, Clarkson, Rosenkrantz, and Vogel 1970; Lakoff 1975; Shakeshaft 1987). Indeed, some scholars, in arguing for the superiority of male communication patterns, have suggested that women develop a more "neutral" (that is, male) speech style to become more competent communicators and leaders (Lakoff 1975).

Some researchers have suggested that female leaders play unwitting roles in their own devaluation. Women do this by communicating in manners that are natural to them; for example, answering a question with a question and using a higher-pitched voice. Scholars have found that female intonation is perceived as subordinate and as proof of a speaker's uncertainty (Holmes 1984; Lakoff 1973; Papalewis and Brown 1989). Mannes (1969) has stated that most people do not associate a higher-pitched voice with serious topics. Female authority is further undermined by women's tendency to be more emotive than men. Some scholars have noted that, because females are often perceived as "emotional," they are seldom seen as strong and decisive (Papalewis and Brown 1989; Shakeshaft 1987; Tannen 1990).

Table 1 summarizes significant findings about male and female patterns of communication.

Table 1: Female and Male Patterns of Communication

FEMALE PATTERNS	MALE PATTERNS
Correct speech forms (Labov 1972; Scott 1979)	More frequent use of joking (Coser 1960; Shakeshaft, 1987)
Dynamic intonations, wide range of pitch (McConnell-Ginet 1978; Shakeshaft 1987)	Hostile verbs (Gilley and Summers 1970; Scott 1979; Tannen 1990)
Polite cheerful intonation (Brend 1975; Scott 1979)	Interrupts conversations with females (Scott 1979; Tannen 1990; Zimmerman and West 1975)
Use of expressive intensifiers (Baumann 1976; Lakoff 1975; Scott 1979)	Greater amount of talking Scott 1979; Swacker 1975
Use of questions to express opinions (Dubois and Crouch 1976; Holmes 1984; Lakoff 1973; Preisler 1986; Shakeshaft 1987)	Lower pitch levels (Sachs, Lieberman, and Erickson 1973; Scott 1979)

Female Patterns of Leadership Derived from Other Fields

The very same communication patterns that women are sometimes criticized for are, ironically, what often make them such effective leaders as long as the definition of leadership effectiveness does not exclude these communication patterns from consideration a priori. Research and scholarly discussions on female leadership have taken place primarily in the fields of linguistics, communications, and business. Weller (1988) has found that female leadership revolves around abilities that encourage cooperation, open communication, and team-building. In general, females tend to be vulnerable and open, and to operate through mutual interests rather than through manipulation. They also tend to approach problem solving with a "win-win" mentality, and to take an active interest in the personal growth and professional development of others. Weller noted, however, that this does not mean that women cannot be assertive or competitive. Nor does it mean that males cannot be cooperative or operate through mutual interests. It also does not mean that women's general leadership patterns are ineffective. Baird and Bradley (1979), for instance, in their study of sex differences in the communication styles of organizational managers, found that women were generally viewed as concerned and attentive. Men, on the other hand, were perceived as dominant, directive, and quicker to challenge others. The significance of these differences becomes clear when one considers another finding of Baird and Bradley's study: that the perceived quality of superior-subordinate communication was positively related to employee perceptions of supervisor receptiveness, encouragement, concern, attentiveness, and approval.

In her study of 22 female and 18 male managers and their secretaries, Statham (1987) found that the females and males she studied exhibited similar patterns to those described by Baird and Bradley. For example, she found that women expressed more concern about the welfare of others, whereas males were more concerned with their status in the company. Statham also described female managers as more people-oriented and male managers as more image-engrossed. Moreover, in delegating tasks, female managers preferred to remain involved in the work while male managers preferred to be less involved.

Some scholars have suggested that women, more than men, need to be encouraged to pursue careers in administration (see, for example, Simone 1987). In this regard, it has been argued that perhaps the most significant connections that women establish during their careers are the relationships they form with their mentors (Papalewis 1983).

Women and the Field of Educational Leadership

The literature on women in educational administration has tended to focus on either the inadequacies of women when measured against male-based norms of effective leader behavior as noted above, or on the barriers would-be female leaders confront when they consider entering the profession. This latter body of research is a response to a rather obvious situation: Historically, males have dominated school leadership positions and females have dominated teaching positions. Researchers (Nostrand 1993; Smith and Piele 1989; Weller 1988) have stated several possible reasons for the lack of females in leadership and administrative roles, among them that females have been denied equal opportunity; females are not brought up to consider leadership careers; females lack experience and are denied access to experience: and, of prime import, female leaders have little access to networks and to mentors. The assumption that females fear success, and the pervasiveness of negative stereotypes of women, have also been cited as possible reasons for the lack of female leaders and administrators.

Leonard and Papalewis (1987) identified several other factors that keep women from attaining educational leadership positions. These factors, or "barriers," fall into two categories, intrinsic and extrinsic. Intrinsic barriers include few advancement opportunities, little training, poor self-image, low self-confidence, and lack of determination and motivation. Extrinsic barriers include lack of influential contacts and discrimination. The researchers concluded that, although intrinsic variables may limit the aspirations and potential of certain females, extrinsic variables are the major conditions inhibiting the access of females to educational leadership positions.

To summarize, although we know much of female leadership styles from other fields, research about female educational leaders has tended to revolve around their dilemmas rather than their contributions. We know what obstacles they face, but we know comparatively little about how they administrate. We know even less about the contributions their different approach to leadership may reveal.

Implications

There are at least four implications that can be drawn from the literature that was briefly reviewed here that are relevant to current attempts to articulate a knowledge base for the field. First, there is a need for more research on the contributions women can and do make when they assume leadership positions. Shakeshaft and her students have begun pioneering studies on the topic and their findings are consistent with findings from studies in other fields. There is a need for other researchers to contribute to this worthwhile endeavor.

Another area that needs to be investigated is the area of mentoring. Given what we know about women's orientation toward relationships, it may be that mentoring relationships—particularly certain kinds of mentoring relationships—may be even more important than a formal knowledge base in helping women grow and develop as educational leaders. The existing research on mentoring from other fields and the very limited work on this topic in our own indicates that both males and females tend to view mentoring as a career development activity ("Tell me how to succeed"). However, females additionally tend to view mentoring as an opportunity for emotional development and personal well-being ("Describe to me the process," "How can this enhance my life?").

Table 2: Literature Specific to Female Mentoring Relationships

1. Very often females were unaware that their first relationship was a mentoring relationship (Jewell 1990).

2. Often females do not trust the mentoring relationship until proof of attaining the professional goal is made, such as getting the job desired, graduating, etc. (Papalewis 1983).

3. Females who had been mentored (in this particular study) had established a career direction of demonstrated competence before the benefactor appeared (Jewell 1990).

4. Females who had advanced in their careers without a patron, traveled as fast, but they did it with greater self-doubt (Jewell 1990).

5. Cross-sex mentoring relationships for females have considerable potential to be exploitative and that the introduction of sex and sexuality into mentoring relationships has a distinctively negative impact on equitable opportunities (LaFrance 1987; Paludi and Hidore-Haring 1987).

6. Mentored females felt that "success and power" were one and the same thing, therefore increasing their sense of personal empowerment (Jewell 1990).

7. Being a mentor and helping to develop the careers of others can effect a females' career in some of the same positive ways as having a mentor (Keele and DeLamare-Schaeffer 1984).

8. Female mentors can increase female identification with successful role models, provide valuable information, and create incentives through illustrative success (Hidore-Haring 1987).

9. Females see mentoring responsibilities as relationships that encourage not only career development, but also emotional development and well being (Keele and DeLamare-Schaeffer 1984; O'Leary 1988).

Table 2 summarizes much of what we know about mentoring, but there are many issues that still need to be discussed on this topic. For example, scholars disagree as to whether women's mentors should be female or male (Gilligan 1982; McElhiney and Bennington, 1990; Miller 1984). Some believe that women should be mentored by females. Others contend that women should be mentored by males, due to the generally more elevated status of men in the professions. Of course, if males and females become sensitive to gender differences in communication and leadership patterns and develop a repertoire of communication and leadership patterns as a result, it is possible that this whole question will become moot.

This possibility leads us to a third implication: Existing research that has been reviewed in this chapter and the research that has been called for here must become part of educational administration's knowledge base and be presented in educational administration courses. Only if we do this will women be able to see themselves in the material taught and build upon the various talents they already possess. Similarly, inclusion of this literature is necessary to insure that women *and* men are exposed to a broad repertoire of leadership options and strategies.

To insure that these things happen, let me draw a fourth and final implication from what has been presented here: We must continue to be sensitive to language's potential to promote both inclusion and exclusion. To maximize the former potential and minimize the latter, I propose considering the adoption by the field of a new term, "fe/male," which more accurately reflects the range of communication patterns and administrative styles that exist in the field of educational leadership. The term "fe/male" places equal emphasis on female and male perspectives. Moreover, its use encourages those in the field to acknowledge the existence—and, in turn, the value—of differing points of view, ways of communicating, and manners of conduct.

References

Baird, J. E., and P. H. Bradley. 1979. "Styles of management and communication: A comparative study of men and women." *Communication Monographs* 46 (2), 101–111.

Baumann, M. 1976. *Two features of women's speech*. In B. Dubois and Crouch (eds.). Proceedings of the Conference on Sociology of Languages of American Women. San Antonio, Texas: Trinity University.

Borisoff, D. and L. Merrill. 1985. *The power to communicate; Gender differences as barriers.* Prospect Heights, Ill. Waveland Press.

Brend, R. N. 1975. "Male-female intonation patterns in American English." Proceedings of the Seventh International Congress of Phonetic Sciences. In B. Thorne and N. Henley (eds.). *Language and sex: Difference and dominance.* Rowley, Mass.: Newbury

Broverman, I., D. Broverman, F. Clarkson, Rosenkrantz, P. and S. Vogel. 1970. "Stereotypes and clinical judgments of mental health." *Journal of Consulting and Clinical Psychology* 34, 1–7.

Coser, R. L. 1960. "Laughter among colleagues." *Psychiatry* 23, 81–95.

Dubois, B. L. and I. Crouch. 1976. "The question of tag questions in women's speech: They don't really use more of them, do they?" *Language in Society, 4.*

Gilley, H. M. and C. S. Summers. 1970. "Sex differences in the use of hostile verbs" *Journal of Psychology,* 33–37.

Gilligan, C. 1982. *In a different voice: Psychological Theory and Women's Development.* Cambridge, Mass.: Harvard University Press.

Hanson, E. M. 1991. *Educational administration and organizational behavior,* (3rd ed.). Boston, Mass.: Allyn and Bacon.

Hidore-Haring, M. 1987. "Mentoring as a career enhancement strategy for women." *Journal of Counseling and Development* 66, 147–148.

Holmes, J. 1984. "Hedging your bets and sitting on the fence: Some evidence for hedges as support structures." *Te Reo* 27, 47–62.

Jewell, S. 1990. "Mentors for women: Career necessity or hype?" *Career Planning and Adult Development Journal* (Summer) 13–15.

Kahn, L. S. 1984. "Group process and sex difference." *Psychology of Women Quarterly* 8 (3), 261–281.

Keele, R. L. and DeLamare-Schaeffer. 1984. "So what do you do now that you didn't have a mentor?" *Journal of the National Association of Women's Deans, Administrators and Counselors* 47 (2), 36–40.

Kotthoff, L. 1984. "Conversational humor: Observations of sex specific behavior." *Women and Language* 8 (1/2), 14–15.

Kramer, C. 1974. Women's speech: Separate but unequal? *Quarterly Journal of Speech, 60* (1), 14–24.

Labov, W. 1972. *Sociolinguistic patterns.* Philadelphia: University of Pennsylvania Press.

LaFrance, M. 1987. *The paradox of mentoring.* Paper presented at the Interdisciplinary Congress on Women, July, Dublin, Ireland.

Lakoff, R. 1973. Language and woman's place. *Language and Society, 1* (2), 45–80.

Lakoff, R. 1975. *Language and woman's place.* New York: Harper and Row.

Leonard, Y. P. & Papalewis, R. Fall, 1987. The underrepresentation of women and minorities in educational administration: Patterns, issues, and recommendations. *Journal of Educational Equity and Leadership, 7* (3), 188–207.

Lynch, K. K. August, 1990. *Women in school administration: Overcoming the barriers to advancement.* Women's Educational Equity Act Publishing Center, 1–5.

Mannes, M. 1969. Women are equal, but. . . . In J. Bachelor, R. Henry & R. Salisbury (Eds.), *Current Thinking and Writing.* New York: Appleton-Century-Crafts.

McConnell-Ginet, S. 1978. Intonation in a man's world. *Signs, 3,* 541–559.

McElhiney, A. & Bennington, A. Summer, 1990. Genesis of a planned mentoring program for re-entry women. *Career Planning and Adult Development Journal,* 13–15.

Miller, J. B. 1984. *The development of women's sense of self* (work in progress). Wellesley, MA: Stone Center for Developmental Services and Studies, Wellesley College.

Nostrand, C. H. V. 1993. *Gender Responsible Leadership.* London: Sage Publications.

O'Leary, L. 1988. Women's relationship with women in the work place. In B. A. Gutek, A. H. Stromberg & L. Larwood (Eds.). *Women and Work.* Newbury Park, GA: Gray, 189–214.

Paludi, M. & Hidore-Haring, M. 1987. Sexuality and sex in mentoring and tutoring: Implications for women's opportunities and achievement. *Peabody Journal of Education,* 164–171.

Papalewis, R. 1983. The mentoring relationship between major advisors and doctoral degree advisees. University Microfilms International, DAQ 56766, Ann Arbor, Michigan.

Papalewis, R. April, 1989. *Gender characteristics of teaching and evaluation measures of instruction.* A paper presented at the annual meeting of the American Educators Research Conference, San Francisco, California.

Papalewis, R. & Brown, R. August, 1989. *Gender communication style and student evaluation of instruction.* Colloquium, University of Sidney, Australia.

Preisler, B. 1986. *Linguistic sex roles in conversation: Social variation in the expression of tentativeness in English.* Berlin: Mouton de Gruyter.

Sachs, J., Lieberman, P. & Erickson, D. 1973. Anatomical and cultural determinants of male and female speech. In R. Shuy & R. Rasold (Eds.). *Language and Attitudes: Current Trends and Prospects.* Washington, D. C.: Georgetown University Press, 74–84.

Scott, K. P. 1979. *Language and gender: Stereotypes revisited.* Paper presented at the annual meeting of the American Educational Research Association, San Francisco, CA.

Shakeshaft, C. 1991. *A cup half full: A gender critique of the knowledge base in educational administration.* A paper presented at the Annual Meeting of the American Educational Research Association, Chicago, Ill.

Shakeshaft, C. 1987. *Women in educational administration.* Beverly Hills, CA: Sage Publications.

Simone, A. 1987. *Academic women working towards equality.* South Hadley, MA: Bergin & Garvey.

Smith, S. C. & Piele, P. K. (Eds.). 1989. *School leadership, handbook for excellence.* Eugene, OR: ERIC Clearinghouse on Educational Management.

Statham, A. 1987. The gender model revisited: Differences in the management styles of men and women. *Sex Roles, 16* (7/8), 409–429.

Swacker, M. 1975. The sex of the speaker as a sociolinguistic variable. In B. Thorne & N. Henley (Eds.). *Language and sex: Difference and dominance.* Rowley, MA: Newbury.

Tannen, D. 1990. *Women and Men in Conversation.* New York: Ballantine Books.

Weller, J. 1988. Women in educational leadership. *Monograph of the Center for Sex Equity, The Ohio State University, 3* (4), 1.

Zimmerman, D. H. & West, C. 1975. Sex roles, interruptions and silences in conversation. In B. Thorne & N. Henley (Eds.). *Language and sex: Difference and dominance.* Rowley, MA: Newbury.

PART III

Adding New Points of View: Alternative Theoretical Approaches and Models

The Micropolitics of Education

Joseph Blase

In recent years, significant theoretical and empirical work in the micropolitics of education has produced strong linkages between this new knowledge base and affiliate areas such as the politics of education, organizational theory, and critical theory. However, the general area of inquiry has developed slowly over the last several decades. This chapter briefly examines the origins of micropolitics, along with some major approaches to micropolitics in education, political interactions between principals and teachers, and other political research in education. Research methodologies and theoretical perspectives, recommendations for research, and implications of the micropolitical perspective for practice are also discussed.

Origins of Micropolitics

Much of the early work in micropolitics began in the fields of public administration and management as a direct challenge to traditional-rational (consensus) models of organization discussed by Weber (1947), Taylor (1947), and Fayol (1949), and to systems approaches developed by Parsons (1951) and Getzels and Guba (1957). Burns (1961) was among the first theorists in public administration to offer a model of organizations as political systems. He noted that life in organizations naturally consists of both cooperative and conflicting elements; individuals and groups are "at one and the same time cooperators in a common enterprise and rivals for the material and intangible rewards of successful competition with each other" (261). Burns contended that both aspects of organization are necessary to achieving organizational goals. Political coalitions and political obligations were considered the "exchange currency" of organizational behavior.

The early accomplishments of researchers such as Strauss (1962), Cyert and March (1963), and Pettigrew (1973) challenged the traditional apolitical models of organizational functioning. Cyert and March (1963), for instance, addressed the problem of choice under uncertain and complex conditions. They discovered that organizational decision making frequently occurred in a context of disparate goals, which precipitated the development of political coalitions and attempts to achieve individual political goals.

Further examination of the literature reveals a host of theoretical approaches to micropolitics. Wamsley and Zald's (1973) political economy approach to public organization focused on the structure of authority and power in order to define organizational goals, directions, and the boundaries of organizational economy. In the field of management, Mayes and Allen (1977) presented a political approach to organization that extended beyond formal decision processes regarding the allocation of resources. In contrast to earlier work, politics was defined in terms of the pursuit of goals and the use of means not sanctioned by the organization. The writings of Schein (1977), Mangham (1979), and Pfeffer (1981) present other significant views of organizational politics.

Micropolitics of Education: Early Work

It was not until the 1980s, several years after Iannaccone (1975) first introduced his concept of micropolitics, that scholarly work on micropolitics was begun in education. Ball (1987), Bacharach and Mitchell (1987), Bacharach and Lawler (1980), Blase (1987b), and Hoyle (1986) were early pioneers in this new area of educational inquiry. Ball, Bacharach and Lawler, and Bacharach and Mitchell offered comprehensive theoretical perspectives on schools as political organizations. Bacharach and Lawler developed a political approach to organization that focused on meso-level analysis, that is, on group coalition processes and the bargaining relationships and tactics employed in the formal decision-making process. Politics was viewed as "the tactical use of power to obtain or retain real or symbolic resources" (1). This approach assumed a dialectical relationship among organizational structure, environment, and the development of organizational interest groups and coalitions.

Ball's political theory of school organization was developed from studies of British schools. His approach stressed group-level analysis and conflictive interactions; it was grounded in understanding the interests of organizational actors, the maintenance of organizational control (particularly the control styles of school heads), and conflicts over school policy. He states, "I take schools, in common with virtually all other social organizations, to be *arenas of struggle*; to be riven with actual or potential conflict between members; to be poorly coordinated; to be ideologically diverse. I take it to be essential that if we are to understand the nature of schools as organizations, we must achieve some understanding of these conflicts" (19). Ball provides valuable research-based findings about the politics of leadership, age and gender, career, race, gossip, rumor, and the relationship, existing between factors external to the school and school site politics.

Despite the importance of Ball's contribution to the emerging micropolitical knowledge base, certain limitations are apparent in his approach. His focus on conflictive, "darkside" political processes ignores consensual/cooperative political dynamics (Blase 1991b; Burlingame 1988; Townsend 1990). A focus on meso-level (group-level) politics fails to account for the individual's political relationship to the organization (Burlingame). For some, Ball's emphasis on the secondary-school data (Burlingame) and a tendency to overgeneralize from his data (Townsend) raise questions about the validity of his political model of school organization. To deal with these and other issues, Blase (1991b) has constructed a broad-based perspective on micropolitics drawn from a comprehensive review of the extant micropolitical and social power literature:

> Micropolitics refers to the use of formal and informal power by individuals and groups to achieve their goals in organizations. In large part, political actions result from perceived differences between individuals and groups, coupled with the motivation to use power to influence and/or protect. Although such actions are consciously motivated, an action, consciously or unconsciously motivated, may have political "significance" in a given situation. Both cooperative and conflictive actions and processes are part of the realm of micropolitics. Moreover, macro- and micropolitical factors frequently interact. (11)

This definition of micropolitics centers on understanding both legitimate and illegitimate forms of power, the disparate goals (that

is, interests) of individuals and groups, consciously and uncon-
sciously motivated actions conflictive and cooperative/consensual
processes and structures, and the interaction of environmental
factors (extra-organizational) and internal political processes. (See
Blase [1991b] for a full discussion of this definition of micropolitics.)

The Politics of the
Principal-Teacher Relationship

Although research in the micropolitics of education is still in its
infancy, there have been significant accomplishments during the
last several years, particularly with regard to understanding
political relationships between school principals (and school heads)
and teachers.

Ball's (1987) work has provided a number of useful insights into
the micropolitics of school leadership vis-á-vis teachers. Ball
discussed three major styles—interpersonal, managerial, and
political (adversarial and authoritarian)—used by school heads to
control teachers; such control typically resulted in satisfaction,
fatalism, or frustration. Most significant, Ball indicated that all
school heads, regardless of political style, sought to "control"
teachers; consequently, he viewed teacher involvement in program
and policy decisions in the schools studied as "pseudo-participation"
at best.

In another publication, Ball and Bowe (1991) assessed the
impact of certain provisions of the 1988 Education Reform Act in
Britain. The authors analyzed the tensions that arose (between
market concerns of the school's senior management team and the
education preferences of teachers) when new principles of financial
management were applied to schools. Ball and Bowe concluded that
the separation of financial and educational planning significantly
diminished the importance of professional concerns related to
student and collegial needs.

Radnor (1990) also investigated the effects of the 1988
Education Reform Act; however, her study focused on curriculum
changes in one comprehensive high school. Radnor demonstrated
how a school head justified an autocratic political approach to
leadership based on externally imposed changes and assumptions
about teachers' ability to contribute to school-wide program and
policy decisions. Radnor discussed how school structure was
bureaucratized as a result of the Reform Act, how curriculum

decisions were centralized, and how curriculum leaders (heads of departments) were transformed into curriculum managers (rather than initiators).

In two studies that included wide samples of teachers, Blase described relationships that existed between so-called "closed" school principals (that is, principals described as authoritarian, inaccessible, inflexible, nonsupportive) and teachers (1991a) and between control-oriented principals (manipulative, self-serving principals focused on eliciting teacher compliance) and teachers (1990). Blase demonstrated that closedness in principals provoked accommodative, reactive, protective political responses from teachers. A control orientation in principals, expressed through the use of strategies such as sanctions, rewards, harassment, and manipulation of access, in order to achieve self-serving goals, was linked to profound negative outcomes in teachers, including feelings of anger, depression, and a sense of resignation.

From both studies, Blase concluded that although principals typically did not exceed the limits of positional authority, their actions often had devastating effects on teachers because such actions violated organizational and professional values and norms. Blase also found little evidence of collective resistance by teachers to either closed principals or control-oriented principals; instead, teachers' political responses tended to be highly individualized, privatized, and reactive. He argued that such responses on the part of teachers seemed to reinforce the adverse administrative political styles identified above. In another article, Blase (1988a) attributed the development of negative forms of control in administrators, in part, to the school's general vulnerability to hierarchical organizational and environmental factors.

In a study of a varied sample of teachers, Blase (1989) found that the leadership approach of open school principals contributed to the development of a relatively open political orientation in teachers, characterized by the use of such strategies as diplomacy, conformity, extra work, and visibility. Exchange processes were seen as providing the infrastructure for political interaction. School principals' emphasis on interpersonal interactions, Blase noted, contributed to teachers' relatively individualistic (versus collective) political stance.

Anderson (1991) studied how school administrators (in one suburban school) influence teachers through the manipulation of language and ideological control. He described the subtle but powerful effects of "cognitive politics" and its ability to contain and marginalize collective action by teachers in that school district.

Anderson suggested that such forms of political manipulation appear to result in "safe" decisions because organizational premises are shared by all. He argued that subtle means of organizational control of teachers may be used more extensively in the future.

Corbett (1991) studied the effects of community influence on one high school's discipline policy and how a principal's attempts to preempt central office and parental intrusions changed the nature of micropolitics in the school. The principal's inconsistent enforcement of student discipline policy was a means of avoiding confrontation with parents; however, this approach inadvertently led to a redistribution of political power away from teachers to parents and students. Corbett's study made visible some of the salient differences between the micropolitical world of administrators and that of teachers.

At this writing, only a few studies of cooperative (consensual) political relationships between school principals and teachers have appeared in the micropolitical literature. Relationahips established between principals and teacher-leaders, between open/effective principals and teachers are described in the following stuidies.

Smylie and Brownlee-Conyer's (1990) study of innovative working relationships between school principals and teacher-leaders (in one school district) described strategies employed by both groups to shape working relationships. These researchers reported that principals used political influence primarily to control and manage teachers' work and, to a lesser extent, to address interpersonal relationship issues. Teacher-leaders used political influence to advance their ideas, to avoid conflict, and to enhance interpersonal relationships with principals. Smylie and Brownlee-Conyers concluded that establishing working relationships between principals and teacher-leaders involved negotiation and accommodation more than competition; yet, difficulties inherent to working together in collegial relationships (in contrast to superordinate-subordinate relationships) were reported by both principals and teachers.

In a study of the micropolitics of leadership in an elementary school, Greenfield (1991) discovered that effective leadership by both the school principal and teachers relied heavily on moral sources of influence. In effect, a commitment to serve children dramatically affected the development of cooperative political relationships between the principal and teachers and also among teachers themselves. From his data, Greenfield conceptualized a new form of political leadership—the "professional" style—based on moral/value congruence. This style constitutes a fourth type in terms of Ball's (1987) political taxonomy of leadership styles, which included the interpersonal, managerial, and political styles.

Blase's large-sample study (in press) of teachers' perspectives on effective school leadership also demonstrated the significance of a common moral/value base to viable political interactions with teachers. Principals' uses of normative strategies to achieve normative goals (that is, goals and strategies consistent with professional and organizational values) accounted for the political influence of effective principals and their positive impact on teacher work involvement. Blase emphasized that effective principals were primarily control-oriented; however, such control was transacted through an equitable process of exchange and consistent with the normative structure of the school.

Other Micropolitical Research in Education

The studies discussed above investigated political relationships between school principals and teachers. The following studies focus on micropolitical relationships between and among other educational actors: new assistant principals and teachers; a superintendent, principals, and teachers; a department head and teachers; teachers themselves; and teachers and students.

Marshall (1991) and Marshall and Mitchell (1991) employed a socialization perspective to examine the assumptive worlds (that is, shared understandings about what is appropriate) of a group of new assistant principals in one school district. They described explicit and implicit norms—limits on risk taking, avoidance of moral dilemmas, demonstration of loyalty and commitment—that influence assistant principals' evolving political perspectives. The authors argued that the assumptive worlds of fledgling administrators help maintain the myths, beliefs, and structure of schools, and work to resist school restructuring and empowerment efforts.

In a study of the micropolitics of the superintendency, Kline-Kracht and Wong (1991) explored the deleterious effects of a school superintendent's strong top-down political style—a style designed to motivate subordinates by keeping them "off balance"—on a school principal, middle-level administrators, a teacher's union, and individual teachers in one upper middle–class suburban high school. The authors learned that the superintendent's designation of curriculum directors as managers reduced their credibility as curriculum leaders and this, in turn, decreased their ability to influence teachers. Of particular significance was the finding that increases in teachers' collective power (vis-á-vis the union) failed to satisfy teachers' individual needs for power and efficacy.

Lindle's (1991a) micropolitical study of a school merger described how one superintendent used evaluation and race as protective political stratagems. Her study highlighted the point that, to gain credibility, political actors frequently attempt to define political goals in positive moral terms.

Sparkes (1988; 1990) described the control-oriented political style of a physical education department head in a secondary school who attempted curriculum change and the department staffs resistance to such change. Sparkes discussed intradepartmental politics, that is, the political strategies and competing interests and ideologies of the department's head and its members. He contended that the department head's assumption that innovation was a rational, value-free process resulted in confusion and conflict. Also discussed were political attempts by the department head and the department's members to elevate the status of the physical education curriculum in the school by using different forms of rhetoric (which might be termed strategic rhetoric) in place of substantive curriculum changes.

Blase (1987a) examined cooperative and conflictive political interactions among teachers who had worked, over the course of a decade for several principals in one secondary school. Effective administrative leadership was linked to the development of associative (cooperative, supportive, trusting) political relationships among teachers; ineffective administrative leadership was related to the development of dissociative (uncooperative, nonsupportive) political interactions. Using Erickson's (1986) model of culture, Blase argued that the political culture of the school could be viewed as emerging from tensions surrounding core values (norms) characteristic of a particular school setting. In another study of political interactions among teachers, Osborne (1989) reported how Zuni teachers' attempts to promote culturally responsive pedagogy interacted with Anglo teachers' resistance and actually helped to maintain the political and cultural status quo in one school district.

In a study of collegiality conducted in the elementary schools in one school board district in Ontario, Canada, Hargreaves (1991) found that teacher collegiality was actually a form of administrative control (it was regulated, compulsory, fixed in time and space) and that this resulted in "contrived collegiality" characterized by inefficiency and inflexibility. Hargreaves warned that it remains to be seen whether school administrative control of teachers will ever give way to the empowerment of teachers, wherein teachers have substantial responsibility for the development and implementation of curriculum and instruction.

Other micropolitical research has centered on teachers' political orientations to students (Blase 1991b; Bloome and Willett 1991) and teachers' political perspectives toward parents (Blase 1987b). Blase indicated in both of his studies that variations in the political stance of school principals was related to variations in the quality of teachers' political interactions with both students and parents. Administrator-teacher relationships were highlighted in another article that focused on the politics of favoritism (Blase 1988b). Here, Blase found that the political behavior of school board members and superintendents significantly influenced teachers' political orientations to the classroom and to the school as a whole. A comparative case study of two elementary schools in one school district by Noblit, Berry, and Dempsey (1991) demonstrated the powerful effects of existing school-level micropolitical structures on school reform. This study indicated that hierarchical attempts at school reform provided opportunities for teachers to expand political influence.

Methodologies and Theoretical Perspectives

Most of the empirical work in the micropolitics of education has been conducted in the United States, Britain, and Canada. Qualitative procedures (interviews, observation, open-ended questionnaires) and case studies (particularly of secondary suburban schools) have been salient in micropolitical research; however, Blase (1988a; 1988b; 1989) has also used open-ended questionnaires designed to collect detailed data from wide samples of American public school teachers.

Most of these studies have focused on school (building-level) politics, especially principal-teacher relationships; some studies have also examined the effects of environmental factors such as legislation on the micropolitics of schools. Other points of emphasis include conflicts surrounding formal decision-making processes (in contrast to consensual politics and political interaction outside of formal decision-making processes) and the political strategies and tactics, purposes, and impacts of political action. Several political studies have focused on change and innovation processes in schools. Micropolitics has been explored in the context of a range of topics, including reading education, curriculum innovation, discipline policy, control and compliance, administrator socialization, and contrived collegiality.

Socialization theory, conflict theory, exchange theory, compliance theory, power theory, and leadership theory have been the prominent frameworks used either to conduct research into micropolitics or to interpret data produced by such studies.

Recommendations for Research

Although substantial research has centered on principal-teacher relationships, more research along these lines, from a variety of theoretical perspectives, would be valuable. Few studies of upward influence have appeared in the literature (Mowday 1978). Micropolitical research using an action-participatory approach has not been undertaken (Everhart 1991). Other school relationships, events, processes, roles, and problems have received little attention using a micropolitical perspective. For example, cooperative/consensual political processes and structures (Blase 1991b; Burlingame 1988; Townsend 1990) and forms of subtle conflict discussed by such writers as Bachrach and Baratz (1962) and Lukes (1974) have received little empirical attention. Ball (1987) and Bacharach and Mitchell (1987) have offered viable political theories of school organization to ground future research. The scholarly literature is virtually silent with regard to normative political theories of organization. Future educational research would benefit from the use of these and other approaches, including cognitive (Anderson 1991), dramaturgical (Goffman 1959), and sociolinguistic (Trudgill 1983) approaches (See Blase [1991b] for delineation of a framework for future political research).

Implications for Practice

Before substantial empirical work in the micropolitics of education was available, Hoyle (1985) commented:

> Studies of micropolitics could well bring the area much more into the arena of open discussion, but it is not easy to see in what ways this might improve the quality of administration or the quality of life in educational organizations for participants. It is even more difficult to see how the outcome of the study of micropolitics would

feature in courses for practising administrators other than as a general mirror-raising component and as theory-for-understanding. (1581)

To the contrary, it would seem that micropolitical knowledge and skills relevant to understanding, to working in, and to changing the character of life in schools would be quite useful to educational scholars and administrators alike. Blase (1991b) wrote:

The micropolitical perspective on organization provides a valuable and potent approach to understanding the woof and warp of the fabric of day-to-day life in schools. This perspective highlights the fundamentals of human behavior and purpose. Micropolitics is about power and how people use it to influence others and to protect themselves. It is about conflict and how people compete with each other to get what they want. It is about cooperation and how people build support among themselves to achieve their ends. It is about what people in all social settings think about and have strong feelings about, but what is so often unspoken and not easily observed. (1)

Lindle's (1991b) investigations into the relationship between micropolitical knowledge and skill in dealing with the routine functions of school administration strongly suggest its relevance to administrator training. Lindle found that educational administration students in clinical internship programs valued the micropolitical approach over a traditional administrative approach. Further, in graduate courses in educational administration taught by Lindle, students indicated that, as a result of their experiences in schools, they naturally developed a micropolitical perspective and that this perspective was considered critically important to their work. In effect, coursework focusing on micropolitics allowed these students to expand an already evolving and deeply embedded knowledge base about schools as political organizations (National Policy Board for Educational Leadership 1992). Glatter (1982) notes that the skill and judgments needed to make choices amidst a complex array of values and interests are worth serious attention in administrator training. O'Brien (1987) has described the benefits of micropolitical skills to educational planners, who must find ways to cope with the conflict inevitable in implementing new policy.

In a course on the micropolitics of education recently taught by the author of this chapter, educational administration students (most of whom were practicing administrators) indicated that this indicated that this perspective and knowledge base provided fresh and provocative ways to understand life in school. They reported that such understandings helped them to improve their ability to influence others, to construct effective ways to respond to the influence of others, to anticipate the consequences of political interactions, and to analyze the political structure of schools. Students also emphasized the important role that political perspective plays in developing the knowledge and skill requisite to promoting democratic/collegial forms of school governance. In a course evaluation, a student wrote:

> The micropolitics class has been and continues to be valuable to me not only as a professional interested in quality education but in my personal life as well. A new political awareness has enabled me to analyze and respond more effectively and appropriately to the context of situations that I find myself in daily. I can reach beyond the surface rhetoric and delve into the often hidden layer of social interaction that contains the real issues from the perspectives of the people involved. . . . I think people who are serious about education, who are serious about seeing good things happen in schools, will need to look through the lens of micropolitics to make a difference.

References

Anderson, G. 1991. Cognitive politics of principals and teachers: Ideological control in an elementary school. In J. Blase (Ed.), *The politics of life in schools: Power, conflict, and cooperation:* 120–30.

Bacharach, S. B., and Lawler, E. J. 1980. *Power and politics in organizations: The social psychology of conflict, coalitions, and bargaining.* San Francisco: Jossey-Bass.

Bacharach, S. B., and Mitchell, S. M. 1987. The generation of practical theory: Schools as political organizations. In J. W. Lorsch (Ed.), *Handbook of organizational behavior:* 405–18. Englewood Cliffs, NJ: Prentice Hall.

Bachrach, P., and Baratz, M. S. 1962. Two faces of power. *American Political Science Review 56*(4): 947–52.

Ball, S. J. 1987. *The micro-politics of the school: Towards a theory of school organization.* London: Methuen.

Ball, S. J., and Bowe, R. 1991. Micropolitics of radical change: Budgets, management, and control in British schools. In J. Blase (Ed.), *The politics of life in schools: Power, conflict, and cooperation*: 19–45.

Blase, J. 1987a. Political interaction among teachers: Sociocultural contests in the schools. *Urban Education 22*(3): 286–309.

———. 1987b. The politics of teaching: The teacher-parent relationship and the dynamics of diplomacy. *Journal of Teacher Education 38*(2): 53–60.

———. 1988a. The everyday political perspectives of teachers: Vulnerability and conservatism. *Qualitative Studies in Education 1*(2): 125–42.

———. 1988b. The politics of favoritism: A qualitative analysis of the teachers' perspective. *Educational Administration Quarterly 1*(2): 152–77.

———. 1989. The micropolitics of the school: The everyday political perspective of teachers toward open school principals. *Educational Administration Quarterly 25*(4): 377–407.

———. 1990. Some negative effects of principals' control-oriented and protective political behavior. *American Educational Research Journal 27*(4): 727–53.

———. 1991a. The micropolitical orientation of teachers toward closed school principals. *Education and Urban Society 23*(4): 356–78.

———. 1991b. *The politics of life in schools: Power, conflict, and cooperation.* Newbury Park, Calif.: Sage.

———. (in press). The micropolitics of effective school-based leadership: Teachers' perspectives. *Educational Administration Quarterly.*

———. (forthcoming). *The micropolitics of teacher work involvement: Effective principals' impacts on teachers.*

Bloome, D., and Willett, J. 1991. Toward a micropolitics of classroom interaction. In J. Blase (Ed.), *The politics of life in schools: Power, conflict, and cooperation*: 207–36.

Burlingame, M. 1988. Review of *The micro-politics of the school: Towards a theory of school organization. Journal of Curriculum Studies 20*: 281–83.

Burns, T. 1961. Micropolitics: Mechanisms of institutional change. *Administration Science Quarterly 6*: 257–81.

Corbett, H. D. 1991. Community influence and school micropolitics: A case example. In J. Blase (Ed.), *The politics of life in schools: Power, conflict, and cooperation*: 73–95.

Cyert, R. M., and March, J. G. 1963. *A behavioral theory of the firm.* Englewood Cliffs, N.J.: Prentice Hall.

Erickson, K. 1986. *Everything in its path: Destruction of community in Buffalo Creek Flood.* New York: Simon & Schuster.

Everhart, R. 1991. Unraveling micropolitical mystiques: Some methodological opportunities. *Education and Urban Society 23*(4): 455–64.

Fayol, H. 1949. *General and industrial management.* In Constance Starrs, London: Sir Isaac Pitman.

Getzels, J. W., and Guba, E. G. 1957. Social behavior and the administrative process. *School Reviews 65*(4): 423–41.

Glatter, R. 1982. The micropolitics of education: Issues for training. *Educational Management and Administration 10*: 160–65.

Goffman, E. 1959. *The presentation of self in everyday life.* New York: Anchor.

Greenfield, W. D. 1991. The micropolitics of leadership in an urban elementary school. In J. Blase, ed., *The politics of life in schools: Power, conflict, and cooperation*: 161–84.

Hargreaves, A. 1991. Contrived collegiality: The micropolitics of teacher collaboration. In J. Blase (Ed.), *The politics of life in schools: Power, conflict, and cooperation*: 46–72.

Hoyle, E. 1985. Educational organizations: Micropolitics. In T. Husen and T. N. Postlethwaite (Eds.), *The international encyclopedia of education: Research and studies.* New York: Pergamon Press.

_____. 1986. *The politics of school management.* London: Hodder and Stoughton.

Iannaccone, L. 1975. *Education policy systems: A study guide for educational administrators.* Fort Lauderdale, Fla.: Nova University.

Kline-Kracht, P., and Wong, K. 1991. When district authority intrudes upon the local school. In J. Blase (Ed.), *The politics of life in schools: Power, conflict, and cooperation* 96–119.

Lindle, J. C. 1991a. *The micropolitics of race and governance in a rural school district: A case study.* Unpublished manuscript. University of Kentucky.

_____. 1991b, April. *The usefulness of the micropolitical framework for evaluating clinical experiences.* Paper presented at the annual meeting of the American Educational Research Association. Chicago.

Lukes, S. 1974. *Power: A radical view.* London: Macmillan.

Mangham, I. 1979. *The politics of organizational change.* Westport, Conn.: Greenwood Press.

Marshall, C. 1991. The chasm between administrator and teacher cultures: A micropolitical puzzle. In J. Blase (Ed.), *The politics of life in schools: Power, conflict, and cooperation*: 139–60. Newbury Park, Calif.: Sage.

_____. and Mitchell, B. 1991. The assumptive worlds of fledgling administrators. *Education and Urban Society 23*(4): 396–415.

Mayes, B. T., and Allen, R. W. 1977. Toward a definition of organizational politics. *Academy of Management Review 2*, 672–78.

Mowday, R. T. 1978. The exercise of upward influence in organization. *Administration Science Quarterly 23*(1): 137–56.

National Policy Board for Educational Leadership. (in press). Developing a problem solving repertoire: The micropolitical approach to educational leadership. In S. D. Thomason (Ed.), *Design for leadership.*

Noblit, G., Berry, B., and Dempsey, V. 1991. Political responses to reform: A comparative case study. *Education and Urban Society 23*(4): 379–95.

O'Brien, P. W. 1987. The power to persuade: A working paper in the micropolitics of educational planning. *Educational Planning 5*(4): 3–11.

Osborne, A. B. 1989. Insiders and outsiders: Cultural membership and the micropolitics of education among the Zuni. *Anthropology and Education Quarterly 20*: 196–215.

Parsons, T. 1951. *The social system.* Chicago: Free Press.

Pettigrew, A. 1973. *The politics of organizational decision-making.* London: Tavistock.

Pfeffer, J. 1981. *Power in organizations.* Marshfield, Mass.: Pitman.

Radnor, H. A. 1990, April. *Complexities and compromises: The new era at Parkview School.* Paper presented at the annual meeting of the American Educational Research Association, Boston.

Schein, V. E. 1977. Individual power and political behaviors in organizations: An inadequately explored reality. *Academy of Management Review* 2(1): 64–72.

Smylie, M. A., and Brownlee-Conyers, J. 1990, April. *Teacher leaders and their principals: Exploring new working relationships from a micropolitical perspective* Paper presented at the annual meeting of the American Educational Research Association, Boston.

Sparkes, A. C. 1988. The micropolitics of innovation in the physical education curriculum. In J. Evans (Ed.), *Teacher, teaching and control in physical education*: 157–77. Lewes, England: Falmer Press.

_____. 1990. Power, domination and resistance in the process of teacher-initiated innovation. *Research Papers in Education* 5(2): 153–78.

Strauss, G. 1962. Tactics of lateral relationship: The purchasing agent. *Administrative Science Quarterly* 7(2): 161–86.

Taylor, F. W. 1947. *Scientific management.* New York: Harper.

Townsend, R. G. 1990. Toward a broader micropolitics of schools. *Curriculum Inquiry* 20(2): 205–24.

Trudgill, P. 1983. *Sociolinguistics: Introduction to language and society.* rev. ed. Harmondsworth, Middlesex, England: Penguin.

Wamsley, G. L., and Zald, M. N. 1973. *The political economy of public organizations: A critique and approach to the study of public organizations.* Lexington, Mass.: Lexington Books.

Weber, M. 1947. *The theory of social and economic organization.* New York: Free Press.

Developments in Theory and Practice: An Opportunity to Examine the Impact of the Environment on School Organizations

Rodney T. Ogawa

Scholars of educational administration have long accepted the view that school organizations, like other types of organizations, are open systems. That is, school organizations are heavily affected by actors and forces in their external environments. Despite broad acknowledgement of this view's validity, scholars continue to ignore what we might call "openness" in their research and writing.

This criticism, of course, is hardly new. Indeed, it is troubling that, nearly a half century after social scientists first began applying general systems theory to the study of organizations, we continue to ignore the relationship between schools, school systems and their environments. However, this may be about to change. Developments in organizations theory and in public education could finally focus the attention of scholars of educational administration on the interplay of school organizations and their environments.

Some Recent History

Critics have for a long time bemoaned the failure of scholars to attend to the impact of the environment on school organizations. In 1979, for example, Griffiths assessed the intellectual turmoil that had gripped organizations theory, a field he credited with spawning the field of educational administration. He concluded that theorists had paid too little attention to the effect of the environment on organizations. Three years later, Hoy (1982) reviewed "Recent Developments in Theory and Research in Educational Administration" in his introduction to a special issue of *Educational Administration Quarterly* devoted to that topic. He amplified

Griffiths's point, arguing that research and theory that ignored the impact of the environment on educational organizations were "simply insufficient."

A decade after Hoy's assessment, scholars generally continue to ignore the environments of school organizations. The *Handbook of Research on Educational Administration*, a recent compendium of scholarship in the field, devotes a sizeable section to organizations. The seven chapters in that section rarely mention organizational environments, devoting their attention, instead, to intra-organizational systems, including leadership, work motivation and satisfaction and decision making. Even more recently, Nicolaides and Gaynor (1992) revealed the relative lack of emphasis given to organizational environments in doctoral-level theory courses in educational administration. Although they acknowledged that general and social systems theories—which do attend to systems' environments—informed theory development in educational administration, they concluded: "The most important roots of educational administrative and organizational theory lie in bureaucratic theory and the concept of scientific management" (Nicolaides and Gaynor 1992, 251), neither of which focuses on the impact of the environment on organizations.

Over a decade has now passed since Griffiths and Hoy observed that theorists and researchers in the field of educational administration were not paying sufficient attention to the impact of environments on school organizations. And, yet, writing and teaching by scholars in our field continue to give only limited attention to organizations' environments.

Help, however, may be on the way. In fact, it already may have arrived. That help takes the form of developments in organizations theory and in American public education. Together, these developments may encourage and perhaps even force scholars to examine the relationship between school organizations and their environments.

Developments in Organizations Theory

Developments in organizations theory can provide the conceptual foundation for examining the relationship of school organizations and their environments. A theme in organizations theory has been a search for the answer to the question of why and how organizations develop and change their structures. Structure, Scott (1987b, 15) noted, "refers to the patterned or regularized aspects of relationships existing among participants in an organization." To the extent that organizations are characterized by the patterned actions and interactions of their members, structure arguably is organization. Thus, the issue of structural development and change lies at the heart of organizations theory.

Over the years, theorists have generated several competing explanations, or theories, for why and how organizations develop and change structure. The more recent theories emphasize the impact of the environment on organizational structure. While these theories are nascent, theorists are debating their conceptual merits and researchers are beginning to test them empirically. These theories and the debate that they have spawned could inform studies of school organizations, and such research could inform the debate and, thus, contribute significantly to organizations theory.

In this chapter, I discuss four theories. Three theories are commonly compared in the current debate over which theory best explains the development of organizational structure. The three theories are contingency theory, institutional theory and transaction-cost theory. The fourth theory—a theory of public bureaucracy—has been used to provide the conceptual rationale for educational choice, the currently controversial approach to educational reform. The four theories characterize organizations very differently and, thus, describe the impact of the environment on organizational structure quite differently.

Contingency Theory

Contingency theory[1] is the earliest and, thus, probably the most familiar of the four theories to scholars of educational administration. It depicts organizations as being technically rational entities; that is, they are primarily oriented towards goal attainment through the production of goods or services. From this perspective, organizations develop or change structures to enhance the effectiveness and efficiency with which their production processes, or technologies, operate.

The external environment is a major source of threats to organizational effectiveness and efficiency, because it presents uncertainties that can affect organizations' technologies in several ways. The environment includes suppliers of resources that fuel production, consumers who use organizations' products, and competitors and regulatory agencies. Each of these aspects of the environment can compromise organizational effectiveness and efficiency. For example, an uncooperative supplier of a necessary resource or a highly restrictive government regulation could shut down an organization's production.

Contingency theory explains that organizations develop or alter structures to enhance their technical effectiveness and efficiency in the face of environmental uncertainty. This means that organizations develop structures to correspond to crucial elements of their environments. Thus, organizations that operate in highly complex environments will tend to have highly differentiated structures (Lawrence and Lorsch 1967). For example, a large metropolitan school district may have a legal department to handle the many legal actions with which it is faced, a purchasing department to manage relations with suppliers, and a school-business partnership program to manage its relations with local businesses.

It also means that organizations develop structures to buffer the work of the organization from environmental intrusions, thus enabling production to continue unhindered by uncertainties presented by the environment (Thompson 1967). For example, most school districts have policies requiring parents to check in at the school office before visiting classrooms, thus reducing the possibility of uninvited interruptions of instruction. Similarly, districts have central purchasing, which saves teachers from having to deal directly with salespeople hawking supplies and instructional materials.

Institutional Theory

Institutional theory[2] emerged as an alternative to rational conceptions—such as contingency theory—of organizations. It is familiar to scholars of educational administration because it was used to explain why educational organizations are loosely coupled systems (Meyer and Rowan 1977), a popular topic in the late 1970s and early 1980s.

Institutional theory characterizes organizations like all social actors, as basing their actions on institutions in the environment rather than on internally derived goals (Scott 1987a). Institutions are general, societal rules which take the form of cultural theories and prescriptions. For organizations, these rules specify appropriate purposes and identify legitimate means for attaining them.

Thus, organizations adopt structures because they mirror institutions, not because they enhance organizational effectiveness or efficiency (Zucker 1987). This is particularly true of organizations that have unclear technologies and that do not operate in competitive markets (DiMaggio and Powell 1983). By adopting structures that reflect institutions, organizations can gain legitimacy with stakeholders in their environments without having to demonstrate the effectiveness and efficiency of their technical operations. Because stakeholders are more likely to provide resources to organizations viewed as legitimate, institutional strategies may contribute to organizational survival or effectiveness. For example, public education is faced with the loss of public confidence. Many school systems are responding by adopting school-based management programs that reflect the nation's longstanding faith in participatory governance. Perhaps some of these school districts have adopted school-based management to enhance their legitimacy in the eyes of local constituents rather than to improve the effectiveness and efficiency of their operations. This may help to explain why there is little empirical evidence of school-based management's impact on student achievement.

Transaction-Cost Theory

Transaction-cost theory[3] is a fairly recent contribution of the discipline of economics to organizations theory and, thus, is probably less familiar to scholars of educational administration than either contingency or institutional theories. Transaction-cost theory treats organizations and organizational structures as mechanisms to govern transactions and, thus, reduce transaction costs (Williamson 1975; 1981).

A transaction involves the exchange of goods, services or other assets between two or more parties. Transaction costs are costs that are associated with completing a transaction but that do not reflect the value of the assets being exchanged. Among the many possible transaction costs, theorists have been particularly concerned with those that stem from opportunism and asset specificity.

Opportunism occurs when one party takes advantage of information that is pertinent to a transaction but not available to the other party (Akerlof 1986). Faced with the threat of opportunism, parties to transactions may take measures to protect themselves, measures that have costs associated with them. These are transaction costs. For example, the seller of a used automobile might not tell a prospective buyer that the automobile has been plagued with a series of mechanical failures, that it is a "lemon". Given this possibility, however, the seller offers and the buyer purchases an extended service warranty.

Asset specificity is the degree to which a good or service has value to only one or a limited number of possible transactions (Klein, Crawford, and Alchian 1986). Both parties to such transactions may take measures, which bear costs, to insure the completion and continuation of the transaction. For example, an auto manufacturer may require a special tire for one of its products. The auto manufacturer is vulnerable because it cannot easily switch suppliers; the supplier is vulnerable because it cannot sell the tire to another manufacturer. Thus, to insure continuation of the transaction, the auto manufacturer and the supplier agree to a long-term contract.

Transaction-cost theory explains that parties engaged in transactions will, in the long run, adopt mechanisms that reduce transactions costs. When the uncertainty and complexity surrounding transactions reach a certain level, organizational mechanisms can govern transactions at less cost than the competitive market can. Thus, when transaction costs of obtaining a particular good or service exceed a given point, an organization will cease doing business with suppliers in the open market and organize its own capacity to produce the needed good or service. On the other hand, when an organization finds that the cost of producing a good or service itself exceeds a certain level, it will purchase the needed good or service in the market. For example, in an effort to cut costs, some school systems have eliminated their in-house food service operations and purchased the service from outside vendors.

Theory of Public Bureaucracy

A theory of public bureaucracy is a recent contribution to organizations theory[4] Despite its recency, this theory should command the interest of educational administration scholars. It serves, after all, as the conceptual grounding for educational choice, one of the most controversial approaches to educational reform currently being proposed (Chubb and Moe 1990).

The theory of public bureaucracy seeks to explain the structure and operation of organizations that exist to implement programs created by legislative bodies. The theory explains that legislators initiate and support programs that serve the interests of their constituents. These legislators understand that their ability to initiate programs is based on their "political authority", which is only temporary (Moe 1989). Legislators can lose political authority every time they face reelection. Thus, legislators construct programs and the organizations to implement them so that the programs' political enemies cannot tamper with them. Legislators accomplish this by making the organizations impenetrable, even to themselves. The theory also explains that, because legislation is the product of compromise, program's enemies can include in its enabling legislation elements aimed at limiting the program's success. Thus, the effectiveness of legislated programs can be seriously compromised, and legislators cannot gain access to the organizations charged with implementing the programs in order to make the programs more effective. This results in a proliferation of programs that are operated by nonelected public officials, whose accountability to the public or its representatives is limited.

Some proponents of educational choice argue that such legislative gridlock explains why public school systems have had such difficulty in improving their academic performance, despite having adopted numerous programs aimed at doing exactly that. Using the theory of public bureaucracy, advocates of choice claim that schools would be more responsive to patrons and, thus, more effective, if they were governed by the marketplace rather than by disjointed and well insulated bureaucracies, which, themselves, are the products of policies and programs adopted by local and state school boards, state legislatures and Congress.

Summary

The four theories discussed here provide very different explanations for why organizations, including educational ones, develop and change their structural features. While all of the theories acknowledge the importance of the external environment, each depicts the environment's impact on organizations' structures differently. Contingency theory explains that organizations react to environmental conditions that affect their technical effectiveness and efficiency by developing structures that respond to or act as a buffer against the environment. Institutional theory suggests that organizations develop structures that reflect institutions, or broad cultural rules, in order to gain legitimacy in the environment, not to enhance the effectiveness and efficiency of their operations. Transaction-cost theory reveals that organizations will either develop an internal structure to produce a needed asset or rely on suppliers in the marketplace, depending on which alternative is least costly. Finally, the theory of public bureaucracy argues that organizations that implement programs produced by constituency-based legislation are characterized by fragmented, highly buffered programs whose effectiveness is compromised by design.

Currently, theorists are arguing the merits of these competing explanations and researchers are beginning to test and compare them empirically. Recent developments in public education in the United States provide opportunities to apply these theories to research on school organizations. Such research could provide the dual benefits of adding to our understanding of educational organizations and contributing to the debate in organizations theory.

Developments in School Organizations and Their Environments

Two related developments in American public education provide opportunities to study the relationship of school organizations and their external environment, in general, and the process by which school organizations develop and change structures, in particular. The first development is occurring in school organizations; the second is occurring in the environment in which those organizations operate.

Educational Reform: Changes in Organizational Structure

A major development in American public education is the emergence of reforms whose avowed purpose is the "restructuring" of school organizations. This use of the term "restructuring" by educational reformers is consistent with the concept of "structure" within organizations theory. As noted earlier, in organizations theory "structure" refers to "the patterned or regularized aspects of relationships of participants in an organization" (Scott 1987b, 15). Current educational reforms, indeed, are aimed at altering the patterned relationships of people involved in public schools. Examples abound. School-based management aims to alter the relationships, existing between schools and district officials, as well as those existing between administrators, teachers and parents. Careers ladders, along with other efforts to enhance the professionalism of teachers, are attempting to change the relationship of teachers and administrators as well as to affect the relationships among teachers. School-business partnerships are aimed at enhancing relationships that exist between school districts and businesses in their communities. As Elmore (1990) has noted, restructuring is affecting three of the major dimensions of school organizations: their core technology, the occupational conditions of teaching and the relationship between schools and their clients.

However, my purpose here is not to discuss restructuring in detail. Rather, it is to make the general observation that restructuring is producing changes in the structure of school organizations, changes that provide researchers with an opportunity to study the role that the environment plays in shaping the structure of school organizations.

The Environment: A Shift to Markets?

While most current approaches to educational reform concentrate on the interior of school organizations, one proposed strategy would deeply affect the environment in which public schools operate. Educational choice, if implemented in its most open form, would move schools from operating within what has been characterized as a domesticated environment into a competitive market. That is, public schools, by virtue of mandatory attendance laws and attendance areas, have been assured of having students and the financial resources, however limited, that serve those students. In an unrestricted system of educational choice, public schools would compete with each other and with private schools for students and the funds that would accompany them. Obviously, this would mean a fundamental change in the character of public schools' environment.

Presently, several states and school districts are considering or beginning to implement choice programs. Existing plans tend to be fairly restrictive. For instance, some allow parents to select only from the public schools that serve the district in which they reside. Again, my purpose here is not to offer an expansive or detailed discussion of choice. Rather, it is to suggest that changes in the environment of public schools produced by choice programs will provide researchers with an unprecedented opportunity to study the environment's impact on the structural features of school organizations.

Implications for Research

The developments in organizations theory and in schools and the environment that I have outlined in this chapter have important implications for research on school organization. In the most general terms, these developments provide the conceptual grounding and empirical opportunity to move research on school organization beyond a closed-system conception and toward a truly open-systems perspective. In more specific terms, these developments provide an opportunity to examine the impact of the environment on the structure of school organizations.

Current efforts to restructure schools and school districts provide an opportunity to contribute to answering the question of why school organizations develop and change structures. Researchers can use contingency theory, institutional theory, transactions-cost theory and the theory of public bureaucracy to frame their studies. These studies could either test hypotheses deduced from a single theory or test the relative explanatory power of two or more theories.

Beyond the general question of which theory best explains why school organizations develop or change structures, researchers could identify the conditions under which different theories best explain the behavior of school organizations. For example, research could seek to determine if different theories explain the development or adoption of structures, depending on the organizational function served by the new structure. Perhaps one theory offers a better explanation of the adoption of structures having to do with support services and another better explains the adoption of structures having to do with instruction.

The fundamental change that choice programs might bring to the environment in which schools operate would provide us an unprecedented opportunity to research the impact that the environment has on the structure of school organization. If public schools move from a domesticated environment to a competitive one, will their reasons for developing and changing structure undergo a concomitant shift? Both the theory of public bureaucracy and institutional theory would predict as much, but for very different reasons. Advocates of choice contend that, as control shifts from the hands of politicized bureaucracies to consumers, schools will jettison unproductive practices and adopt more effective ones. Institutional theory can be inferred to predict a similar outcome. Because it claims that the absence of a competitive market is one condition contributing to the tendency of organizations to adopt structures for symbolic purposes, the removal of that condition should contribute to organizations developing structures to enhance productive efficiency. In any case, both theories suggest that schools operating in a competitive market would behave more in keeping with contingency theory—that is, they would seek to improve their technical effectiveness and efficiency—than would schools in the current, domesticated environment. This, of course, remains an empirical question, a question that choice programs would provide an opportunity for researchers to answer.

Scholars of educational administration, then, have the opportunity to move beyond dominant closed-system conceptions of school organization. By doing so, they could contribute significantly to what we understand about schools as organizations. In addition, they would contribute to the debate within organizations theory over the question of why and how organizations develop and change structures.

Notes

1. For early, comprehensive treatments of contingency theory see the following: P. R. Lawrence and J. W. Lorsch, *Organization and Environment: Managing Differentiation and Integration*, Boston: Graduate School of Business Administration, Harvard University (1967); J. D. Thompson, *Organizations in Action*, New York: McGraw-Hill (1967).

2. For comprehensive treatments of institutional theory see the following: P. J. DiMaggio and W. W. Powell, "The Iron Cage Revisited: Institutional Isomorphism and Collective Rationality in Organizational Fields," *American Sociological Review*, 48 (April 1983); J. W. Meyer and B. Rowan, "Institutionalized Organizations: Formal Structure as Myth and Ceremony," *American Journal of Sociology*, 83 (September 1977); W. R. Scott, "The Adolescence of Institutional Theory," *Administrative Science Quarterly*, 32 (1987); L. G. Zucker, "Institutional Theories of Organization," *Annual Review of Sociology*, 13 (1987).

3. For comprehensive treatments of transactions-cost theory see the following: J. B. Barney and W. G. Ouchi, *Organizational Economics*, San Francisco: Jossey-Bass (1986); O. E. Williamson, *Markets and Hierarchies: Analysis and Antitrust Implications*, New York: Free Press (1975); O. E. Williamson, "The Economics of Organization: The Transaction Cost Approach," *American Journal of Sociology*, 87 (November 1981).

4. For early discussions of a theory of public bureaucracy see the following: T. M. Moe, "The Politics of Bureaucratic Structure," in J. E. Chubb and P. E. Peterson, *Can the Government Govern?*

Washington, D.C.: Brookings Institute (1989); T. M. Moe, "The Politics of Structural Choice," in O. E. Williamson, *Organization Theory: From Chester Barnard to the Present and Beyond*, New York: Oxford University Press (1990); T. M. Moe, "Politics and the Theory of Organization," *The Journal of Law, Economics, and Organization*, 7 (April 1991).

References

Akerlof, G. A. "The Market for 'Lemons': Quality Uncertainty and the Market Mechanism." in J. B. Barney and W. G. Ouchi (eds.) *Organizational Economics*. San Francisco: Jossey-Bass, 1986: 27–39.

Chubb, J. E., and Moe, T. M. *Politics, Markets and America's Schools*. Washington, D. C.: Brookings Institute, 1990.

DiMaggio, P. J., and Powell, W. W. "The Iron Cage Revisited: Institutional Isomorphism and Collective Rationality in Organizational Fields." *American Sociological Review* 48 (1983): 147–60.

Elmore, R. F. "On Changing the Structure Public Schools." in R. F. Elmore and Associates. *Restructuring Schools: The Next Generation of Educational Reform*. San Francisco: Jossey-Bass, 1990.

Griffiths, D. E. "Intellectual Turmoil in Educational Administration." *Educational Administration Quarterly* 15 (1979): 43–65.

Hoy, W. K. "Recent Developments in Theory and Research in Educational Administration." *Educational Administration Quarterly* 18 (1982): 1–11.

Klein, B., Crawford, R. G., and Alchian, A.A. "Vertical Integration, Appropriable Rents, and the Competitive Contracting Proces." In J. B. Barney and W. G. Ouchi (eds.) *Organizational Economics*. San Francisco: Jossey-Bass, 1986: 39–71.

Lawrence, P. R. , and Lorsch, J. W. *Organization and Environment: Managing Differentiation and Integration*. Boston: Graduate School of Business Administration, Harvard University, 1967.

Meyer, J. W., and Rowan, B. "Institutionalized Organizations: Formal Structure as Myth and Ceremony." *American Journal of Sociology* 83 (1977): 340–63.

Moe, T. M., "The Politics of Bureaucratic Structure." In J. E. Chubb and P. E. Peterson, *Can the Government Govern?* Washington, D.C.: Brookings Institute, 1989: 267–329.

Nicolaides, N., and Gaynor, A. K. "The Knowledge Base Informing the Teaching of Administration and Organizational Theory in UCEA Universities: A Descriptive and Interpretive Survey." *Educational Administration Quarterly* 28 (1992): 237–65.

Scott, W. R. "The Adolescence of Institutional Theory," *Administrative Science Quarterly* 32 (1987a): 493–511.

———. *Organizations: Rational, Natural, and Open Systems.* Englewood Cliffs, N.J.: Prentice-Hall, 1987b.

Thompson, J. D. *Organizations in Action.* New York: McGraw-Hill, 1967.

Williamson, O. E. *Markets and Hierarchies: Analysis and Antitrust Implications,* New York: Free Press, 1975.

Williamson, O. E. "The Economics of Organization: The Transaction Cost Approach." *American Journal of Sociology* 87 !1981): 548–77.

Zucker, L. G. "Institutional Theories of Organization," *Annual Review of Sociology* 13 (1987): 443–64.

The Preparation of Educational Leaders and Rational Choice Theory

Tyll van Geel

How should school leaders behave? Ethics, morality, religion, and the law offer one set of answers. School administrator courses in organizational theory, organizational psychology and school politics offer a different set of answers. Yet another set of answers is suggested by the fast-emerging body of work grouped together under the rubric of "rational choice theory." In other words, social science paradigms do affect the choice of prescriptions to guide the administration of the schools, and affect as well the kinds of skills needed by the effective school leader. Rational choice theory has very speciflc implications for management behavior and policies that are dramatically different ftom the perspectives traditionally offered in school administrator preparation courses.

Consider, for example, the problem of fostering cooperation among school personnel. A standard perspective on this problem offered in administration courses is the Getzels-Guba (1957) psychosociological model. This model conceives of the social system as consisting of two major independent dimensions that interact. The first dimension consists of the roles and associated expectations that are intended to form a cooperative system, which is designed to fulfill the goals of the system. In other words, this normative dimension consists of a set of complementary roles, and each role has associated with it a set of prohibitions, requirements, goals, duties and rights. Failure to meet these expectations exposes the holder of the role to sanctions. The second, so-called "ideographic" dimension consists of the individuals who fill these roles with their own unique needs and personalities. These needs determine that person's interactions with the environment. Behavior within the school system is, therefore, a consequence of the interaction between the role and the personality of the incumbent in that role. Roughly speaking, the cooperative system of roles breaks down when the incumbents do not fulfill the expectations associated with their role; the special job of the administrator is to assure that cooperation still occurs, by integrating the demands of the organization and the needs of the staff. The kinds of problems that administrators may confront include conflicts occurring between an incumbent's needs and the role expectations the incumbent faces; conflicts occurring among the expectations brought to bear upon an incumbent; internal conflict occurring within an individual; and conflict occurring between and among incumbents. The lesson the model teaches the practitioner is that there are several ways to deal with these conflicts. Defining roles more clearly, socializing the personnel into their roles, meeting the social-psychological needs of role incumbents and allowing more individual initiative to reduce role-personality conflict are among the steps leading to a more effective school that are suggested by this paradigm. (Kimbrough and Nunnery 1988; Lipham 1988).

Social-psychological models of conflict, on the other hand, offer a somewhat different description of the causes and solutions of conflict. Dean Pruitt and Jeffrey Rubin define conflict as "a belief that the parties' current aspirations cannot be achieved simultaneously" (Pruitt and Rubin 1986). Whether this conflict escalates so that the two parties adopt "contending" strategies rather than less contentious ones, such as problem solving, depends upon how much each party is concerned about the well-being of the other party. The more each party wants the other party to realize its aspirations, the more each party will be willing to adopt noncontentious tactics. The prescription that emerges for educational leaders in a supervisory position is thus clear: the leader should seek to foster mutual concern among the employees, thereby reducing the likelihood of their resorting to contentious practices. The popular research and writing of Roger Fisher and his associates points to similar lessons for people engaged in bargaining. According to this research, parties are more likely to "get to 'yes'" if they work on building their relationship in the course of the bargaining (Fisher and Brown 1988). A third party, such as a supervisor, can play a crucial part in helping the parties "understand how the world looks through the eyes of the other." Two additional lessons emerge for administrators from the work of these social psychologists: trust among the parties is an important ingredient to obtain cooperation and reduce conflict; and contentious tactics such as "tit-for-tat" are seen as very damaging. This tactic will not produce cooperation, according to these theorists, but will only cause the relationship to deteriorate in a downward spiral.

The prescriptions for action suggested by rational choice theory are in some respects directly opposed to those emerging from social psychology and organizational theory. Take the specific example of "tit-for-tat." According to an important piece of rational choice research, the tit-for-tat strategy is precisely that tactic most likely to produce cooperation. (Axelrod 1984). Thus, how one looks at the social world makes a big difference in how one is led to act in that world. As it turns out, the important field of "rational choice" is missing ftom most school administrator preparation programs and ought to be included. The usefulness of the rational choice perspective for school administration will be demonstrated in this chapter.

An Overview of the Field

Rational choice theorists attempt to make sense of the complexity of human inaction by starting with a few simple but ultimately powerful assumptions, or axioms, about human motives and behaviors. Working deductively from these assumptions, they develop logical implications to explain and predict behavior, taking into account the behavior of others, as well as different "institutional" constraints such as voting rules, agenda-setting rules, and incentive systems. As a social science perspective resting on "methodological individualism," rational choice theory claims that all social phenomena are derivable ftom the properties of individuals, as long as one takes into account, in certain ways, the setting in which those individuals are located. Rational choice theory presumes as well that all political actors—voters, professional politicians, bureaucrats—have preferences, and make rationally calculated decisions that maximize the realization of their preferences at the lowest possible cost. Thus, the different branches of rational choice theory assume that people have preferences and act to attain them. The study of people acting to attain their preferences makes use of four concepts: (1) preferences, (2) strategies, (3) action, and (4) outcomes. Rational political actors develop and execute strategies designed to bring about the outcomes they prefer.

The most well-developed of the rational choice theories is, of course, economics, the concepts and tools of which have been used to study not just standard behavior in the marketplace but also bureaucracies and even families (McKenzie 1975; Putterman 1986). The other branches of rational choice theory that seem to hold the most interest for educational administration are those branches that deal with modeling social life in terms of so-called "games" of coalition formation, public choice and voting processes, bargaining, the forecasting of political decisions, and conflict (Riker 1962; Hamburger 1979; Mueller 1989; Brams 1990; Raiffa 1982; Bueno de Mesquita 1985; Dixit and Nalebuff 1991).

The richness and diversity of rational choice theory and research is far too extensive to review in depth in this short chapter; instead, I will illustrate its usefulness for educational administration by concentrating on the work that seeks to analyze social phenomena in terms of games. Before turning to that task, however, I will indicate briefly the kind of problems addressed by the other branches of the theory and some of the findings of this body of work.

Coalition theorists deal with questions of which coalitions form, what the political goals of a particular coalition will be, the size of the coalitions, and how the members of the coalition divide the booty they win by becoming a winning coalition. The general approach is to assume that potential coalition partners will join the coalition that leads to the greatest pay-off for them, and this is when the division of the booty among the members of the winning coalition becomes crucial. One of the principal findings of this body of theory is that if a coalition is big enough to win, it has no need to take on additional members, a finding known as the minimum winning coalition principle (Riker 1962).

The theorists who examine public choice and voting process address a variety of topics, including the effect of different voting rules on the outcomes of voting processes. What we learn ftom this work is that different voting rules—Condorcet, Broda, Bentham— can yield totally different winners when fused with the same group of voters, who hold the same preferences ftom voting process to voting process (Riker 1982). Other important findings include the median voter theorem and the existence of the so-called "voting cycle" or "paradox." The median voter is that voter whose preference is located at a position where fifty percent of the voters are located to the left and fifty percent to the right. The median position is, thus, determined by the point where there are an equal number of voices on each side. It is not necessarily the average position. The median position is the dominant or winning position and, based on this understanding, many predictions can be made about the behavior of politicians; in effect, the best policy position for a politician is the median position (Brams 1975).

The voting cycle is called a paradox because in this case rational voters collectively produce an irrational result, that is, a set of intransitive preferences. Rationality is defined here to mean that if a voter prefers A to B and B to C, then the voter also prefers A to C. These preferences are transitively ordered. But suppose three voters, James, Sidney, and Lynn, are faced with three alternatives A, B, C, upon which they vote in a pairwise comparison (A is pitted against B, B, against C and A against C). Suppose the preferences of the voters are ranked as follows:

James	Sidney	Lynn
A	B	C
B	C	A
C	A	B

The preference ranking of these three voters means A gains a majority against B; B wins against C; but C beats A. Collectively, the preference pattern is intransitive or circular; thus, any given alternative is defeated by one of the others. In this case, it is not possible to know which alternative the voters will select. The existence of this possibility opens the door to agenda manipulations and other sophisticated moves, which can be used by the astute politician to achieve preferred outcomes (Riker 1986; Strom 1990).

Bargaining theorists have worked on predicting the outcomes of bargaining, the effect of certain bargaining tactics on the otherwise predicted outcome, and the dynamics of the bargaining process when there are more than two players at the table (Raiffa 1982; Brams 1990).

Some of the most interesting and advanced work on forecasting political conflict is being done today by Bruce Bueno de Mesquita based on an "expected utility" approach to understanding human choices. Based on his mathematical models and using a minimum of political data, Bueno de Mesquita has predicted the outcomes of such political decision-making processes as the negotiations between Great Britain and the Republic of China over the fate of Hong Kong, and the negotiations among the members of the European Economic Community over the year that certain pollution control requirements will go into effect on automobiles. (Bueno de Mesquita 1985). Bueno de Mesquita has developed related models, which he uses to forecast the outcomes of international conflicts, for example, whether two nations will go to war, bargain, and even whether one or the other side will yield or capitulate to the other (Bueno de Mesquita 1992). These models can be used in connection with domestic conflict and domestic political decision-making at the level of the local school board.

Institutions and Game Theory

Schools are a form of institution characterized by durability, by formal rules that allocate roles, resources of power, constraints on the choices of the role incumbents and clients, and enforcement mechanisms. Institutions (of which schools are one example) are established in part to resolve coordination and collective action problems by obtaining contributions, in the form of work, from individuals. But setting up an institution in order to elicit a coordinated effort from a group of people does not mean that coordination will always be forthcoming from those who are in the institution.

One way to study the possibilities for and the obstacles to cooperation is to turn to that branch of rational choice theory dubbed "game theory." When rational choice theorists use the word *game* they do not mean games such as football or chess: nor are they referring to simulations or the so-called "games people play." What they do refer to are situations in which people, known as the "players," make choices that affect each other. Game theory itself has different dimensions to it. One branch looks at people as decision makers who calculate the expected utility of the outcomes connected with each of the action choices they have available. Without going into the details of this theory, one example of how it can be used goes as follows below.

Everybody recognizes that people are tempted to break the rules: to speed, to fudge data reported to the Internal Revenue Service, and to take advantage of personal leave and sick leave provisions built into contractual agreements. We also know that no organization, indeed no government, can possibly compel all the people to obey all the rules all the time. There simply are not enough rule enforcers on the job at every minute of the day to assure universal compliance. Thus, given the huge temptation to break the rules, and the inability on the part of the enforcers to mount a total enforcement effort, how is rule compliance achieved?

The answer is that rules are enforced through a random and unfair policy. This is one of the important insights developed by rational choice theorists. Take the case of a rule prohibiting smoking in a school's rest rooms. Full enforcement of such a rule could require the permanent, full-time assignment of a monitor to the toilet facilities. But creating an enforcement policy that assured a 100% chance of apprehending every violator would be too costly for the school. The alternative would be to move to a policy that would decrease a student's chance of being caught smoking; if the smoker got caught, however, the penalty would be so severe that taking a chance and breaking the rule would not be a rational choice. (In the language of game theory, the expected utility of smoking in the toilets is less than the expected utility of compliance with the rules.) This policy combines random checks of the rest rooms with heavy penalties for the unfortunate few who do get caught (Hamburger 1979).

Because random enforcement of organizational expectations is such a cost-effective and powerful means for obtaining compliance, one can predict that those who wish not to be controlled will seek ways to take this tool away ftom the organization. Thus, teachers have persistently resisted the randomized visits of principals to their classrooms by arguing the unfairness of surprise entrance. Random enforcement will clearly remain a persistent bone of contention.

Cooperation Is Preferred

Rule enforcement and coercion are not the only reasons that cooperation emerges within an institutional setting. To describe the emergence of cooperation without coercion, it is useful to introduce a standard way in which game theorists graphically depict the set of choices two individuals may face. The graphic device is a matrix composed of intersecting rows and columns.

		Player # 1	
		Column # 1	Column #2
P l a y e r #2	Row # 1	B, S	T, T
	Row # 2	T, T	S, B

One player has the option of choosing between the left- and right-hand columns; choosing a column is called a "move." The other player chooses between the top row or the bottom row. The intersection of a column and row forms a cell in which there are letters or numbers representing what we might call the "payoff," or outcome, for each player. Thus, the top left cell contains the payoffs for the two players when the "column player" chooses the left column and the "row-player" chooses the top row. According to convention, the row player's payoff is listed first and the column player's payoff is listed after the comma. The absolute value of the numbers used in the matrix is not significant. What is important is the relative value of the numbers; for example, (1, 0) is equivalent to (5, 4), in that the first number is marginally greater than the second number in each set of parentheses. Letters may also be substituted for illustrative purposes, hence B = best payoff; S = second best payoff; T = third best; W = worst payoff.

This matrix format is used to describe a variety of social situations, including those in which getting cooperation among the players is a central problem of their relationship. Take the case of two friends who want to do something together on Saturday evening; Will wants to see a movie and Joe wants to shoot some pool (Luce and Raiffa 1957). Both would prefer to do something together rather than go their separate ways, even if, for example, Will must play pool to be with Joe.

This situation is represented in the next matrix.

		Joe	
		Movies	Pool
W i l l	Movies	2, 1	0, 0
	Pool	0, 0	1, 2

Reading the matrix we can see that if Will and Joe agree to go to the movies (Will chooses the top row and Joe chooses the left column) then Will receives a payoff of 2 and Joe a payoff of 1. The situation is different if they agree to play pool, because Will receives a benefit of 1 and Joe a benefit of 2. If they go their separate ways, they receive no benefit (0, 0). Clearly the advantage for both is to cooperate, but how should they do so? The terms of the agreement is the point on which they disagree. They could seek to solve the problem by bargaining. One form such bargain might take is an agreement to go to the movie this Saturday and play pool the next Saturday. Note also that either of the two players could make a forcing move: "I'm going to the movies; join me if you want." If Will makes this move, Joe will rationally calculate that it would be to his immediate advantage to join Will, because he has more to gain by joining Will then by going his separate way (compare Joe's payoff in the left and right columns). Thus, given this situation, we might predict the possibility of a "forcing move"; we can predict as well that they will cooperate in some way, even if the precise terms of the cooperation are not certain without more information about the players and their long-term relationship.

Notice that this is not a zero-sum game, in which one person's gain is another's loss. There are possibilities for mutual advantage in this game (and in another game to be discussed later), as well as for conflict of interest. The game is a mixed-motive one, in which there is a mixture of conflict and agreement of interests. A significant feature of this situation is that each party can only gain if the other also gains.

Many situations within the school setting that can aptly be described by this game (sometimes called "Battle of the Sexes"). School board-union relationships are sometimes described in these terms, as might be the relationship between a supervisor and teacher. Or take the case of teachers, engaged in team teaching, who need to cooperate to develop the next project the students will undertake. A more political example is the case of a seven-person school board voting on an issue that requires a two-third's majority. Suppose four members of the board are willing to vote for a bond issue necessary to raise the money to construct two new buildings; these board members are indifferent regarding, the location for the larger of the two new buildings. Two more votes are needed to pass the bond issue, but the two board members who are willing to cooperate by voting "yes" disagree on the location of the buildings. Not to vote "yes" dooms the project, in that everybody goes their separate ways and payoffs are zero. But to vote "yes" and to pass the bond creates the problem of the terms of the agreement regarding the location of the buildings. One way one of the two board members could force the issue would be to turn in a proxy vote which specified that his "yes" vote was contingent upon the larger building be located in a certain place, and then leaving on a vacation where he could not be reached. If the bond issue is to pass, the other rationally calculated "yes" vote would have to agree, or suffer the consequence of a zero payoff.

Altruism is not always the best policy. Take the case of two teachers whose classroom teaching methods create noise and interfere with the teaching that goes on in the nearby class. In one case, teacher A uses video tapes, the soundtrack of which invade the other room. Teacher B likes to have some of the students sing and play music. If both teachers are altruistic and refrain from doing what annoys the other, neither obtains a benefit (lower right cell). If teacher A refrains, but teacher B does not (upper right cell), then A suffers the noise of the other class but does not get the benefit of using video tapes. If teacher B refrains, but teacher A does not, then B suffers noise from A without being able to instruct her pupils in music (lower left cell). However, if both do their thing, each suffers the noise of the other, yet gets the benefit of his or her respective teaching tools.

| | | Teacher A | |
		Tapes	Refrains
Teacher B	Music	2, 2	3, -1
	Refrains	-1, 3	0, 0

Hamburger (1979) notes that in this game of "convergence" the interests of the two players converge but do not coincide, because each player harms the other by pursuing his own interest. Yet each has a dominant strategy; regardless of what the other teacher does, it is best for each to do his own thing. Ironically, the two teachers do better by continuing to annoy the other than by being altruistic. This leads us to other situations in which a refusal to cooperate is the better strategy for each player.

Noncooperation as the Rational Choice

One game is so well-known that its name, "chicken," has entered the popular culture. This game asks the question "who is the chicken?" In the popular mind, the game is best illustrated by two automobiles driving at great speed directly at each other. The first driver to swerve is the chicken, but failure of either to swerve spells disaster for both. This game can also be illustrated in matrix form, using the notation discussed earlier.

| | Driver A | |
	Swerve	Drive
D r i v e r B Swerve	S, S	T, B
Drive	B, T	W, W

This game is a useful way to illustrate the kind of difficult confrontations that occurred between the school board for the City School District of Rochester, New York, and the teacher's union headed by Adam Urbanski. The confrontation arose over the district's need for the board to make a mid-year reduction in the school budget. The board favored cutting salaries and services at the school building level (for example, reducing the number of elementary school librarians, and implementing a give-back of teacher salaries), while the union favored making reductions in central office staff. Failure of either party to swerve would send the board, union, and community into further debt, the need to borrow money and a downgrading of the district's credit rating. Yet for each party, the rational choice may be to stay hard-nosed. School board members faced legal and other pressures, which made it impractical to engage in a full scale elimination of central office jobs. Union officials faced loss of position at the next union election. But, certainly, the pressure to reach an agreement was severe, for failure to do so would have landed the two players (as well as the community) in the bottom right cell. Negotiations dragged on for some months, until finally the board was forced to act unilaterally, imposing a variety of steps that led to approximately 150 layoffs. The board's relationship with the union remains difficult a year after these events.

Even when a compromise can be reached, agreement is not necessarily a comfortable position for the two parties, who still face severe temptations to cheat on that agreement, and thus to end their cooperation. This temptation is illustrated by the best known strategic game called the "prisoner's dilemma." The game gets its name from a situation in which two prisoners find themselves. Suppose two thieves, Mo and Flo, agree before the heist that if either one is caught he will not incriminate the other. The theft goes badly, and both are arrested and kept apart so that they may not communicate while being interrogated. If both stick to their bargain, and neither talks, they might at most be successfully prosecuted for petty theft, which carries a sentence of three years. If, however, one confesses, tells the police where the stash is, and blames the other for being the ring-leader, he will get a light sentence of one year, and the other will get the maximum of five years. If they both end up confessing, each will receive a four year penalty.

Now consider Mo's calculations. Mo knows that Flo is either confessing (defecting from the agreement) or sticking to the agreement (cooperating). If Flo confesses, Mo will get five years by sticking by the agreement and four years by confessing. Thus it is better for Mo to confess if Flo confesses. If Flo sticks by the agreement, Mo gets one year by confessing, and three years by not confessing. Thus, it is still better for Mo to confess, regardless of what Flo does.

Flo, of course, is going through the same calculations and reaching the same conclusion. If Mo confesses, Flo is better off confessing; and if Mo does not confess, the better move is still for Flo to confess. Hence both Mo and Flo confess. If they had been able to maintain solidarity and stand by their agreement, they both would have gotten away with shorter sentences.

This situation is modeled in the next matrix, where one can see that if Flo had chosen the bottom row and Mo the right column they would have ended up with 3 year sentences. But each player is afraid he will be the sucker who sticks by the agreement while the other guy confesses. (See lower left cell and upper right cell.) Not surprisingly, both players, seeking to avoid being the sucker, confess, with the predicted result being the upper left cell. In this case, the numbers in the matrix refer to the years each is sentenced to jail.

		Mo	
		Cooperate	Defect
F l o	Cooperate	S, S (3) (3)	W, B (5) (1)
	Defect	B, W (1) (5)	T, T (4) (4)

Like the "battle of the sexes," this game describes a situation of mixed motives; cooperation is good, but so is defection. Yet there exists here what theorists call a dominant strategy for each player—defection. To repeat, Mo knows that if Flo sticks by the agreement, Mo's better choice is to confess; and if Flo does not stick by the agreement, again Mo's better payoff will come from confessing. Flo also finds that the better of his choices is to defect from the agreements. Thus, unless some other factors enter the picture, the predicted result of situations described as prisoner's dilemma is noncooperation.

Unfortunately, the dilemma depicted in this game is an inherent aspect of the human condition. Let's return to the agreement reached between the union and board to reduce the midyear budget. While the board may have agreed to some reductions in central office staff, it in fact may implement the agreement via cosmetic changes, such as shifting staff positions off the central office budget, allocating the positions to other budget categories and retaining the personnel at the central office. Meanwhile, the real budget savings are achieved through similarly covert moves that affect staffing at the school building level; that is, positions go unfilled. Though the union may have fewer opportunities to cheat in this way on the budget deal, it still has some weapons available. For example, it can continue its open and public attack on the size of the central office staff. Ironically, in the case just described, that attack would in fact be justified, although unbeknownst to the union officials, because the cheating done by the board would have taken place covertly and out of view of union officials.

Of course, unions and boards are not the only players who find themselves on the horns of the prisoner's dilemma. Take the situation in which a school building's administrative staff and teachers have repeatedly engaged in bureaucratic "warfare" over a variety of issues. The toll has been severe on both sides, so they agree to "cool" it. Yet each side is worried that it will be played for the sucker. Administrators and teachers worry that the other side could be laying the groundwork for a final political assault by lining up evidence and wooing supporters. Not willing to be trapped into being the honest dupe, the two sides secretly break the agreement and continue to solicit ammunition and gather support. Of course, the continuing preparation for political combat cannot remain secret for long, and soon both parties find themselves back where they were prior to their treaty. The same matrix used to describe the problem Flo and Mo faced can be constructed to demonstrate that, despite initial best intentions, the teachers and administrators find themselves in the bottom right cell, because each has chosen to defect from the agreement.

Preemptive cheating on agreements, which occurs out of fear that the other side is cheating, is a central obstacle to cooperation on a wide range of matters, including such life-and-death issues as arms reduction treaties. How, then, is cooperation possible? I will return to a more complete answer in a later section of the paper, but one answer is that if the parties perceive a good probability that they will be repeatedly working together—if the parties see that the prisoner's dilemma is an infinitely repeated game for them—then the parties will rationally conclude that cheating or defection is, in the long term, more costly than is cooperation. By constantly cheating, they would never cooperate and achieve the benefits of the upper left cell, and if those benefits are big enough in the long term, it makes sense to attempt to achieve a level of trust, to hold to the agreements, and thus stabilize a cooperative relationship. (Axelrod 1984; Sober 1992) However, the temptation to cheat remains strong. The benefits of being the deceptive party, which are represented in upper right and lower left cells are very large—thus it remains important to "trust and verify."

Because agreements and compromises are hardly any guarantee of ultimate success, the very process of trying to reach an agreement is difficult as each party tries both to get the best deal and as part of the deal to obtain verification procedures that will help to detect cheating and punishment procedures for the party who cheats.

A different way of presenting the prisoner's dilemma game is a useful perspective from which to analyze the problems of cooperation even when the parties are not hostile antagonists. For example, site-based management creates a situation in which it may be useful to explain and predict the dynamics of the management team using the prisoner's dilemma. Suppose central office has told the school-based team to pull together in the development of a new program for the school. The team members now have a lot of hard work ahead of them including investigating model practices in other school districts, examining research, determining the level of resources they have available, and working toward consensus.

The three graphs shown on page 250 together provide a demonstration of the value of not-cooperating. (Hamburger, 1979) The graphs depict the relationship among three players—Jane, Sam, and Lesley.

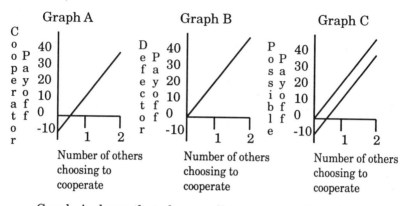

Graph A shows that the payoff to a cooperating player (e.g., Jane) increases as the number of other players who also cooperate increases, that is, as Sam joins in and then also Lesley. Thus, if no one else cooperates, Jane sustains a net loss from all the efforts she puts to develop the plan by herself. When other people join in, however, her payoff jumps up. Graph B shows the benefits that, for example, Sam accrues by not chipping in. If no one else chips in, Sam's payoff is zero; but as Jane and Lesley join in the effort to develop a school-based plan, Sam gets more and more benefits, for which he did nothing. Graph C combines Graphs A and B and shows that an individual is always better off not cooperating, regardless of how many other people actually offer to cooperate.

These graphs represent a prisoner's dilemma, because noncooperation is the dominant strategy no matter what the other participants do. This conclusion emerges for all the players. Yet the players would be better off if they cooperated. Total noncooperation among the players yields each players zero payoff, but if they cooperate, they receive a handsome payoff (See Graph A). Unfortunately, mutual cooperation is an unstable state, because each player is sorely tempted to defect, an individually rational move.

Let's assume, however, that the team manages to get its act together and develops a plan that includes acquiring better playground equipment for the school. (A vote on this and other alternatives of course, could raise cyclical majority problems discussed earlier.) In the absence of a sufficient budget, the school professionals suggest to the parents' advisory board that it might take on as a project the purchase of playground equipment. It is now the parents who find themselves on the horns of the prisoner's dilemma. The financial situation they face is as follows:

Total Cost of Construction of the New Playground	$2500
Cost Per Family (assume five families)	$500
Gross Benefits Per Family	$1000
Net Benefit Per Family	$500

Though it is rational for these families to cooperate in the construction of the new playground, it is also individually rational to defect, to be a free rider and to let the other families build the playground that one's children will make use of. The next matrix illustrates the problem:

		All Other Families	
		Pay In	Free Ride
B u r t o n	Pay In	500, 500	-1500, 1000 each family
	Free Ride	1000, 375 each family	0, 0

If everybody collaborates, the net benefit for the Burtons and the other families is $500 (upper left cell). If only the Burton family contributes to the construction of the playground, the Burtons would suffer a net loss of $1500 ($1000–$2500). Each of the other families obtains a pure gain of $1000, as their children will be able to use the playground. If only the Burton's are the free rider, they obtain a pure benefit of $1000, while other families will net only a benefit of $375 after paying construction costs. If no one contributes, there are no benefits.

A close look at the matrix reveals it as the prisoner's dilemma. Unless some way is found to overcome the temptation to be a free rider, the playground will not be constructed. Problems of obtaining cooperation for joint projects are ubiquitous in social life. Unions have solved the free-rider problem by establishing the agency shop rule, under which everybody in the unit represented by the union, pays union dues, even if they do not join the union. In fact, the playground equipment problem is a metaphor for any project that creates benefits that noncontributors can enjoy and cannot be prevented from enjoying. Projects that involve such "collective good" benefits (or positive externalities) are difficult to get off the ground without some form of mandatory contribution, hence the justification for government and systems of taxation (Head 1974).

Even more troubling for bureaucracies is the observation that activities of individual employees entail costs in time and effort, to the employee personally and benefits, some of which the employee personally enjoys and some of which are "collective" and publicly enjoyed. These external or collective benefits, which are associated with each person's work, create a prisoner's dilemma as surely as the example of building the playground. Like the free-riding parent, employees may want to enjoy the benefits without paying the cost. And while everybody would prefer an organization in which no one shirked, everybody is likewise tempted to be a free rider (Alchian and Demsetz 1972).

Adding to the difficulties of obtaining cooperation is the fact that supervisors are also self-interested rational calculators. A self-interested supervisor does not trust those employees, who may shirk their work, and the employees do not trust the supervisor, who is probably trying to get them to do more work, or take more risks, with no increase and perhaps even a decrease in pay.

Incidentally, getting large numbers of people to cooperate who are not subject to hierarchical controls involves similar problems. Thus, encouraging commuters to forgo driving and to use public transportation, getting people to restrain their use of air conditioners during extremely hot weather in order to avoid brown-outs, and getting people to reduce water usage during a drought all involve similar problems of social coordination. The heart of the matter is that the rational individual is tempted to be a free rider, tempted not to restrain himself and to go ahead with the use of the car and unreduced consumption of electricity and water: "With everybody else limiting their water use, there is no harm in my using a bit more." Analogous problems arise with regard to such matters as teachers' consumption of school supplies and the monopolizing of meeting time.

Limitations and Implications for Preparation of School Leaders

The research program of rational choice theorists is beyond early infancy, but is likewise still far from maturity. Much has been learned and should be included in the programs for preparing school personnel. But vast possibilities exist for further development of the field, as well as for the formulation and testing of propositions about behavior within public school institutional arrangements.

What are some of the things we can teach that will provide leaders with a solid basis for action? The literature on public choice explains the effects of voting rules, cyclical majorities, agenda setting rules, and insincere or sophisticated voting on election outcomes. This information is indispensable for anybody working with collective choice processes. Similarly, there is much we know from game theory that is highly suggestive of what organizational leaders should do to induce cooperation and to lower or eliminate the barriers to cooperation.

From game theory we know that incentives are crucial to obtaining cooperation. A central task of management should be to devise incentive systems that make cooperation the rational choice for subordinates. For example, the more superiors can develop institutional incentives that throw employees into "battle of the sexes" games, the more cooperation will occur among the employees. Even if the creation of incentives is not always possible, an understanding of the problems created by the ubiquitous prisoner's dilemma can help the administrator. For example, the more often school personnel must act together, the more they see that they are involved in a repeated prisoner's dilemma game, and the more likely it becomes that cooperation will emerge. Leaders can also help in the setting up of verification mechanisms to reduce the temptation to defect in secret from agreements. Improving communication is another important step in eliminating likelihood of defection and noncooperation among those caught in the dilemma. The existence of smaller working groups also makes it more difficult for defection and free riding to go undetected; thus, site-based management is likely to work better in schools with smaller faculties. Good monitoring, reporting, and supervisory systems increase the probabilities of continued cooperation simply by making defection more difficult. Couple these steps with a tit-for-tat management style—management sanctions for each employee defection—and one has a prescription for a cooperative working relationship, which will evolve over time. Yet if monitoring the possibility of shirking is not easily accomplished, it is only logical for organizations to turn instead to agreements with employees that hold employees accountable for performance outcomes.

These so-called "tough" or "hard-nosed" implications of rational choice theory have been questioned by scholars, who continue to develop the theory, test its propositions, and explore its implications. Gary J. Miller, in a review and discussion of this body of literature, argues that cooperation can and must be encouraged by other methods than those I have outlined above. He argues that norms, along with organizational culture and a willingness of management to give more to employees than the labor market dictates, can help develop a willingness on the part of employees to work when they would rather shirk. Though there is no way to turn an organization into a machine, with each employee doing exactly what is expected of him or her, the "best [managerial] response to this problem is to inspire among their own employees a willingness to cooperate and trust each other by setting an example of being concerned and trustworthy themselves" (Miller 1990, 345). Miller believes the latest research shows that "the choices of 'homo economicus' in repeated, personal, norm-constrained, social interactions becomes virtually indistinguishable from the behavior attributed to 'homo sociologicus'" (Miller 1990, 343). Robert H. Bates and William T. Bianco disagree with Miller, however, saying that "the leader of a team possesses far less ability to initiate and sustain team production than Miller would seem to claim" (Bates and Bianco 1990, 349).

Rational choice theory is a vibrant field that has already solved many problems and provided a way to address many others. For example, research based on this paradigm promises to shed light on school politics broadly conceived, for example, by forecasting public sector union strikes, and school board decision making. In addition, rational choice theories promise to illuminate what might be called bureaucratic politics, micropolitics or inter-organizational dynamics. Thus, rational choice theory should be able to explain the reasons why school administrators decide or decide not to bring dismissal proceedings against incompetent teachers, why school administrators seem unable or unwilling to actively supervise to achieve educational productivity, and why there is a tendency for school personnel to form "treaties" and establish peaceful but unproductive relationships (Boyd and Hartman 1988; Bridges 1990). This powerful way of illuminating the real problems of public school officials ought to be a standard part of the preparation of school leaders and a part of the research agenda of schools of education.

Bibliography

Alchian, A., and Demseta, H. 1972. "Production, Information Costs, and Economic Organization." *American Economic Review* 62: 777–95.

Axelrod, R. 1984. *The Evolution of Cooperation*. New York: Basic Books.

Bates, R. H. and Bianco, W. T. 1990. "Comment: Applying Rational Choice Theory: The Role of Leadership in Team Production." In K. S. Cook and M. Levi, eds. *The Limits of Rationality*. Chicago: University of Chicago Press, 349–57.

Bridges, E. M. 1990. *Managing the Incompetent Teacher*. Eugene, Or., ERIC Clearing House on Educational Management.

Boyd, W. L., and Hartman, W. T. 1988. "The Politics of Educational Productivity." In David H. Monk and Julie Underwood, eds. *Microlevel School Finance*. Cambridge, Mass.: Ballinger Publishing Company.

Brams, S. J. 1990. *Negotiation Games*. New York: Routledge.

―――. 1975. *Game Theory and Politics*. NY: The Free Press.

Bueno de Mesquita, B. 1985. *Political Forecasting: The Case of Hong Kong*. New Haven: Yale University Press.

Dixit, A., and Nalebuff, B. 1991. *Thinking Strategically*. New York: W.W. Norton & Company.

Fisher, R., and Brown, S. 1988. *Getting Together*. New York: Penguin Books.

Hamburger, H. 1979. *Games as Models of Social Phenomena*. San Francisco: W.H. Freeman and Company.

Kimbrough, R. B., and Nunnery, M. Y. 1988. *Educational Administration*. 3rd ed. New York: McMillian Publishing Company.

Lipham, J. M. 1988. "Getzel's Models in Educational Administration." In Norman J. Boyan, ed. *Handbook of Research on Educational Administation*. New York: Longman.

Luce, R. D., and Raiffa, H. 1957. *Games and Decisions*. New York: Wiley.

McKenzie, R. B., and Tullock, G. 1975. *The New World of Economics*. Homewood, Ill.: Richard D. Irwin Inc.

Miller, G. J. 1990. "Managerial Dilemmas: Political Leadership in Hierarchies." In K. S. Cook and M. Levi, eds. *The Limits of Rationality*. Chicago: University of Chicago Press, 324–48.

Mueller, D. C. 1989. *Public Choice II*. Cambridge, Mass.: Cambridge University Press.

Pruitt, D. G., and Rubin, J. Z. 1986. *Social Conflict*. New York: Random House.

Putterman, L. 1986. *The Economic Nature of the Firm*. Cambridge. Mass.: Cambridge University Press.

Raiffa, H. 1982. *The Art and Science of Negotiation*. Cambridge, Mass.: The Belknap Press of Harvard University Press.

Riker, W. H. 1962. *The Theory of Political Coalitions*. New Haven, Conn.: Yale University Press.

_____. 1982. *Liberalism Against Populism*. San Francisco, Calif.: W.H. Freeman Company.

_____. 1986. *The Art of Political Manipulation*. New Haven, Conn.: Yale University Press.

Strom, G. S. 1990. *The Logic of Lawmaking*. Balitmore, Md.: The Johns Hopkins University Press.

Needed: A Knowledge Base that Promotes Creativity—Toward a Rhetorical Knowledge Base for Educational Administration

Jane Clark Lindle

All jobs in education are noted for their spontaneity given the nature of the clientele. Gather growing children into masses, and there is ample opportunity for unpredictable and potentially combustible events (Metz 1978). Teachers, for example, must make multiple judgments in a short period of time. Estimates suggest thousands of decisions are made in the span of a school day (Berliner 1986; Jackson 1990; Joyce and Weil 1986; Pasch, Sparks-Langer, Gardner, Starko, and Moody 1991).

While all educators must display mental agility, educational administrators in particular must be able to think on their feet in a variety of settings. Furthermore, the kind of thinking in which they engage is not limited to that which merely matches predetermined routines and responses to clearly identifiable structure. The idiosyncracies of schools and people, what Schön (1990) calls the "indeterminate zones of practice—uncertainty, uniqueness, and value conflicts" (p. 6), frequently require newly invented, atypical responses. In this chapter, I will focus on inventive or creative thought and begin to consider what must be included in educational administration's knowledge base if that knowledge base is to help promote, or at least not inhibit, school leaders' creativity and inventiveness.

Educational Administration's Traditional Knowledge Base

The dominant source of knowledge for many educational administration programs over the last two decades has been organizational theory. Lifted from psychology and sociology by business administrators, school administrators purloined the concepts and adapted the prescriptions for corporate board rooms to elementary and secondary faculty meetings. Frequently these prescriptions have been oriented toward organizational control and routinization. Yet the relentlessly chaotic conditions of practice in educational administration have challenged the field to a continual search for ever more rational, manageable, and predictable ways of leading schools. Even as business and industry have turned toward more innovative practices, educators have remained oddly focused on seeking and adopting conventional and conservative practices in an abiding effort to calm the always volatile conditions of schooling.

These attempts to routinize the often-syncopated rhythms of schools have been roundly criticized by others in this volume and elsewhere (e.g., Immegart and Boyd 1977; Murphy and Hallinger 1987). Rather than repeating their charges, we will acknowledge such as basic assumptions for pursuing a quest for a missing or additional knowledge base, one that will facilitate the development of creative or inventive thinking in current and prospective school leaders.

Creativity: Definitions and Research

Definitions of creativity are not hard to find. Although they differ in some of their details, most definitions emphasize originality and the individual's fluency in accessing or producing the unique (Guilford 1959; Lefrancois 1985; Mednick 1962). Guilford's (1959) early distinction between convergent and divergent forms of thinking has had a sustaining influence on most conceptions of creativity (Lefrancois 1985). Convergent thinking is a closed process routinely producing "right" answers. Divergent thinking is an open, inventive process. Guilford's definition of divergent thinking can be applied to school leadership. Certainly any profession with "indeterminate zones" (Schön 1990, p. 6) of uniqueness requires practitioners with divergent, inventive insight.

The study of creativity languished among psychologists over the 1970s and 1980s, as cognitive psychologists focused on the structure of intelligence, various thinking styles, and the physiology of the brain (Gardner 1976; Lefrancois 1985; McCleary 1993; Telzrow 1987; Whalen and Mann 1987). However, the essence of invention—professionals playing with ideas—enjoyed some appeal and experimentation in corporate environments (McCleary 1993; Rickards 1993).

One of the pioneers in the exploration of corporate creativity was William J. J. Gordon (McCleary 1993; Weaver and Prince 1990). Gordon, in his work (1961), employed a classical rhetorical concept known as the dialectic (McCleary 1993). A dialectic involves synthesizing contradictory states, assumptions, or conditions (Kneller 1984). In Gordon's case, dialectical reasoning was enhanced by the use of analogics and the conflicts inherent in them (Gordon 1961; Gordon and Poze 1972; Joyce and Weil 1986; McCleary 1993; Weaver and Prince 1990).

Gordon's contributions occurred following the Second World War. His goal was to spark the problem-finding and problem-solving capacity of engineers and eventually other scientists and corporate research and development (R&D) specialists. Gordon and his colleagues focused on the amazingly productive outcomes of seemingly disorderly, messy collaboration (McCleary 1993; Rickards 1993; Weaver 1993; Weaver and Prince 1990). Despite the myth that the scientific process is an orderly incremental progression of discovery, scientific breakthroughs depend on radical shifts in perspectives and thinking (Kuhn 1970; McCleary 1993; Popper 1959).

Gordon stimulated this messy process through a series of mind-stretching exercises he dubbed *Synetics* (Gordon 1961; Weaver and Prince 1990). A group of problem solvers were brought together with a clear, but very general definition of a problem or opportunity. The definition included factors that led to the problem, locus of problem ownership among decision makers and implementers, and a general definition of the ideal outcome for the meeting (McCleary 1993; Weaver 1993). Then, by the use of analogies that forced new understandings of familiar dilemmas, creative solutions were invented by the groups (Gordon 1961; Gordon and Poze 1972; Joyce and Weil 1986).

For example, a common problem requiring creative thinking in companies is how to get new product ideas accepted by, first, the sales force and, then, the general public (Rickards 1993). Part of the process involves selecting an appropriate network of participants in the synetics exercises. So rather than just having R&D personnel or only the engineers or scientists, the clients, members of the sales force, and servce/repair personnel are included with the R&D people in product design or refinement. The ground rules include specific instructions to open up the climate and avoid competitive behavior or retaliation. Each participant is asked to help clarify the definition of the problem; for example, how can we get people to buy our new multisensory, educational widget? Then the facilitator leads the group through some warm-up mind-stretching exercises that are fairly simple analogies: "Name something that is like the sun." "How is what you've named like the sun?" "How is it not like the sun?

After the warm-up, the facilitator returns to the defined/clarified problem and begins asking the group for more complex analogies. "Name an animal that is similar to our problem." The group generates a list of animals and the facilitator asks them to come to consensus on which animal is most like the problem. Once the animal is selected, the group is then asked to focus on the animal and personalize its characteristics, "If you were this animal, how would you feel?" Once again, a list of responses is recorded so that all participants can read and review it.

The facilitator then turns to a phase known as "compressed conflicts" by asking the participants to reflect on pairs of adjectives that are opposites among the listed personal characteristics. The group is then asked to come to consensus on the most vivid conflict represented among all the conflicts that have been identified. The process is then recycled. Beginning with the identified conflict, the facilitator asks for another direct analogy, "What machine is most like the conflict you have chosen?" Once the group has generated another list and come to consensus on one response, the facilitator then refocuses attention on the originally identified problem. "What do the machine you chose, the compressed conflict you identified, and this problem have in common? How might you resolve these issues?" Groups led through this process are frequently successful in making the leap from fanciful thinking to concrete solutions (Joyce and Weil 1986; Rickards 1993; Weaver 1993).

The success of these analogical dialectics illustrates intrinsic conflicts found in the analogies (McCleary 1993). These conflicts tap into the human mental capacity of holding, even linking strongly contradictory thought—the quintessence of divergent thinking (Guilford 1959; Weaver and Prince 1990).

Although synectics has been successful in the corporate world, educational administrators have not really explored their creative sides (Hooper 1992). On the other hand, these techniques have been converted to applications in problem solving and creative writing for elementary and secondary school students (Gordon and Poze 1972; Joyce and Weil 1986; Weaver and Prince 1990).

Another pioneer in the development of corporate creativity—albeit in a somewhat different area—is Gareth Morgan (1986; 1989a; 1989b). Morgan's focus is on organizational theory. Morgan transformed the traditionally stodgy approach to organizational theory by employing metaphorical thinking, another manifestation of dialectics, in the analysis of organizational life. For example, he marshalled the complex and diverse literature on organizational theory into managable and historically accurate explanations by suggesting that organizations be thought of alternately as machines, organisms, brains, cultures, political systems, psychic prisons, and instruments of domination (Morgan 1986). In a similar manner to Gordon's work, Morgan's approach suggests strategies for leaders' thinking that go beyond linear efficiency rules for problem solving and decision making.

In contrast to educational administration's neglect of Gordon's promotion of analogical invention, metaphorical thinking has enjoyed quiet acceptance among scholars in the field. Morgan's (1986) suggestion that metaphors could enhance the understanding of organizational problems has spawned a proliferation of metaphorical discussions of a variety of educational processes. Perhaps no more fitting a tribute to the power of metaphorical thinking in education can be found than the wealth of articles addressing metaphorical illustrations and solutions to problems in education. A recent electronic search of ERIC revealed nearly 400 of these works since 1988. From descriptions of schools' governance (Behn 1992; Bredeson 1988; Hogsett 1993; Steinhoff and Owens 1989) to explorations of leadership style and processes (Blumberg 1989; Conway 1991; Dana and Pitts 1993; Kerchner 1988; Prestine 1993b; Rogers 1992) to critiques of business-education linkages (Sztajn 1992), educational theorists and practitioners have embraced the imaginative stimulation of metaphors.

What the literature does not address, however, is how to promote metaphorical thinking or any other form of creative problem solving among prospective and practicing school administrators. The discussion now turns to this question.

Promoting Creative and Inventive Thought

Instructional practices that might develop inventive and creative thought can easily be inferred from what has been said above. Already some administrator preparation programs make assignments requiring students to characterize their own educational organizations in metaphors (Bredeson 1988). Also, we could adapt Gordon's synectics techniques and use them in educational administration classes (Lindle 1990). Just imagine how delightful a school leadership course might be if students were encouraged to explore analogic incongruities. Certainly it takes practice for rusty adults to be more inventive and imaginative. From personal experience, I can testify that mid-career adults maintain long moments of embarrassed silence when their professor asks them a simple question such as "What is an orange like?" But these mind-stretching activities eventually pay off when an imagination exercise for children, "Put your mother on the ceiling" (DeMille 1973), is converted to an educator's mind-bender "macramé your school board president to the rafters." Laughter ensues. With laughter comes relaxation. With relaxation comes mental freedom. With mental freedom comes the agility of mind so necessary for reflection on and invention of new definitions and solutions to changing problems of school leadership.

For additional approaches, we might look to the rather substantial knowledge base of rhetoric. The connection between the rhetorical arts and inventive thinking is as old as the identification of rhetoric as an art. Before today's popular understanding of the term "rhetoric" as a political, dissembling, semantic swamp, rhetoric was a respected field of Classical letters. The ancient arts of rhetoric included the practical applications of argument, persuasion, and debate, and the interpretive arts of poetry, drama, and storytelling.

The practical applications of rhetoric seem particularly germane to the field of educational administration (Billig, 1991; Floyd and Jacobs 1993; Jacobs 1993; Kahane 1992; Keough 1992; Kuhn 1992). For instance, inclusion of argumentation and debate as part of the educational administration curriculum would be a welcome addition for beleaguered school leaders. In many cases, school leaders are not prepared for the dialectical nature of decentralized governance or constructivist classrooms (Brooks and Brooks 1993; Hallinger, Leithwood, and Murphy 1993; Prestine 1993a; Prestine and Legrand 1991; Strike 1993). They need the opportunity to practice taking a position and defending it. They need to experience the dialectical tensions of arriving at a consensus in a group. They also need to cultivate and apply the inventive thinking derived from dialectics.

Indeed the dialectical process is a powerful metaphor for educational change. Rapid change is a consistent condition of the world of schools because that world is full of contradictory, conflicting expectations. By including the knowledge base of rhetoric, especially of dialectics, students of educational administration can become accustomed to the topsy-turvy moments of practice. As future school leaders turn assumptions upside down and inside out in an effort to redefine problems and search for innovative solutions, they will not only have opportunities to practice inventive and creative thinking; they will also practice the very necessary skills of thinking on their feet in the increasingly contested realm of educational decision making.

Summary

Here I have argued that the field of educational administration must move beyond the knowledge bases it has employed in the past. The development and practice of school leadership must incorporate knowledge and skills that will promote inventive, creative thinking. Specific strategies and techniques developed in the corporate world have been discussed. At a more general level, I have argued for the need to look to the classical field of rhetoric for a fundamental awareness of dialectical and divergent processes inherent in creativity and invention.

References

Behn, R. D. (1992). "Management and the neutrino: The search for meaningful metaphors." *Public Administration Review* 52 (5), 409–19.

Berliner, D. C. (1986). "In pursuit of the expert pedagogue." *Educational Researcher* 15 (7), 5–13.

Blumberg, A. (1989). *School administration as a craft: Foundations of practice.* Boston: Allyn and Bacon.

Billig, M. (1991). *Ideology and opinions.* Newbury Park, Calif.: Sage Publications.

Bredeson, P. V. (1988). "Perspectives on schools: Metaphors and management in education." *Journal of Educational Administration* 26 (2), 293–310.

Brooks, J. G. and M. G. Brooks. (1993). *The case for constructivist classrooms.* Alexandria, Va.: Association for Supervision and Curriculum Development.

Conway, J. (1991). "Clarifying the coaching roles: Principal, department head, teacher." *NASSP Bulletin* 75 (538), 16–23.

Dana, N. F. and J. H. Pitts. (1993). "The use of metaphor and reflective coaching in the exploration of principal thinking: A case study of principal change." *Educational Administration Quarterly* 29 (3), 323–38.

DeMille, R. (1973). *Put your mother in the ceiling: children's imagination games.* New York: The Viking Press.

Floyd, K. and R. M. Jacobs. (1993). " 'School communication'—An elusive variable?" *Journal of Management Systems* 5 (2), i–iv.

Gardner, H. (1976). *Frames of mind.* New York: Basic Books.

Gordon, W. J. J. (1961). *Synectics.* New York: Harper & Row.

———— and T. Poze. (1972). *Strange and familiar.* Cambridge, Mass.: Porpoise Books.

Guilford, J. P. (1959). "Three faces of intellect." *American Psychologist* 14, 469–479.

Hallinger, P., K. Leithwood, and J. Murphy. (eds.). (1993). *Cognition and school leadership.* New York: Teachers College Press.

Hogsett, C. (1993). "A new paradigm for schools." *Educational Forum* 57 (3), 246–55.

Hooper, D. W. (1992). "Success depends on leaders' 'whole brain' thinking." *The School Administrator* 49 (6), 14–17.

Immegart, G. L. and W. L. Boyd. (eds.). (1977). *Problem-finding in Educational Administration.* Lexington, Mass.: Lexington Books, D.C. Heath and Co.

Jackson, P. W. (1990). *Life in classrooms.* New York: Teachers College Press.

Jacobs, R. M. (1993). "Road maps to understanding communication." *Journal of Management Systems* 5 (2), 1–15.

Joyce, B. and M. Weil. (1986). *Models of teaching* (3rd ed.) Englewood Cliffs, N.J.: Prentice Hall.

Kahane, H. (1992). *Logic and contemporary rhetoric: The use of reason in everyday life* (6th ed.). Belmont, Calif.: Wadsworth.

Keough, C. M. (1992). "Bargaining arguments and argumentative bargains." In L. L. Putnam and M. E. Roloff (eds.). *Communication and negotiations*, vol. 20 of *The Sage Annual Review of Communications Research*. Newbury Park, Calif.: Sage Publications, 109–27.

Kerchner, C. T. (1988). "Bureaucratic entrepreneurship: the implications of choice for school administrators." *Educational Administration Quarterly* 24 (4), 381–92.

Kneller, G. F. (1984). *Movements of thought in modern education.* New York: John Wiley and Sons.

Kuhn, D. (1992). "Thinking as argument." *Harvard Educational Review* 62 (2), 155–78.

Kuhn, T. S. (1970). *The structure of scientific revolutions* (2nd ed.). Chicago: University of Chicago Press.

Lefrancois, G. R. (1985). *Psychology for teaching* (5th ed.). Belmont, Calif.: Wadsworth Publishing.

McCleary, D. (1993). *The logic of imaginative education.* New York: Teachers College Press.

Mednick, S. A. (1962). "The associative basis of the creative process." *Psychological Review* 69, 220–32.

Metz, M. H. (1978). *Classrooms and corridors: The crisis of authority in desegregated secondary schools.* Berkeley, Calif.: University of California Press.

Morgan, G. (1989a). *Teaching organizational theory.* Newbury Park, Calif.: Sage Publications.

Morgan, G. (1989b). *Creative organization theory.* Newbury Park, Calif.: Sage Publications.

———. (1986). *Images of organizations.* Newbury Park, Calif.: Sage.

Murphy, J. and P. Hallinger. (eds.). (1987). *Approaches to administrative training in educational administration.* Albany, N.Y.: SUNY Press.

Pasch, M., G. Sparks-Langer, T. G. Gardner, A. J. Starko, and C. D. Moody. (1991). *Teaching as decision making.* New York: Longman.

Popper, K. R. (1959). *The logic of scientific discovery.* London: Hutchinson.

Prestine, N. A. (1993a). Appreticeship in problem-solving: Extending the cognitive apprenticeship model. In P. Hallinger, K. Leithwood, and J. Murphy (eds.) *Cognition and school leadership.* New York: Teachers College Press, 192–212.

———. (1993b). "Extending the essential schools metaphor: Principal as enabler." *Journal of School Leadership* 3 (4), 356–72.

Prestine, N. A. and B. LeGrand. (1991). "Cognitive learning theory and the preparation of educational administrators: Implications for practice and policy." *Educational Administration Quarterly* 27 (1), 61–89.

Rickards, T. (1993). "Creative leadership: Messages from the front line and the back room." *Journal of Creative Behavior* 27 (1), 46–56.

Rogers, J. L. (1992). "Leadership development for the 90s: Incorporating emergent paradigm perspectives." *NASPA Journal* 29 (4), 243–52.

Schön, D. A. (1990). *Educating the reflective practitioner.* San Francisco: Jossey-Bass.

Steinhoff, C., and R. G. Owens. (1989). "The organisational culture assessment inventory: A metaphorical analysis in educational settings." *Journal of Educational Administration* 27 (3), 17–23.

Strike, K. A. (1993). "Professionalism, democracy, and discursive communities: Normative reflections on restructuring." *American Educational Research Journal* 30 (2), 255–75.

Sztajn, P. (1992). "A matter of metaphors: Education as a handmade process." *Educational Leadership* 50 (3), 35–37.

Telzrow, C. (1987). "Left brain, right brain." In C. R. Reynolds and L. Mann (eds.). *Encyclopedia of special education,* vol. 2, 944–45. New York: John Wiley and Sons.

Weaver, W. T. (1993). "Anatomy of a creative problem-solving meetings." *Journal of Creative Behavior* 27 (4), 236–69.

——— and G. M. Prince. (1990). "Synectics: Its potential for education." *Phi Delta Kappan* 71 (3), 378–88.

Whalen, E., and L. Mann. (1987). "Cognitive styles." In C. R. Reynolds and L. Mann (eds.). *Encyclopedia of special education,* vol. 1, New York: John Wiley and Sons. 364–66.

A Constructivist View of the Knowledge Base in Educational Administration

Nona A. Prestine

> The task is to produce a changed environment for learning—an environment in which there is a new relationship between students and their subject matter, in which knowledge and skill become objects of interrogation, inquiry, and extrapolation. As individuals acquire knowledge, they also should be empowered to think and reason (Glaser 1984, 103).

Many of the differences and disagreements that exist about the form and function of a knowledge base in educational administration rest on underlying epistemologic and ideologic differences. Each extant perspective on the knowledge base of educational administration grows out of a particular way of understanding, a bias of convention or discipline; each highlights some aspects while ignoring others. If one accepts the proposition that the danger for any field lies in its potential trivialization by a single paradigmatic view, then the discourse and even discord presented in this volume can be taken as a distinct sign of a robust and vital field of study. As noted by Shulman, it is likely that "for the social sciences and education, the coexistence of competing schools of thought is a natural and quite mature state" (1986, 5). This would seem to suggest that the richness of the field can only be enhanced by such debate.

The controversy surrounding the knowledge base in educational administration is no trivial matter. When deciding explicit questions of "what knowledge," implicit questions of "whose knowledge" are also part of the equation. The establishment of a knowledge base, however construed, sets a course that holds profound implications about who we are, what we do, and what we value. Little can remain untouched, simply because educational administration is a marvelously ambiguous term, enjoying multiple permutations of meaning across different contexts of use. It describes a process engaged in by individuals and names both a field of study and an occupational role that occupies the energies and commitments of many people over the course of their adult lives. It is a course of study and a field of study. All elements are interconnected by a complex web of relationships. Change one thing of substance and all others will necessarily be affected.

Giving attention to the interconnected nature of educational administration holds important ramifications for consideration of the knowledge base. If the practice of educational administration is considered a normative enterprise, then the delineation of preparation programs (and the knowledge domains undergirding them) must also be thought of as a normative, not a descriptive, enterprise. Debates and decisions about a knowledge base can be seen as socially constructed exercises and take meaning within the particular ideological and ethical framework of those who have the power to define wisdom for a profession. These judgments and decisions necessarily hold important implications about what needs to be learned in preparatory programs and how it should be learned; what knowledge is necessary for practice and how it is used in practice; and, what knowledge domains should be emphasized in scholarly inquiry and how such inquiry should proceed.

The current UCEA-endorsed proposal for a knowledge base cannot be faulted on any technical basis, but needs to be understood and examined in the context of the functionaltst framework in which it ts embedded. There is much to be said in favor of this particular framework, which has traditionally identified the knowledge base (at least as informally evidenced and translated through course content and program offerings) as conceptualized around discrete, functional managerial areas of concerns, namely, law, finance, organization, leadership, supervision. The regularities of an identified knowledge base go a long way toward supporting the rationality of a more orderly task structure for preparation programs. These knowledge domains are already reflected in the chapter contents of numerous educational administration texts (See Hanson 1991; Hoy and Miskel 1991; Owens, 1991). Several states' certification and administrator competency test requirements appear to reinforce these same content areas. With intense competition for "syllabus space" and "program space," the functionalist approach offers what can be characterized as a standardized system of access to content areas (Rowan 1990). The focus on transmitting this domain knowledge may, in fact, be a most efficient means to this end and certainly has thus far dominated preparation program content and practices.

However, this regularity, routinization, and efficiency also creates several sticky issues. Although noted as important to the eventual establishment of expert practice (Glaser 1984; 1987; Spiro, Coulson, Feltovich, and Anderson 1988; Spiro, Vispoel, Schmitz, Samarapungavan, and Boerger 1987; Shulman 1986; 1987; 1988), domain knowledge, by itself, provides insufficient clues for many students about how to actually use it in solving problems and carrying out tasks in practice. Such knowledge tends to remain inert in situations for which it is appropriate (Collins, Brown, and Newman, 1989). Despite the numerous issues that have enlivened the debate about the appropriate form and structure of a knowledge base for educational administration, little has been said about professional knowledge use: that is, about the knowledge that professionals actually use in their practice and, more importantly, about the ways in which they acquire and use such knowledge. Little if any consideration has been given to issues surrounding initial knowledge acquisition in preparation programs, the accessibility and use, nonuse, or modification of such knowledge in practice, and the contribution of such knowledge to the development of professional expertise. Yet, without such considerations, attempts to codify a knowledge base for educational administration are likely to be misdirected and misspent.

Of course, there are always inherent difficulties in establishing a relationship between the administrator preparation program received by students and the quality of their actual administrative practice. Prescribed courses can be noted, number of courses taken can be counted, grades received can be recorded, but little can be deduced about the character or quality of those courses or the manner in which grades were awarded. Scores on competency or certification exams can be examined, but again, those kinds of tests may well assess knowledge that is not of great value to practicing administrators. Nonetheless, it would seem likely that issues surrounding knowledge acquisition need to be examined.

A final possible danger in using the functionalist approach lies in students construing their notions of preparation programs around the assumption that a given knowledge base represents "the truth" and all that they need to do is write it down, study it, and pass a test on it to be competent administrators. Representing the knowledge base as separate knowledge domains perpetuates this notion of administrative knowledge as a collection of discrete, monolithic structures. "Discrete skill [areas] for administrators are certainiy identifiable and entire preparation programs have been built around them. This makes eminent sense if one views administrator preparation programs as 'training' and driven by distinct and separate job demands. Yet, [this] extraction fractionates and trivializes the act of administration and serves to narrow rather than expand practitioner knowledge-in-use" (Prestine and LeGrand 1991, 73). In this view, possession would be all that counts. In essence, when all the marbles have been picked up, the game is over.

This chapter argues that educational administration must be understood as more than just the sum of the separate parts (or domains) of a knowledge base. There are other important types of knowledge for practitioners that cannot be neatly slotted within the traditional functionalist conception of the knowledge base and other equally important considerations as to knowledge acquisition for accessibility and use in the indeterminate problems of practice that must be considered. The goal of educational administrator preparation programs cannot be limited to a knowledge accumulation function, but rather must encompass assisting practitioners to use such knowledge to reason soundly about their practice as well as to perform skillfully; in short, to empower individuals to think and reason as they acquire knowledge (Glaser 1984). Sound reasoning requires that we engage with a process of thinking about actions as well as that we maintain an adequate base of facts. principles, and experiences from which to reason.

Acknowledging an inherent bias, this chapter presents an alternative conception of a knowledge base in educational administration, one that is informed by a cognitive learning theory perspective. Briefly, this perspective emphasizes three interrelated aspects of learning that hold important implications for construing understandings of knowledge: "First, learning is a process of knowledge *construction*, not knowledge recording or absorption. Second, learning is *knowledge-dependent*; people use current knowledge to construct new knowledge. Third, learning is highly tuned to the *situation* in which it takes place" (Resnick 1989, 1). A traditional (and functionalist) view of instruction as the direct transfer of knowledge from the instructional setting to the context of practice does not fit this constructivist perspective. Rather, instruction is viewed as an intervention in a continuous-construction process.

A key tenet of this constructivist theory is that people learn by actively constructing knowledge, weighing new information against their previous understanding, thinking about and working through discrepancies (on their own and with others), and coming to a new understanding, which implies an emphasis on comprehensive understanding involving the whole person rather than 'receiving' a body of factual knowledge about the world. . ." (Lave and Wenger 1991, 33). In harmony with other cognitive learning theories, the constructivist perspective posits that knowledge is situated, a product of both context and activity. Knowledge is "situated in activity" and used "within specific contexts and cultures" (Brown, Collins, and Duguid 1989, 11). The important point ts that "situatedness" means that knowledge and, by extension, the knowledge base, are not context-free concepts and, in fact, have no meaning except within a given context and culture.

The rest of this chapter continues this conversation about a constructivist view of the knowledge base in educational administration. In an effort to understand the context for the knowledge base, the first part presents a characterization of the domain of educational administration from a constructivist perspective. The concept of educational administration as an ill-structured domain is linked with issues concerning the specification of a knowledge base. The second part goes on to consider related issues of the different types of knowledge and knowledge acquisition and their accessibility for use. This section also attempts to clarify some different types of professional knowledge and different approaches for conceptualizing a knowledge base for educational administration. The last section presents some conclusions and considerations about a constructivist view of the knowledge base in educational administration.

Educational Administration as an Ill-Structured Domain

> Compartmentalization of knowledge components is an effective strategy in well-structured domains, but blocks effective learning in more intertwined, ill-structured domains which require high degrees of knowledge interconnectedness. . . .Well-structured domains can be integrated with a single unifying representational basis, but ill-structured domains require multiple representations for full coverage. (Spiro, Feltovich, Jacobsen, Coulson 1991a, 27)

The foundation of a constructivist view is built on a bedrock assumption that a hallmark of the profession of educational administration is the presence of enormously complex and ill-defined "problem situations." Thus, educating or preparing prospective administrators cannot be thought of as a mere matter of inculcating formal, abstract, and decontextualized knowledge, since such static and prescriptive knowledge will have little applicability (or transferability) across the complex and fluctuating problems of practice. Rather, to educate an administrator is to influence the very premises that undergird an administrator's understandings and actions in specific practitioner contexts. This conception implies an examination of issues that is not limited to identification of a knowledge base, but that extends as well to understanding the ways in which methods of knowledge acquisition provide accessibility and flexibility of action.

The relevance and efficacy constructivist ideas offer to instructional design in educational administration have been argued more fully elsewhere (see Prestine, in press; Prestine and LeGrand 1991); other important implications, drawn from this perspective, can also be examined and discussed in terms of the knowledge base. A large part of administrative practice can be characterized by situations in which ill-defined and messy problems present multiple and uncertain solution paths. Schön characterizes this ill-defined nature of professional practice as the "unfamiliar situations where the problem is not clear and there is no obvious fit between the characteristics of the situations and the available body of theories and techniques" (1987, 34). Prescriptive, formulistic, and preemptive organizations of knowledge have little applicability in these ambiguous and complex contexts. Moreover, the generalizability of knowledge structures is usually insufficient for transfer across differing problem contexts.

The implicit assumption that knowledge is independent of the situations in which it is acquired and used, "that once a person learns something, she hows it no matter where she is" (Resnick 1989, 11), is a serious point of contention for a constructivist perspective of educational administration. The assumption that knowledge, once acquired, is transportable and remains in immutable form across different contexts justifies the current organization of preparation programs. If knowledge can be acquired in one context and then freely moved for use in a variety of contexts (what Lave (1988) characterizes as the "toolbox" approach to knowledge transfer), then it makes eminent sense to designate special, encapsulated, and decontextualized environments as places where people will acquire knowledge and then compartmentalize and structure that knowledge into discrete entities.

However, the lack of well-defined problems witnessed in the practitioner context precludes the a priori identification of appropriate relevant knowledge structures that can be readily transferred across the possible permutations of problems as they occur in the contexts of practice (Prestine, in press). When set structures of knowledge necessary for competent practice cannot be predetermined across possible applications, the knowledge domain is considered an ill-structured one.

> In an ill-structured domain, individual cases can be reasonably interpreted from different conceptual perspectives, each adding something useful that the others miss. The domain as a whole will be inadequately characterized by any fixed organization of superordinate and subordinate conceptual structures. . .any overly limited version of what is 'correct' will miss too much of the complexity that must be mastered for sufficiency of rich conceptual understanding. (Spiro et al. 1991b, 22)

Berliner (1986) identifies teaching as one example of an ill-structured domain; another likely candidate would appear to be educational administration.

Because solution paths are not clear in ill-structured domains, the ability to revise problem representations in order to access and reconstruct knowledge structures into multiple configurations for possible solution strategies becomes not only highly desirable, but absolutely necessary. "Because knowledge will have to be used in too many different ways for them all to be anticipated in advance, emphasis must be shifted from the retrieval of intact knowledge structures to support the construction of new understandings, to the novel and situation-specific assembly of prior knowledge drawn from diverse organizational loci of preexisting mental representations" (Spiro et al. 1991a, 28).

Knowledge that will need to be used in many different ways needs to be presented in many different ways (Spiro et al. 1987; 1988). The interconnectedness existing between dfiferent aspects of domain knowledge and multiperspective representations of examples/cases should be highlighted. Emphasis needs to shift away from the retrieval of a priori, prepackaged knowledge structures, which usually are rigid and provide little opportunity for adaptation to diverse contexts of use. Rather, the focus must be on the assembly of situation-sensitive schema from knowledge structures that can be taken apart, moved about, and reassembled to fit the needs of a given context of application. "Purpose-sensitive situational schemata are constructed, thus allowing knowledge to be used in different ways on different occasions for different purposes. . . .Storage of fixed knowledge is devalued in favor of the mobilization of potential knowledge (Spiro et al. 1987, 181). According to this perspective, knowledge domains must be treated as a "landscape" that one comes to know by exploring it from many directions (Spiro et al. 1987). Because of the breadth, complexity, and irregularity of the content domain, limiting knowledge acquisition to a single point of view or a single system of classification will produce a relatively closed knowledge system instead of one that is open to context-dependent variability and flexibility.

The knowledge that we want learners to acquire is not and cannot be fully and explicitly codified within a knowledge base. This does not imply that no knowledge can be prespecified. It is important, however, that prespecified not be understood as some final product, as a package of reified knowledge that all learners must then assimilate. A knowledge base is certainly required, but since the nature of the ill-structured problems that any given practitioner might encounter may not be predictable, the content of the knowledge base cannot be clearly specified (Federiksen 1984). In an ill-structured domain, where ambiguity and complexity abound, where routine, formulistic prescriptions for practice are minimally effective, and where the contexts of the practice are uncertain and constantly shifting, the extent of knowledge prespecification should be limited to rough guideposts or starting points from which to begin thinking about the domain; the emphasis should be on flexibility rather than on rigidity of structuration and use.

Domain-Specific and Strategic Knowledge

> Attempts to map out knowledge requirements of a profession are associated with the design of training courses. . . .The language of syllabus construction prevails, accompanied perhaps by some homilies about the aims of the profession. . . .Thus knowledge is likely to be labelled and packaged according to traditional assumptions about where and how it will be acquired (Erault 1985, 119)

In this constructivist perspective, content (in other word, knowledge) cannot be separated from either process or context. Knowledge is not addressed as a singular, static object one possesses, but is examined in concert with issues concerning how knowledge is acquired and how knowledge is used in practice contexts. As Leithwood and Steinbach (1991) aptly state, "In the absence of domain-specific knowledge, one has nothing to think about. In the absence of reasonably well-developed, general thinking skills, one's knowledge may not be applied in circumstances where it has potential use. For instructional purposes, it seems reasonable to approach the matter in a conditional way. The probability that a person will successfully solve a problem is a function of both the availability of problem-relevant knowledge and general thinking skills. . . ." The intertwined nature of both domain-specific and strategic knowledge and the critical emphasis on empowering individuals to use domain-specific knowledge needs further discussion.

Domain-specific knowledge can be categorized as the declarative and procedural knowledge (the explicit factual or conceptual, theoretical knowledge and identtfied procedures) that are identified with a given subject or domain. Strategic knowledge encompasses the goal-directed techniques and approaches that intentionally control the problem-solving activity. "Strategic knowledge involves strategies and heuristics, as well as strategies for control of the problem-solving process that involve reflection in order to determine how to proceed, and finally, strategies experts have about how to learn new concepts, facts, and strategies" (Prestine and LeGrand 1991, 69).

There is little doubt that domain-specific knowledge is essential to development of expertise. As Herbert Simon (1978; 1980) and others (Berliner 1986; Glaser 1984; 1987; Chi, Glaser, and Farr 1981; Lesgold 1984) who have compared the performance of experts to that of novices have noted, there can be no such thing as expertise without a knowledge base: "The performances of highly competent individuals indicate the possession of, rapid access to, and efficient utilization of an organized body of conceptual and procedural knowledge; . . . a major component of expertise is the possession of this knowledge" (Glaser 1987, 82). However, three important corollaries are frequently overlooked in this general celebration of domain-specific knowledge. The first is that a knowledge base for expertise, especially in ill-structured domains, will be extensive and dynamic, not rigid or formulistic, and will have multiple sources. Second, this knowledge base must be available for flexible use across varying contexts of practice; the means by which knowledge is acquired will influence its later accessibility. Finally, there exists a powerful relationship between domain-specific and strategic knowledge, especially in ill-structured domains.

To acknowledge that, for a profession like educational administration, one must conceive of a knowledge base that is extensive, dynamic, and drawn from multiple sources, on the surface seems reasonable and hardly contentious. Yet, a functionalist map of the knowledge base tends to focus narrowly on discipline-based, "academicised" knowledge. As Erault (1985) notes, such a map reminds one of "a fifteenth-century eurocentric map of the world, in which people and lands beyond the confines of Renaissance culture are barely acknowledged" (119). In this conception, the profession of administration is narrowed, the interconnected nature of practice-world complexities are ignored, and alternative knowledge perspectives are marginalized.

For example, much of what could be called practice-based knowledge has been excluded or systematically ignored by preparation programs. In part, this can be attributed to efforts to "elevate" the status of educational administration within academe by distancing the professional image from that of the retired superintendent using "war stories" as the basis of preparation. However, much is lost when the "wisdom of practice" is ignored. Only recently has some interest arisen in exploring this untapped area of professional knowledge, within the form of studies that examine administrative thinking and problem solving (Leithwood and Stager 1986; Leithwood and Stager 1989; Leithwood and Steinbach 1991) within the practitioner context. Undoubtedly, as this practice-based knowledge accumulates, it most likely will be unwieldy, erratic, and difficult to codify. Administrators themselves find it difficult to articulate what they know and how they know it. As Polanyi (1966) so eloquently put it, "We know more than we can tell" (4). Yet, this tacit knowledge, which undergirds practice, represents an important and often overlooked source for the knowledge base.

In the final analysis, the functional relevance of any knowledge base will likely depend less on its presumed validity than on the ability and willingness of people to use it. This will be determined mainly by the individual professional and his or her work context, factors which would seem to recommend the inclusion of practice-based knowledge. However, this relevance will also be affected by the way in which the knowledge is introduced and linked to ongoing professional concerns.

One of the problems encountered in any discussion of *knowledge* or *knowledge base* is that both terms refer to something external as well as to something internal. On the one hand, the terms knowledge and knowledge base connote an identifiable, durable intellectual framework of a domain, inclusive of theories, abstractions, and systems of belief that transcend individuals and interpretations, and which exist prior to them, and, to a large extent, beyond their control. This functionalist conception is the one used most frequently in the debates swirling around the establishment of a knowledge base for educational administration. On the other hand, knowledge and a knowledge base can be conceptualized as internalized phenomena that are experienced, understood, and constructed in different ways by different individuals. This constructivist understanding is crucial, in that it posits that knowledge can only be understood by the individual as it is constructed by the mind. In this view, knowledge is not so much an external object for possession as it is a web of connections actively and continually reconstructed by the individual to form a fabric of internalized meaning.

Since it is not possible to control the meanings that individuals will construct as new knowledge is added to prior knowledge, our concern should not be so much with the transmittal of intact knowledge structures but with the ways in which knowledge structures are acquired. "[K]nowing how experts structure their thinking about a problem tells us little about how they use those knowledge structures in practice...[and] cautions us to pay attention to how experts acquire whatever knowledge might be said to characterize their thinking about the problems of practice" (Lampert and Clark 1990, 22). What this suggests is that the ways in which knowledge is acquired will affect its later accessibility and use in novel problem situations encountered in professional practice. While the use of domain-specific knowledge is very much evident in expert performance, the ability to access and apply it remains "very much a matter of how the knowledge and skill [were] acquired" (Perkins and Salomon 1989, 22). Thus, knowledge or a knowledge base cannot be considered in isolation from issues concerning how that knowledge is acquired and used by practitioners.

Finally, a constructivist perspective argues that strategic knowledge is as significant and important as domain-specific knowledge. "Strategic knowledge refer(s) to the usually tacit knowledge that underlies an expert's ability to make use of concepts, facts, and procedures as necessary to solve problems and carry out tasks" (Collins, Brown, and Newman 1989, 477). Strategic knowledge provides the means of accessing and flexibly reconstructing the domain-specific knowledge needed for expert problem solving, while domain-specific knowledge provides for the efficient and effective utilization of strategic knowledge. In a constructivist view, the two types of knowledge form a reciprocal relationship or dialectic, which enables the individual to access and flexibly reconstruct knowledge for use in practitioner contexts.

Recent research in expertise has even suggested that the relative importance of either domain-specific and strategic knowledge may be a function of the nature of the domain itself. General strategic methods and techniques appear to be less important in such well-structured domains as physics or genetics, where one can rapidly access learned and intact knowledge structures and procedures (declarative and procedural knowledge) to manipulate a problem situation (Glaser 1984). In less well-structured domains, where a priori identification of knowledge structures needed for problem solving is not possible, a more strategic approach ts needed. "More general, managerial, or heuristic strategies seemed to have more power in those domains that we perceive to be more ill-structured" (Alexander and Judy 1988, 393). Thus, it would seem imperative that strategic knowledge be given at least equal consideration with domain-specific knowledge in establishing a knowledge base for an ill-structured domain like educational administration. "In solving ill-structured problems, experts employ general [heuristic] methods and their thinking is less immediately driven by the principles and procedural aspects of their specific knowledge structures" (Glaser 1987, 91).

Conclusions

> We must avoid the creation of rigid orthodoxies. We must achieve standards without standardization. We must be careful that the knowledge base approach does not produce an overly technical image of teaching, a scientific enterprise that has lost its soul. (Shulman 1987, 20)

Shulman's timely and insightful comments about the development of a knowledge base for teaching serve well as a cautionary marker at this juncture of our own journey toward establishing a knowledge base for educational administration. As this chapter has argued, we should work to develop the broadest of knowledge outlines, but these must serve as guides to help structure discourse or as markers that offer departure points for alternative routes. The idea of working toward a conclusively final product, a journey's end for the knowledge base, seems illusionary and self-defeating. Returning to Shulman's persuasive arguments once more, "A knowledge base for teaching is not fixed and final. . . .We may be able to offer a compelling argument for the broad outlines and categories of the knowledge base. . . . It will, however, become abundantly clear that much, if not most, of the proposed knowledge base remains to be discovered, invented and refined" (1987, 12). It is likely that much the same is true for educational administration.

The guiding metaphor for our work in conceptualizing a knowledge base must be likened more to that of explorers in a vast and largely uncharted country than of tourists following the same conventional, bounded, and established routes to a predetermined destination. We must think of ourselves as mapmakers, not map-readers. That we have only begun this task should not daunt us. The invaluable efforts of those who have preceded us can serve as departure points for new initiatives and as fertile ground for further elaboration and refinement. This conception of the knowledge base is more analogous to exploring or crisscrossing a landscape rather than it is reflective of a rigidly fixed, linear, and unidirectional design.

Much remains to be explored and mapped. Sticky issues of how administrators make use of their preparation in the problematlc world of practice have yet to be conclusively addressed. Whether the meaning of "being an administrator" can be separated from the culture of the school, that is, from the practitioner's actual experience of working in administration, is another issue yet to be resolved. The experience of women and/or minority groups who work in administration and the contributions of poststructural analyses remain largely untapped and underrepresented.

The debate over knowledge base issues needs to be continued. Basic questions regarding what "knowing" administration means need to be raised, along with political questions such as, "Whose knowledge is legitimated?" and "Why is such knowledge being legitimated?" The establishment of a knowledge base strikes most directly at preparation programs. When the knowledge base is construed narrowly, with predetermined categories of knowledge imposed on learners, the opportunity is lost for reflection on and, most certainly, for the challenging of, conventional wisdom. Established content becomes something to be "delivered" to students by teaching them "what they need to know." This delivery-of-services model, inherent in an established knowledge base, treats students as deficient, or at best, as consumers—a much narrower role than that played by reflective, thoughtful administrators in a democratic society (Erdman 1987).

Implicit in the knowledge base argument is the notion that the standardization of knowledge across programs will bring about some uniformity, at least of intent, if not of results. The catch with this argument is that no benevolent deity has ordained that these supposedly parallel programs, all of which draw on a uniform knowledge base, will be in any way more consistent with one another than they are at present. Any notion that incorporating the knowledge base as a benchmark of program status and approval will push other institutions into conformity seems illusory at best.

This chapter has argued that a conception of administrative practice and preparation must be necessarily ambiguous, that the question of the establishment of a knowledge base must be open to question, and that continued research on administrators and institutional structures as they mutually influence practice must be a priority. Attention needs to be given to the meanings preparation programs hold for learners, for knowledge-in-use, for divergent thinking, and for conceptual analysis. This multifaceted conception of knowledge contrasts sharply with a convergent, linear, and hierarchical approach to knowledge, which distorts practice. These and other issues caution us that in the debate over the establishment of a knowledge base, it would seem to be wise to err on the side of inclusion rather than exclusion, divergence rather than convergence. If educational administration is to remain a vibrant and dynamic field, one that pushes the edge of the envelope, as it were, we must not be confined by rigid prespecification of boundaries or meticulous categorization of knowledge. "The damage done by the specification of particulars may be irremediable;...the belief that, since particulars are more tangible, their knowledge offers a true conception of thing is fundamentally mistaken" (Polany 1966, 19).

References

Alexander, P. A., and Judy, J. E. 1988. The interaction of domain-specific and strategic knowledge in academic performance. *Review of Educational Research* 58(4): 375–404.

Berliner, D. C. 1986. In pursuit of the expert pedagogue. *Educational Researcher* 15(7): 5–13.

Brown, J. S., Collins, A. and Duguid, P. 1989. Debating the situation: A rejoiner to Palincsar and Wineburg. *Educational Researcher* 19(4): 10–12.

Chi, M. T. H., Glaser, R., and Farr, M. J. 1988. *The nature of expertise.* Hillsdale, N.J.: Lawrence Erlbaum Associates.

Collins, A., Brown, J. S., and Newman, S. E. 1989. Cognitive apprenticeship: Teaching the craft of reading, writing and mathematics. In L. B. Resnick, ed., *Knowing, learning, and instruction: Essays in honor of Robert Glaser:* 453–94.

Erault, M. 1985. Knowlege creation and knowledge use in professional contexts. *Studies in Higher Education* 10(2): 117–33.

Erdman, J. 1987. Reflecting on teaching and adult education. *Lifelong Learning: An Omnibus of Practice and Research* 10(8): 18–21.

Frederiksen, N. 1984. Implications of cognitive theory for instruction in problem solving. *Review of Educational Research* 54(3): 363–407.

Glaser, R. 1984. Education and thinking: The role of knowledge. *American Psychologists* 39(2): 93–104.

_____. 1987. Thoughts on expertise. In C. Schooler and K. W. Schaie, eds., *Cognitive functioning and social structure over the life course:* 81–94. Norwood, N.J.: Ablex Publishing.

Hanson, E. M. 1991. *Educational administration and organizational behavior.* 3rd Ed. Boston, Mass.: Allyn & Bacon.

Hoy, W. K., and Miskel, C. G. 1991. *Educational administration: Theory, research, practice.* 4th Ed. New York: McGraw-Hill.

Lampert, M., and Clark, C. M. 1990. Expert knowledge and expert thinking in teaching: A response to Floden and Klinzing. *Educational Researcher* 19(5): 21–23.

Lave, J. 1988. *Cognition in practice: Mind, mathematics and culture in everyday life.* Cambridge. Mass.: Cambridge University Press.

Lave, J., and Wenger, E. 1991. *Situated learning: Legitimate peripheral participation.* Cambridge, Mass.: Cambridge University Press.

Leithood, K. A., and Stager, M. 1986, April. Differences in problem-solving processes used by moderately and highly effective principals. Paper presented at the Annual Meeting of the American Educational Research Association. San Francisco, Calif.

Leithwood, K. A., and Stager, M. 1989. Expertise in principals' problem solving. *Educational Administration Quarterly 25*(2): 126–61.

Leithwood, K. A., and Steinbach, R. 1991. Improving the problem-solving expertise of school administrators: Theory and practice. *Education and Urban Society.*

Leithwood, K. A., and Steinbach, R. 1991. Indicators of transformational leadership in everyday problem solving of school administrators. *Journal of Personnel Evaluation in Education 4*(3): 221–24.

Lesgold, A. M. 1984. Acquiring expertise. In J. R. Anderson and S. M. Kosslyn, eds., *Tutorials in learning and memory: Essays in honor of Gordon Bower*: 31–60. San Francisco: Freeman Press.

Owens, R. G. 1991. *Organizational behavior in education.* 4th edition. Englewood Cliffs, N.J.: Prentice Hall.

Perkins, D. N., and Salomon, G. 1989. Are cognitive skills context-bound? *Educational Researcher 18*(1): 16–25.

Polanyi, M. 1966. *The tacit dimension.* Garden City, N.Y.: Doubleday.

Prestine, N. A. (In press). Apprenticeship in problem solving: Extending the cognitive apprenticeship model. In P. Hallinger, K. Leithwood, J. Murphy, eds., *Cognition and School Leadership.* New York: Teachers College Press.

———, and LeGrand, B. 1991. Cognitive learning theory and the preparation of educational administrators: Implications for practice and policy. *Educational Administration Quarterly 27*(1): 61–89.

Resnick, L. B. 1989. Introduction. In L. B. Resnick eds., *Knowing, learning and instruction: Essays in honor of Robert Glaser*: 1–24. Hillsdale, N.J.: Lawrence Erlbaum Associates.

Rowan, B. 1990. Commitment and control: Alternative strategies for the organizational design of schools. In *Review of Educational Research.* Vol. 18: 353–89. Washington, D.C.: American Educational Research Association.

Schön, D. A. 1987. *Educating the reflective practitioner.* San Francisco: Jossey-Bass.

Shulman, L. S. 1986. Paradigms and research programs in the study of teaching: A contemporary perspective. In M. C. Wittrock, ed., *Handoook of Research on Teaching.* 3rd Ed.: 3–36 New York: MacMillan.

_____. 1986. Those who understand: A conception of teacher knowledge. *American Educator 10*(1): 9–15.

_____. 1987. Knowledge and teaching: Foundations of the new reform. *Harvard Educational Review 57*(1): 1–22.

_____. 1988. The wisdom of practice: Managing complexity in medicine and teaching. In D. Berliner and B. Rosenshine, eds., *Talks to teachers:* 369–86. New York: Random House.

_____. 1978. Information-processing theory of human problem solving. In W. K. Estes, ed., *Handhook of learning and cognitive processes, Vol. 5, Human Information Processing.* Hillsdale, N.J.: Erlbaum.

_____. 1980. Problem solving and education. In D. T. Tuma and R. Reif, eds., *Problem Solving and Education: Issues in Teaching and Research.* Hillsdale, N.J.: Erlbaum.

Spiro, R. J., Feltovich, P. J., Jacobson, M. J., and Coulson, R. L. 1991a. Cognitive flexibility, constructivism, and hypertext: Random access instruction for advanced knowledge acquisition in ill-structured domains. *Educational Technology 31*(5): 24–33.

_____, Feltovich, P. J., Jacobson, M. J., and Coulson, R. L. 1991b. Knowledge representation, content specification, and the development of skill in situation-specific knowledge assembly: Some constructivist issues as they relate to cognitive flexibility theory and hypertext. *Educational Technology 31*(5): 24–33.

_____. Coulson, R. L., Feltovich, P. J., and Anderson, D. K. 1988. Cognitive flexibility theory: Advanced knowledge acquisition in ill-structured domains. In *Tenth Annual Conference of the Cognitive Science Society:* 375–83. Hillsdale, N.J.: Erlbaum.

―――, Vispoel, W. P., Schmitz, J. G., Samarapungavan, A., and Boerger, A. E. 1987. Knowledge acquisition for application: Cognitive flexibility and transfer in complex content domains. In B. C. Britton, ed., *Executive control processes*: 177–99. Hillsdale, N.J.: Erlbaum.

An Otherist Poststructural Perspective of the Knowledge Base in Educational Administration

Colleen A. Capper

The knowledge base study teams promise that "the conceptual sufficiency of each [knowledge domain] map will be analyzed using multiple perspectives on inquiry, e.g., functionalist, interpretive, radical structuralist, radical humanist" (UCEA 1992, 7), and "to that end, [they] intend to include multicultural and emergent frameworks, and identify gaps in the knowledge base for educational administrators" (UCEA 1992, 13). The purpose of this chapter is to analyze the knowledge base from emergent frameworks, with an emphasis on what might be labelled the *otherist* poststructural perspective. In so doing, the chapter clarifies the otherist poststructural perspective by comparing and contrasting it with other emerging approaches in educational administration (critical theory, feminist theory, and poststructural theories). The chapter specifically considers the ways each of these approaches would critique the knowledge base and the recommendations they would make in relation to it. Sacrificing specificity for the sake of brevity and simplicity, I paint each approach in broad strokes, ignoring variations that exist within each theoretical perspective.

Critical Theory and the Knowledge Base

A Critique of the Project

Critical theorists could agree on at least three aspects of the knowledge base. First, the stated assumptions for the knowledge base do acknowledge diversity, race, ethnicity, and social class. Second, the authors of the knowledge base project also mention that the knowledge base fails to reflect the "knowledge gains" in subfields like sociology and organizational theory, and they acknowledge that the current focus on technical aspects of school management is not satisfactory by noting that "a narrow focus on the position-related skills required for the job is insufficient" (UCEA 1992, 5). Third, critical theorists would probably agree with the purpose of the knowledge base, that is, that we do need to determine "critical problems of practice" and what is "essential" for school leaders to know.

Regardless of these potential points of agreement, however, critical theorists would find several chinks in the content armor of the knowledge base project. First, critical theorists would question some central assumptions of the knowledge base project. For example, they would question the assumption that so-called "administrator training" programs are a random system of courses, and that these programs need to conform to a unified standard. Critical theorists would argue that the field of educational administration currently claims a knowledge base and that the vast majority of preparation programs probably adhere to the seven proposed domains. Critical theorists would argue also that these domains are based on existing structures and cultures, not on nontraditional perspectives of education, learning, organizations, or administration. Thus, critical theorists would argue that the knowledge base will serve only to confirm current preparation and practice as "right," chiselling them in the stone of a computerized dissemination system. Critical theorists would also call into question the assumption that school administration is necessary, that it is necessary to have "training" at the university, that this training include specific aspects of "knowledge," and that this objective "knowledge" be transmitted from professor to the student in the context of the university classroom.

Second, although the authors writing about knowledge base theory call for a revolution—"Astonishing problems and conditions of contemporary life scream for attention and require a *revolution* (emphasis added) in schooling, especially in the ways educators define their work and organize institutions to serve children" (UCEA 1992, 4)—the purpose, development, and implementation of the knowledge base project, seen from a critical theory perspective, would seem more likely to cement traditions into place and legitimize current educational administration theory, practice, and preparation, and thereby perpetuate systems of domination and oppression. Moreover, the knowledge base project frames the "problem" with some nebulous allusions to power, but does not make power a core issue. Thus the "solution" to be found in the knowledge base lacks an awareness of power issues.

Third, although the authors of the knowledge base project also acknowledge that "the curriculum in schools continues to be inauthentic: it does not include the experiences and contributions of all people" (UCEA 1992, 5), the project does not recognize that preparation programs suffer from the same inauthenticity, and the proposal does not clearly articulate how the knowledge base will include experiences and contributions of all people.

Fourth, critical theorists would also be concerned about the scope of implementation and the implications of control, and would ask whether universities will be required to adhere to the knowledge base in order to be members of UCEA, whether compliance checks will be made to see if it is being taught, and whether faculty hiring will be dependent on the candidates' signing an agreement to adhere to the knowledge base in their courses.

Finally, critical theorists would probably agree with the UCEA (1992) authors that we need to determine what is "essential for school leaders to know to solve critical contemporary problems of practice" (p.6). Critical theorists' greatest point of disagreement, however, would occur in the context of determining "critical. . . problems of practice," which would then determine what is "essential" for school leaders to know (p. 8). For critical theorists, critical problems of practice would be those which constrain the so-called "empowerment" of all students and staff toward the transformation of social inequities. This transformative philosophy, which underpins the purpose of the project, would then shape the content, development, and implementation of the knowledge base in ways quite different from the proposed version.

Recommendations from a Critical Theory Perspective

Critical theorists would suggest that all seven domains of the knowledge base should include a concern for suffering and oppression, a critical view of education, goals of empowerment and transformation, and an emphasis on morals and values (Burrell and Morgan 1979; Foster 1986; Smyth 1989). A critical theory perspective would suggest also that we develop and shape the knowledge base via the deliberate involvement of disempowered people in discussions of education; these people can identify educational "problems," "causes," and "solutions" based on their own personal experiences with inequity. In turn, this involvement would help disempowered people recognize, understand, and act against the objects of their oppression.

Feminist Theories and the Knowledge Base

A Critique of the Project

Feminist theorists would probably agree with nearly all the critiques and recommendations of the critical theory perspective; however, they would cite additional problems and suggestions. For example, with regard to the limitations of critical theory, Luke (1992) argues

> What I have suggested here is the urgent need for a serious skepticism of and critical attention to those contemporary educational narratives that claim to be emancipatory, ideologically critical, self-reflexive, and politically conscientious, and yet remain theoretically entrenched in gender- and color-blind patriarchal liberalism. (49)

The following concentrates on the differences that distinguish feminist perspectives from critical theory perspectives. While this section is relatively short, and does not draw distinctions among the various feminisms (liberal, socialist, or radical), a later section does focus specifically on feminist theories with regard to their connection to poststructural theories.

Feminist theorists would criticize the knowledge base as one that perpetuates patriarchy. They would note, for example, obvious slights to women, such as an absolute lack of attention to gender issues in the knowledge base proposal, as well as the fact that, out of seven study teams formed for the project, only one is chaired by a woman. They would also point out other limitations. For example, although the authors of the project recognize that "most preparation programs focus on hierarchical authority and the development of administrative styles based on bureaucracy" (UCEA 1992, 5), they do not acknowledge the patriarchal foundations of such preparation programs. Feminist theorists would also question the emphasis on particular kinds of knowledge, citing the legitimation of the cerebral, intellectual, and rational (Calás & Smircich, 1991). Indeed, they would argue that the seven domains do not leave room for any affective/social dimensions of knowledge. Ferguson's (1984) feminist view of bureaucracy also aptly describes the knowledge base project, if we consider that the knowledge base represents the patterns of belief about the world dominant in male experience. . . a world made up of essentially physically and socially disembodied 'things,' governed by ultimately predictable laws or rules that can be rationally perceived and controlled by human beings. Knowledge is seen as 'impersonal, abstract, universal and absolute'. (159–160)

Recommendations from a Feminist Perspective

Feminist theorists would recommend gender representation in the knowledge base project. For example, they would recommend equal representation not only for study team chairpersons, but also for study team membership. They would also advocate the inclusion of knowledge that points out gender differences. Differences existing between men and women should be included in all knowledge domains, for example, in studies that point out that women are more willing to engage in dialogue and that they emphasize working with relationships and facilitation rather than "leading," and that men tend to emphasize management, rational thought, policy, and bureaucracy. The study and consideration of feelings, intuition, and emotion, and their relation to educational administration, would also be included.

Poststructural Theories and the Knowledge Base

A Critique of the Project

A poststructural perspective of the knowledge base is preempted by a poststructural view of organizations. A poststructural view of organizations suggests that organizations are based on an antifoundational perspective, in that they do not inherently serve any particular purpose and are socially constructed (Burrell 1988; Cooper and Burrell 1988; Cooper 1989). Thus, poststructuralists would not view the knowledge base as inherently "right" or "wrong," but, instead, would contend that a knowledge base is not even necessary in a world where meanings and perspectives are continually shifting and deferred, without any normative direction that can be taken (Parker 1992).

Poststructuralists would question the very idea of a base, and along with its associated synonyms: foundation, underpinning, bottom, support, basis, core, essence, the fundamental principle or underlying concept (Cherryholmes 1988). Poststructuralists believe that all of the world is socially constructed, without an essential base, or, in other words, that the world is eternally fluid.

Calás and Smircich's (1992) description of poststructural theory can instruct a critique of the knowledge base:

> Different from symbolic or semiotic approaches, where the analysis of signification focuses on the discovery of 'the real meaning,' poststructuralism acknowledges the ambiguity of all meaning. Poststructuralists focus on the activities by which nonambiguity and clarity are *claimed* in the search for 'true knowledge'. (226)

Thus, with regard to the knowledge base project, rather than searching for the so-called "real," "true," or "essential" knowledge base, poststructuralists would proclaim the ambiguity of all knowledge bases, including alternative proposals to this knowledge base.

If poststructuralists could proceed beyond their objections to the need for, or existence of, a knowledge "base," they would also point to concerns within the knowledge domains. For example, in the domain leadership and management processes, the idea of "poststructural leadership" would be an oxymoron—the practice of one precludes the practice of the other. That is, while poststructural perspectives assume an antifoundational stance, definitions of leadership imply decision making based on particular, foundational criteria.

A second example can be found within the legal and ethical dimensions of schooling. A poststructuralist perspective might ask, "whose ethics and whose values will prevail in schools?" A so-called "pure" poststructural view of administration would not necessarily ameliorate the gender bias in the knowledge base project that has been noted by feminist theorists (Blackmore 1988; Shakeshaft 1987).

Recommendations from a Poststructural Perspective

Given their lack of belief in a knowledge base and their view that any suggestion for practice can be deconstructed, poststructuralists would not be concerned about the development or implementation of a knowledge base. From a poststructuralist perspective, identifying the lack of attention to race, gender, sexuality, disability, religion, and other areas of difference in the knowledge base—a goal of critical and feminist theories—is a necessary first step. A poststructural view of the constructed knowledge base, however, in which deconstruction plays a pivotal role, prevents the reifying of these characteristics into reconstructed hierarchies and new oppressive power structures under the name of equity.

Otherist Poststructural Theories and the Knowledge Base

The joining of feminist views with poststructural theories has been explored in the literature under the phrase "feminist poststructural theories" (see Weedon 1987). Even though all the literature in this area refers to "feminist poststructuralism," or poststructural feminisms, in this chapter I prefer to use the term *otherist* rather than the term *feminist*. *Otherist* is used to clarify that the analysis is not confined to and does not reify gendered relations. Rather, otherist theories are views that consider not only gendered relations, but relations from other nondominant group perspectives, such as social class, disability, and sexuality. Although feminist theorists do pay attention to other dimensions of difference beyond that of gender, their central project is gender.

A Critique of the Project

An otherist poststructural perspective of the knowledge base resides at the nexus of critical theory, poststructural, and feminist perspectives (Lather 1991). Unlike poststructural theories, an otherist poststructural perspective recognizes the need for a knowledge base, and unlike critical theorists, is not as eager to cast the knowledge base in stone, nor to view it as unilaterally privileging the dominated against the oppressed. Luke and Gore's (1992) comparison of poststructuralism and otherist poststructural perspectives expresses these theoretical differences:

> A poststructuralist feminist epistemology accepts that knowledge is always provisional, open-ended and relational. Our treks through language and master narratives on the way to this kind of knowing are located in historical and cultural context. This contextual character of all knowledge and knowing suggests that there can be no finite and unitary truths. So, for instance, while we might claim that male rule oppresses women in a near seamless historical

and global patriarchal regime, the specificity of women's
oppression as it intersects with class, color, nationality,
history, [sexuality], and culture implies that one theory, one
method of analysis, or one concept of the subject cannot un-
problematically be applied to all women in all contexts. (7)

In short, an otherist poststructural view of the knowledge base
avoids the limitations of critical theory; moves beyond the gendered
relations of feminist theories; and appreciates the messiness and
complexities of poststructural theories without drowning in a sea
of relativism; and all the while maintains a focus on social change.

An otherist poststructural perspective recognizes, within the
complexity of constructed relations, the pervasiveness of power and
resistance to it and the infinity of meanings inherent in language.
Otherist poststructural perspectives would be concerned with a
combination micro/macro view of administration, and would walk
a tightrope between relating to layers/complexities of oppression
and avoiding essentialist views of this oppression.

From an otherist poststructural perspective, many avenues
could be taken with regard to its critique of the knowledge base.
Of the many facets of otherist poststructural theories, three I
address here are standpoint theories, local/specific knowledges, and
subjugated knowledges.

Standpoint Theory and/or a "Sea of Relativism"

One concern about poststructural views of the knowledge base,
pointed out by advocates of traditional as well as by nontraditional
views of administration, is that if no firm foundation exists, if there
is neither "right" nor "wrong," nor any normative dimensions, then
the knowledge base project will drown in a sea of relativeness and
indeterminacy. Related questions include, "Is there any common
grounding in common values? Is there any normative underpinning? What about social justice and caring as foundational
values, notwithstanding the array of moral dilemmas and interpretive problems?"

Standpoint theory means, in part, that a person "takes a stand"
on an issue or philosophy, and that all positions are recognized.
Otherist poststructural theorists do not shy away from taking a
stand, but they recognize the "undecidability, partiality, and
uncertainty *within* a theoretical commitment" (Luke 1992, 48). In
contrast to the antifoundational poststructural perspective, otherist
poststructuralist theorists claim a foundation, but a foundation of

"difference," beyond gender, social class, and race, that exists to create a

> conceptual space for difference in subject location, identity and knowledges [that] renders such a foundation anti-essentialist and indeterminate. . . . This kind of indeterminacy is not the same as the postmodernist deferment. Rather, it is an indeterminacy that lies in its rejection of certainty promised by modernist discourses, a rejection of a self-certain and singular subject, and a rejection of knowledges that promise answers which lead to closure (Luke and Gore 1992, 7).

The knowledge base does not "take a stand" and then recognize its own partiality and contradictions, at least not seriously. While it says it will constantly "improve," this improvement stems from a positivist, narrowing perspective, one that is convergent rather than divergent. It does not interrogate its own paradigm positions with regard to the knowledge base idea, the domains selected, or the resources cited within the domains. Such a narrow view would be impossible to hold if multiple perspectives/paradigm bases were marginally recognized in the first place.

Standpoint theory would suggest that the knowledge base project "take a stand" within multiple epistemologies, overtly identify the epistemological positions of its development, context, and implementation, then recognize the partiality and contradictions within it, and engage in a constant self-interrogation.

Local and Specific and/or Totalizing Grand Narratives

Otherist poststructuralists would claim that the knowledge base project (and its critical and feminist theory alternatives) constitute "totalizing grand narratives"; that is, the project develops a base or foundation that is total, or all-encompassing. Again, while the knowledge base project claims to be open to continued change and additions, these continued improvements will be grounded in relation to the existing foundation—an accurate description of positivist science. Tierney's (1992) description of modernist research and knowledge production aptly reflects the knowledge base project:

> The modernist believes that we study specific topics and gain knowledge in a cumulative fashion. The more one studies, the greater potential the individual has for becoming an authority on a specialized topic. Indeed, the

specialization of knowledge into disciplines and subfields helps create figures of authority who have obtained much knowledge about a specific narrowly defined concept. (16)

Nicholson (1990) concurs and explains, "Knowledge. . . is supposed to be grounded in experience. But what has counted as knowledge in modern, Western cultures originates in and is tested against only a certain limited and distorted kind of social experience" (95).

Interpretivist and feminist views of the knowledge base often call for knowledge to be locally constructed and situationally and personally contextualized. Prestine's (1991) work on situated cognition and contextualized problem solving, and Anderson and Page's work (this volume) on narrative storytelling by educational administrators as ways to construct "knowledge," are two such examples of interpretivist work. Luke (1992) cautions, however, that it is dangerous to focus on the specific, personal, contextualized experience of individuals as the only form of knowledge.

In contrast, otherist poststructuralist perspectives would encourage the seeking of local and contextualized knowledge and understanding in educational administration, but would cast such experiences against the complex tapestries of the "historical structures of domination and exploitation" (Luke 1992, 49). In short, the knowledge base should be grounded in the local/specific knowledges and experiences of those involved in education, coupled with the complex historical structures of domination and control.

Subjugated Knowledges

A third area of contention existing between the knowledge base and otherist poststructural theories is one of subjugated knowledges (Sawicki 1991). Subjugated knowledges suggest the inclusion not only of local/specific knowledge, but also of knowledges specific to the experience of subjugated individuals and groups who are connected via points of struggle, which can reveal the partiality of the "knowledge base" with which we currently work (Ferguson 1984; Nicolaides and Gaynor 1992).

From a modernist perspective, many would believe the weakness of the knowledge base as it is suggested by subjugated knowledges could be remedied by "adding," within each domain, concerns and issues, such as gender and race, associated with nondominant societal groups. Others would recommend adding a separate knowledge domain focused primarily on nontraditional perspectives. From an otherist poststructural approach, however, some express doubt about the efficacy of "harnessing the traditions" in a way that could, purportedly, advance the educational situations of all students (Harding 1990). The knowledge base project then, should consider subjugated knowledges in its development, content choices, and implementation. The project needs to be careful about including subjugated knowledges and local/specific knowledge without considering how such inclusions would alter the entire project. Similarly, otherist poststructural theorists would question the wisdom of circling the wagons of knowledge around educational administration via the knowledge base, especially during an era of burgeoning scholarship in "subjugated" philosophies and theories such as nontraditional epistemologies (Sedgwick 1990), gender and organizations (Mills and Tancred 1992), sexuality and organizations (Hearn, Sheppard, Tancred-Sheriff, and Burrell 1989), theories of feminism and poststructuralism not directly applied to education or organizations (Nicholson 1990; Sawicki 1991), and the array of brilliant work juxtaposing feminist theories and critical pedagogy in education (Luke and Gore 1992).

Conclusion

The knowledge base project artificially separates epistemology[2] from pedagogy when the two coexist, and then weakly reaches for a link with social context. That is, the knowledge base was developed without regard for its connection with learning and instruction, and only with a slight nod toward the social construction of power. For the authors of the knowledge base, and for those who suggest multiple alternatives, concerns about a "knowledge base" at the macro level of administrator preparation, research, and policy making, cannot be separated from the current context of the micro level. That is, attention needs to be devoted to the position of individuals in roles named, for example, professor and student, researcher and research subject. We must examine those roles and contexts, as well as the content (that is, the knowledge base), instruction, and contexts of social power that affect the lives of persons involved in the education milieu.

Within these multiple positions of practice in relation to a "knowledge base," otherist poststructural perspectives suggest staking one or several epistemological positions; naming the contradictions, constraints, and limitations within this commitment; dignifying local/specific knowledge and a recognition of its historical constraints and enablements; and actively recognizing and cultivating subjugated knowledges.

As with other educational reforms, we need to be concerned about swallowing the knowledge base whole, taking it as the last word for the field of educational administration. Administrator preparation programs need to be careful about legitimating themselves to themselves and to their constituents by adhering to the content within the knowledge domains.

As evidenced by the critique and recommendations in this chapter, it is almost unbelievable and inconceivable to imagine that a project naming itself the "knowledge base" in educational administration could be conceived and birthed without discussing and wrestling with epistemological issues.

Yet, some would ask, what would such a discussion achieve? They would likely question the justification of discussing and soul searching in relation to the epistemologies and philosophies as outlined in this chapter, particularly at a time when education appears to be drowning in a sea of dysfunction. Emerging perspectives in educational administration suggest that even though the knowledge base project promises to consider new approaches, the result is a project that may struggle with its ability to provide a life raft in the turbulent educational seas. We can no longer afford to ignore the need for discussion, sustained critical thought, and self interrogation of our own work.

Regardless of the concerns raised by otherist poststructural theories, the otherist poststructural perspective is not the only way to approach the knowledge base, nor the best way; it is one approach among many to be considered when wrestling with the immensity of a knowledge base. Otherist poststructuralist theories, as well as other emerging perspectives, are not the definitive answer for the knowledge base project, but they call into question the wisdom of seeking definitive answers in the first place.

Notes

1. This chapter was based in part on C. A. Capper's *"Otherist" poststructural perspective of educational administration: A case in point: The proposed knowledge base in educational administration.* Paper presented at the University Council for Educational Administration Conference, Minneapolis, Minn. October 30–November 1, 1992.

2. Epistemology is defined as "the division of philosophy that investigates the nature and origin of knowledge. A theory of the nature of knowledge" (The American Heritage Dictionary: 460).

References

American Heritage Dictionary. 1985. Boston: Houghton Mifflin Company.

Blackmore, J. 1989. Educational leadership: A feminist critique and reconstruction. In J. Smyth, ed. *Critical perspectives on educational leadership*: 93–130. Philadelphia, Pa: Falmer Press.

Burrell, G. 1988. Modernism, postmodernism and organizational analysis 2: The contribution of Michel Foucault. *Organization studies 9* (2): 221–235.

Burrell, G., and G. Morgan. 1979. *Sociological paradigms and organizational analysis*. London: Heinemann.

Calás, M. B., and L. Smircich. 1991. Voicing seduction to silence leadership. *Organization Studies 12*(4): 567–602.

———. 1992. Using the "F" word: Feminist theories and the social consequences of organizational research. In A. J. Mills and P. Tancred, eds., *Gendering organizational analysis:* 222–34. Newbury Park, Calif.: Sage.

Cherryholmes, C. 1988. *Power and criticism: Poststructural investigations in education*. NY: Teachers College Press.

Cooper, R. 1989. Modernism, postmodernism and organizational analysis 3: The contribution of Jacques Derrida. *Organizational studies 10*(4): 479–502.

Cooper, R., and G. Burrell. 1988. Modernism, postmodernism and organizational analysis: An introduction. *Organization Studies 9*(1): 91–112.

Ferguson, K. E. 1984. *The feminist case against bureaucracy*. Philadelphia, Pa.: Temple University Press.

Foster, W. 1986. *Paradigms and promises: New approaches to educational administration*. Buffalo, N.Y.: Prometheus.

Harding, S. 1990. Feminism, science, and the anti-enlightenment critiques. In L. Nicholson, ed., *Feminism/postmodernism*: 83–106. New York: Routledge.

Hearn, J., D. L. Sheppard, P. Tancred-Sheriff, and G. Burrell. 1989. *The sexuality of organization*. Newbury Park, Calif.: Sage.

Lather, P. 1991. *Getting smart: Feminist research and pedagogy with/in the postmodern*. New York: Routledge.

Luke, C. 1992. Feminist politics in radical pedagogy. In C. Luke and J. Gore, eds., *Feminisms and critical pedagogy:* 25–53, New York: Routledge.

—— and J. Gore. 1992. Introduction. In C. Luke and J. Gore, eds., *Feminisms and critical pedagogy:* 1–14.

Mills, A. J. and P. Tancred. 1992. *Gendering organizational analysis.* Newbury Park, Calif.: Sage.

Nicholson, L. J. (Ed). 1990. *Feminism/postmodernism.* New York: Routledge.

Nicolaides, N., and A. K. Gaynor. 1992. The knowledge base informing the teaching of administrative and organizational theory in UCEA universities: A descriptive and interpretive survey. *Educational Administration Quarterly 28*(2): 237–65.

Parker, M. 1992. Post-modern organizations or postmodern organization theory? *Organization Studies 13*(1): 1–17.

Prestine, N. A. Fall, 1991. Problem solving and expertise: A cognitive view of administrative leadership. *Organizational Theory Dialogue.*

Sedgwick, E. K. 1990. *Epistemology of the closet.* Berkeley, Calif.: University of California Press.

Sawicki, J. 1991. *Disciplining Foucault: Feminism, power, and the body.* New York: Routledge.

Shakeshaft, C. 1987. *Women in educational administration.* Newbury Park, Calif.: Sage.

Smyth, J. (Ed). 1989. *Critical perspectives on educational leadership.* New York: Falmer Press.

Tierney, W. 1992. *Self and identity in a postmodern world: A life story.* Unpublished manuscript.

University Council for Educational Administration. 1992. *Essential knowledge for school leaders: A proposal to map the knowledge base of educational administration.* Submitted by the University Council for Educational Administration.

Weedon, C. 1987. *Feminist practice and poststructuralist theory.* New York: Basil Blackwell, Inc.

Theoretical Pluralism in Educational Administration

Daniel E. Griffiths

The purpose of this paper is to explore the concept of theoretical pluralism and relate it to educational administration. I prefer the concept of theoretical pluralism to that of multiparadigm, which is now the hot topic in educational administration, because theoretical pluralism seems to be a step closer to reality. Multiparadigm carries the baggage of ontology, epistemelogy, and metaphysics that theoretical pluralism does not. My argument is simple and straightforward: organizations and organizational behavior are complex phenomena and should be studied from a number of points of view. The most advantageous way of going at this is to use a number of theoretical approaches.

While the term *paradigm* has a multitude of definitions—Kuhn (1970), for instance, is reported to have used it in 22 different ways (Masterman 1970)—Gioia and Pitre (1990, 585) use the term in a way that appears to have current common acceptance. They write that a paradigm is "a general perspective or way of thinking that reflects fundamental beliefs and assumptions about the nature of organizations." Those advocating paradigm research have created classifications of the dimensions they have chosen and have forced theories to fit into their artificial boxes. The most popular scheme is that of Burrell and Morgan (1980), who have devised four different research paradigms: Radical Humanist, Radical Structuralist, Functionalist, and Interpretivist. Theories are then placed in what is considered to be the appropriate box, even though the fit is often awkward. Astley and Van de Ven (1983, 245) also have a four paradigm scheme, composed of Natural Selection View, Collective Action View, System-Structural View, and Strategic Choice View, into which theories are fitted.

The best example of the above point is the Functionalist paradigm of Burrell and Morgan (1979). This box is crammed full of theories of such a varied nature that should one be used, the research results would differ radically from the results of another choice. Both open and closed systems are included as are theories of formal and informal organizations. Mayo, Roethlisberger, Homans, Merton, Parsons, Vroom, Selznick, Gouldner, Blau, Weber, and Barnard and many others are all lumped together to make a mishmash that cannot be justified on the grounds that "all theories of organization are founded upon a philosophy of science and a theory of society, whether the theorists are aware of it or not" (Burrell and Morgan 1979: 119). My contention is, of course, that theorists are not aware of these two assumptions and are not unduly concerned when they are so labeled ex post facto. Researchers investigate problems, use whatever theories are useful (that help to solve the problem), and do not concern themselves with ontological or metaphysical positions (Griffiths 1983). The trouble is that virtually all researchers have a limited repertoire of theories (often only one) and they bend the problem to fit their theory.

As I see it, the major shortcoming of multiparadigm research is that it appears to be confined to theory building rather than problem solving. Two conclusions seem appropriate after reviewing multiparadigm work. The first is that theory creation is the goal and second, that all the theories within a paradigm are considered to be equally useful for purposes of research. Both Burrell and Morgan (1979) and Gioia and Pitre (1990) write at a high level and only occasionally refer to specific theories. Since the only practical use of theories is in research, it is necessary to move from the paradigm level to the theory level. This, it seems to me, is what Weick (1992) does in his article "Agenda Setting in Organizational Behavior: A Theory-Focused Approach." Likewise, making the move from paradigm to theory was my purpose in editing the Special Issue of the *Educational Administrative Quarterly* entitled "Nontraditional Theory and Research" (Griffiths 1991).

Sources for a Research Agenda
Theory-Focused or Problem-Focused?

The Journal of Management Inquiry (1992) included two articles that explored the basis for a research agenda in organizational science. Lawrence (1992) contrasts the way social scientists *should* act with the way physical scientists *do* act. He argues (1992, 140), "The physical sciences start their discovery process with a theory orientation. They first ask what is known and from this they formulate their questions about what needs to be known." Behavioral scientists have an advantage over physical scientists in that subjects can define and describe their own problems. Lawrence sets forth the steps for doing behavioral research as follows:

> Step one: Select an important emerging human problem to study, a selection based on careful listening and observations: be explicit about the value choices involved.
> Step two: Do some initial field scouting of the problem to make an initial assessment of the key parameters.
> Step three: Examine relevant theory to use promising hypotheses and conceptualizations.
> Step four: Be eclectic in research design, choice of data collection techniques, and analytic methods.
> Step five: Collect data systematically.
> Step six: Analyze and generalize.
> Step seven: Present results so that they are useful for action by responsible problem solvers as well as accessible to the academic community (1992, 149).

Weick (1992) attempted to demonstrate that the research should have a theory-focused perspective. I am by now convinced that Weick often writes with a literary tongue-in-cheek and that this is a specific instance. Each time he gets around to identifying how his interest is attracted, he refers to a problem. In fact, toward the end of his argument he says, "My work is no less problem-focused than is Lawrence's. It's just that the problems I focus on are more private, closer in, and more hidden by theory-based overlays" (175). It seems to me that the difference separating Weick and Lawrence is one of style and not substance.

The two do agree on what is a much more important point, that is, the necessity of using a wide variety of appropriate theories to solve the problems being researched. In fact, Weick makes an eloquent plea to stop the fighting among advocates of different theories:

> But I'm not convinced that chronic ethnocentric conflict between warring paradigms has done much to help us consolidate organizational studies into a shared body of knowledge. We need to be subtle and complex in diverse

ways if we want to comprehend significant differences in organizational life. But we also need to match this differentiation with the integration that comes when we articulate connections, themes, and patterns that tie those differences into coherent, memorable guidelines.

I come down on the side advocated by Lawrence, namely, that the research agenda in organizational science should be problem-focused, largely because it seems to me that Weick is as problem-focused as is Lawrence and that the primary reason for research in an applied field such as organizational science is the solving of problems.

What Theories?

The argument between positivists and antipositivists does not go away. It flared again in the November 1992 issue of *Organization Science*. Astley and Zammuto (1992: 443–60) advocated the concept of "language games" and, in so doing, attacked positivist science. Donaldson (1992: 461–66) and Beyer (1992: 467–75) condemned the use of language games and their methodology and advocated the use of what they called positivism. The fact that the term *positivism* has itself changed through its use by social scientists so that it no longer has its original meaning (see Griffiths 1986, 257–72), escapes Donaldson and Beyer and is ignored by Astley and Zammuto. Both sides provide a sufficient number of zingers to keep the reader interested. Donaldson (1992, 464), for instance, called antipositivism, "Voodoo Management or Management by Mumbo Jumbo," while Astley and Zammuto (1992, 443) quote Dean West of the New York University Graduate School of Business Administration as saying of academic research in organizations, "It's often crap." But when the fun is over and one considers the three articles, the impression grows that all say something of value to the research agenda of organizational scientists. Certainly, all organizations have cultures, and messages are interpreted through the screen of the culture. And just as certainly there is an objective world that can be ignored only at great risk to organizational members. Given these facts, it seems to me that the debate between positivists (so-called) and antipositivists only makes a stronger case for the research value of theoretical pluralism.

Criteria for the Selection of Theories

As stated above, Lawrence's third step in doing behavioral research is, "Examine relevant theory to use promising hypotheses and conceptualizations" (Lawrence 1992, 140). Are there any guides or criteria for the selection of appropriate theories? While Lawrence has developed a strong case for examining a variety of theories, he offers no help in selecting them. Astley (1985, 500) observes that Lincoln (1985, 35) "believes there can be no objective choice between alternative perspectives: the validity of the perspective employed depends on the context of inquiry and on the research concerns that guide investigation." Astley then states (1992, 500), "The variety of ways to reconstitute our knowledge of organizational reality is, in this sense, bounded only by theoretical ingenuity in inventing new linguistic constructions." Weick (1992, 172) seems to support Lincoln's contention when he writes, "All theories are about practice and practicality, and the trick is to discover those settings and conditions under which they hold true. . . .The question is, where is the theory true? In what context do events go together the way the theory predicts?"

Astley (1992) broadens the discussion of theories that could be used by introducing ideas of interest and excitement: "Old paradigms fall from grace not because they are wrong but because they are boring" (503). And further, "Successful scientists. . .are intuitively perverse, always ready to question accepted world views and create opportunities for the critical rejection of what is taken as given by others" (504). An acceptable criterion for selecting theories is the fact that one is bored with the usual traditional approach and wants to try something new, or at least different.

Not all theories can be used on all problems. This would appear to be the rule. Griffiths, Hart, and Blair (1991) attempted to use chaos theory to analyze a case study of rapid growth and conflict in a school district. They found that while certain of the chaos concepts were useful in analyzing the case, they were unable to develop the quantitative measures possessing the necessary precision to examine chaotic systems. In a such a case, the question of feasibility must be considered. Is it feasible to obtain the needed measurements and/or observations necessary to test the theory's concepts? The practicality of cost also enters the picture. It may be possible to use a particular theory, but only at too high a cost. Feasibility, then, is a criterion in terms of both possibility and cost.

Lawrence (1992, 141) introduced the concept of "user-friendly" when discussing the analysis and presentation of research. By this he means that the research should be done and the report written in such a way that it could be used by practitioners, organizational managers, and policymakers. Since organizational science is an applied discipline, this is not an unreasonable criterion (although one would never think so from reading the literature).

Beyer (1992, 471), in a discussion of the language that organizational scientists should use, concludes, that it should be, "grounded and tested by some experience of organizations that has some reality about it. Without such grounding, I don't think our language would be of much interest to managers, our students, or our employers and clients" (471). This, of course, is an aspect of the user-friendly idea discussed above. Examples of language abuse abound; for instance, imagine the impact the following gem might have on a group of inner-city school administrators (Jeffcut 1992, 687), "Such a revelation of the ambiguity of postmodernity as becoming explicable through the reinvigoration of a modernizing meta-narrative enables the apparent transposition of postmodern undecidability into late-modern manageability."

The criteria that could be used to select theories appropriate for research include:

Feasibility: Is it possible to utilize the theoretical concepts? Can appropriate measurements and empirical observations be made? Is there a fit between the theory's concepts and the problem?

Excitement: Will the theory lead to new insights or merely reinforce old ones?

Context: Is this the context in which the theory applies? Is there a conceptual overlap between the problem and the theory?

Cost: Even though the theory meets other criteria, can researchers afford the cost in money, time, and effort?

User-Friendly: Is the language of the theory known to principals, superintendents, and teachers as well as to educational administration professors?

Fruitful: Does the theory generate solutions to the problem?

Applications and Implications

Theoretical pluralism has meaning for research and for the management of research that, if implemented, would result in rather dramatic change from present practice.

Theoretical pluralism could influence research in two ways. First, researchers could utilize a wide range of theories in the solution of problems and second, select the most appropriate theory or theories for a particular problem. In the second instance, the selection of the most appropriate theory or theories, the criteria listed above could be used. It is not necessary that a theory meet all of the criteria; rather, the criteria could be used as a basis for making a judgment. The chart on page 309 illustrates the point that certain theories are more appropriate for certain categories of problems than are others. It should be noted that, in all instances, several theories are appropriate for each category of problems, but in no instance are all of the theories appropriate for researching a category of problems. This becomes much more evident when problems within a category are examined.

A common problem, for instance, is the taking of an annual school census to determine how many children are eligible for admission to the public schools. The methodology of a traditional census study is appropriate, while critical theory, chaos theory, or semiotics (and most other approaches) are not. If, however, a school district wishes to interpret the census data, many other theories such as critical, Marxist, semiotics, and feminist might well be used. Gaining the full meaning of the data requires more than a single theoretical approach.

While there have been few applications of theoretical pluralism there have been some. Reilly, Main, and Crystal (1988) offer an example of the use of multiple theories to study a problem. They studied executive compensation using an economic theory and a behavioral model. They found no support for the economic theory; however, "strong associations were found between CEO compensation and the compensation level of outside members of the board of directors, especially those who serve on the compensation committee" (257). They concluded by quoting Baker, Jenson, and Murphy (1988), with whom they agree, "Ultimately, it may be that psychologists, behaviorists, human resource people understand something about human behavior and motivation that is not yet captured in our economic models" (615). In this case, the use of two theories on a single problem led to a much more complete understanding of the factors involved in executive compensation than if either of the theories had been used alone.

A team of researchers reported (Griffiths, ed. 1969) a study in which four theories were used as the bases on which 90 Organizational Taxonomic Units (OTUs) were scored in an attempt to develop a single taxonomy of organizational behavior. They failed

Categories of Problems and Theories Appropriate for Their Study

Categories	*Functionalism	*Contingency Theory	*Getzels-Guba	*Decision Theory	*Historical Theory	*General Systems Theory	Social Judgment Theory	Critical Theory	Chaos Theory	Marxist Theories	Action Research	Feminist Theory	Semiotics	Sense-making Theory	Self-interest Theory	Phenomenology
A. Social and Cultural Influences on Schooling	x				x	x		x		x		x	x			x
B. Teaching and Learning Processes	x			x					x		x					
C. Organizational Studies	x	x	x	x		x	x		x	x	x	x	x	x		x
D. Leadership and Management	x	x	x	x	x	x	x	x		x	x	x	x	x		x
E. Policy and Political Studies	x				x			x		x		x	x		x	
F. Legal and Ethical	x			x	x			x				x				
G. Economic and Financial Dimensions of Schooling	x			x		x			x	x					x	

* Types of traditional theory.

to do so; however, they did demonstrate the feasibility of using theoretical pluralism in research on organizational behavior. What they found was summed up in this manner: "Perhaps these theories are (1) more complete, and (2) more separate than is supposed" (247). If the team had not kept the goal of creating a single taxonomy so firmly in mind, they might have recognized the power of theoretical pluralism.

The second application of theoretical pluralism is discussed by Gioia and Pitre (1990, 598–99), who present some interesting implications for multiparadigm research. They suggest that research teams be composed of devotees of different paradigms, that faculties be likewise composed, and that there be doctoral-level training in philosophies of social science that encourage the use of multiparadigm awareness. Substitute theoretical pluralism for multiparadigm and the advice is equally valuable.

References

Astley, W. G. 1985. Administrative science as socially constructed truth. *Administrative Science Quarterly 30* (4): 497–513.

Astley, W. G. and A. H. Van de Ven. 1983. Central perspectives and debates in organization theory. *Administrative Science Quarterly 29* (2): 245–73.

Astley, W. G. and R. F. Zammuto. 1992. Organization science, managers, and language games. *Organization Science 3* (4): 443–60.

Baker, G. P., M. C. Jensen, K. J. Murphy. 1988. Compensation and incentives: Practice vs. Theory. *Journal of Finance 43*: (593–616).

Beyer, J. M. 1992. Metaphors, misunderstandings, and mischief: A commentary. *Organization Science 3* (4): 467–74.

Burrell, G. and G. Morgan. 1979. *Sociological paradigms and organizational analysis.* London: Heinemann.

Donaldson, L. 1992. The Weick stuff: Managing beyond games. *Organization Science 3* (4): 461–66.

Gioia, D. A. and E. Pitre. 1990. Multiparadigm perspective on theory building. *Academy of Management Review 15* (4): 584–602.

Griffiths, D. E., ed. 1969. *Developing taxonomies of organizational behavior in educational administration.* Chicago: Rand McNally.

———. 1983. Evolution in research and theory: A study of prominent researchers. *Educational Administration Quarterly XIX* (3): 201–21.

———. 1986. Theories in educational administration: Past, present, and future. In B. O. Ukeje, L. O. Ocho, and E. O. Fagbamiye, eds. *Issues and concerns in educational administration.* Ibadan: MacMillan Nigeria.

———, A. W. Hart, and B. G. Blair. 1991. Still another approach to administration: Chaos theory. *Educational Administration Quarterly 27* (3) 430–51.

Jeffcutt, P. 1992. Book Review. *Administrative Science Quarterly 37* (4): 687.

Kuhn, T. J. 1970. *The structure of scientific revolutions.* Chicago: University of Chicago Press.

Lawrence, P. R. 1992. The challenge of problem-oriented research. *Journal of Management Inquiry 1* (2): 139–42.

Lincoln, Y. S. 1985. *Organizational theory and inquiry: The paradigm revolution.* Beverly Hills, Calif.: Sage.

Masterman, M. 1970. The nature of a paradigm. In M. Kochem, ed., *Growth of knowledge.* Cambridge, Mass.: Wiley. Noted in T. Kuhn (1970).

Reilly, C. A. III, G. G. Main, and G. S. Crystal. 1988. CEO compensation as tournament and social comparison: A tale of two theories. *Administrative Science Quarterly 33* (2) 257–74.

Weick, K. E. 1992. Agenda setting in organizational behavior: A theory-focused approach. *Journal of Management Inquiry 1* (3): 171–83.

Contributors

Gary L. Anderson is a former teacher and principal who is currently director of Latin American Programs in Education at the University of New Mexico. He is also an Associate Professor at the University of New Mexico.

Joseph Blase is a professor of educational leadership in the Department of Educational Leadership, College of Education, at the University of Georgia. His research interests include the micropolitics of education, the sociology of teaching/teaching as work, educational leadership, and the school principalship. He recently published *The Politics of Life in Schools: Power, Conflict and Cooperation* and *Bringing Out the Best in Teachers: What Effective Principals Do.*

Paul V. Bredeson is a professor of educational administration at the University of Wisconsin-Madison. His research interests include role transition in restructured schools and personnel selection processes in educational organizations. He taught high-school Spanish and was a high-school principal. He received the Jack A. Culbertson Award (1990) for outstanding contributions to research and leadership in Educational Administration. He is a past President of the National Council of Professors of Educational Administration (NCPEA) and is President-Elect of the University Council for Educational Administration (UCEA).

Colleen A. Capper is associate professor of educational adminis-tration at the University of Wisconsin at Madison. During a five-year term as a missionary for the United Methodist Church, she founded and directed a nonprofit agency, served as a public school administrator for special education and at-risk students, and worked as a college instructor at Union College, all located in the Appalachian region of southeastern Kentucky. She edited the

SUNY Press volume *Educational Administration in a Pluralistic Society* (1993), and is author of the forthcoming *Theoretical and Practical Ruptures: Multiple Approaches to Educational Administration.*

Robert Donmoyer is a professor of educational policy and leadership at Ohio State University. For the past fifteen years, his scholarship has focused on questions related to research utilization. Among other questions, he has explored the implications of the postpositivist critique of knowledge use in applied, public-policy fields like education. In recent years, Professor Donmoyer has expanded his research focus to include studies of the impact of organizational structures on educational practice. This new interest is evident in a SUNY Press book, *At-Risk Students: Portraits, Policies, Programs, and Practices* and in his work as Organization and Policy Research Coordinator of the National Center for Science Teaching and Learning.

William Foster is a professor of educational leadership at Indiana University. He is the author of *Paradigms and Promises: New Approaches to Educational Administration* and a number of articles. His interests lie in the area of critical theories, leadership, and administrator preparation.

Daniel E. Griffiths is dean emeritus and professor emeritus of the School of Education, New York University. He has published widely in administrative theory, educational administration, and education. He has written or edited 11 books and authored over 200 articles, reviews, chapters, and reports. He is the first recipient of the Roald F. Campbell Lifetime Achievement Award.

Vivian W. Ikpa is an assistant professor in the Department of Educational Leadership and Policy Studies at Temple University. Her research interests are the politics of education, school desegregation policies, AIDS and equity issues, and gender and equity issues.

Michael Imber is a professor of educational policy and leadership at the University of Kansas. He is the author of *Education Law* and *A Teacher's Guide to Education Law* and of many publications and presentations on various topics of educational policy and law. Professor Imber has extensive experience advising school board members, educators, and parents on issues of educational policy and law and working with disabled children and adults. He also spent four years as the director of a school for at-risk students.

Jane Clark Lindle is on the faculty in the Department of Administration and Supervision at the University of Kentucky. Her scholarship focuses on the micropolitics of school organizations. Her past positions include the principalship and elementary and secondary teaching positions in regular and special education. Her current professional involvement includes the local school board, school-based, decision-making consulting, and presentations on the implementation of the 1990 Kentucky Educational Reform Act.

Janet Littrell is a college administrator and is completing doctoral studies in leadership at the University of San Diego. Her interests lie in the application of critical thought to higher education.

Joseph Murphy is professor and chair of the Department of Educational Leadership at Peabody College of Vanderbilt University. He is also a senior research associate with the National Center for Educational Leadership. One of his areas of interest is the preparation of school administrators. His recent books in this area include: *Approaches to Administrative Training in Education* (edited with Philip Hallinger, 1987); *The Landscape of Leadership Preparation: Reframing the Education of School Administrators* (1992); and *Preparing Tomorrow's School Leaders: Alternative Designs* (edited, 1993).

Rodney Muth is a professor of educational administration at the University of Colorado at Denver. He writes on various topics in education, including policy issues such as educational reform and school choice and organizational issues such as leadership, power, decision making, and problem solving. Recent articles have appeared in *Planning and Changing*, the *Journal of Educational Administration*, and the *American School Board Journal*. Recent chapters of his have appeared in *Democratic Leadership: The Changing Context of Administrative Preparation, NCPEA: In a new Voice*, and *Educational Reform: Making Sense of It All*.

Rodney Ogawa is an associate professor of education and an associate director of the California Educational Research Cooperative at the University of California, Riverside. His scholarship examines schools from the perspective provided by organizations theory and leadership theory. Most recently, he drew upon institutional theory to study the sources of school-based management.

David Jude Ortiz is a 1992 graduate of the University of California, Riverside, graduating with honors in political science.

He has presented a paper, entitled "Superintending a Multifarious School District: A Case Study in Leadership Style," for the University of California, Riverside, Minority Summer Internship Program, and has collaborated with Flora Ida Ortiz on a book chapter concerning politicizing executive action. A Patricia Robert Harris Fellow, he is currently pursuing a Master of Public Administration degree at California State University, Fullerton.

Flora Ida ortiz is professor of educational administration at the University of California at Riverside. Her recent work includes *The Superintendent's Leadership in school Reform*; "An Hispanic Female Superintendent's Leadership and School District Culture"; and "Politicizing Executive Action: The Case of Hispanic Female Superintendents." These works relate superintendency leadership to race and ethnicity. Her forthcoming book, *Schoolhousing: Planning and Designing Educational Facilities*, analyzes school district and state agencies' interorganizational and interpersonal relationships.

Bonnie Page is director of Project LEAD and interim director of Re: Learning for the State of New Mexico.

Rosemary Papalewis is a professor of educational administration at California State University (CSU), Fresno, and is a co-director of the joint doctoral program in Educational Leadership. She has conducted research and published widely in the area of educational leadership, focusing particularly on issues of gender, equity, and teacher-administrator mentor relationships and programs. Her recent interests include doctoral education programs, gender aspects of leadership, and the dynamics of mentorship. She has, in the past, served as teacher, principal, and superintendent. She has also served as President of the National Council of Professors of Educational Administration (NCPEA). She currently serves as a panel member for the California Commission on Teacher Credentialing, and represents CSU Fresno on the state-level Academic Senate of the California State University system.

Nona A. Prestine is an assistant professor of educational administration at the University of Illinois at Urbana-Champaign. Her research interests include cognitive learning theory and school restructuring. Her most recent publication, "Benchmarks of Change: Assessing Essential School Restructuring Efforts," appeared in the Summer, 1993, issue of *Educational Evaluation and Policy Analysis*.

Jayminn Suler Sanford is an assistant professor of education at Temple University. She teaches courses in the Department of

Curriculum and Instruction and Technology in Education and coordinates the Five Year Teacher Preparation Program and Temple's Professional Development Schools.

James Joseph Scheurich is an assistant professor at the University of Texas-Austin. His scholarly work focuses on school reform, organizational theory, research methodology, critical theory, and poststructuralism. He has recently published in *Educational Research* (in press), the *Educational Administration Quarterly*, the *Journal of Curriculum and Supervision*, and the *Review Journal of Philosophy and Social Science*.

Charol Shakeshaft is a professor and chair in the School of Education at Hofstra University. Since 1979, she has directed an institute to help women move into positions in school administration. Her award-winning book, *Women in Educational Administration*, is in its fifth printing. She is currently completing a book on sexual abuse of students in schools by school personnel and peers.

Tyll van Geel is Taylor professor of education in the Graduate School of Education, University of Rochester, Rochester, New York. Professor van Geel's books include *Education Law, A Teacher's Guide to Education Law, Authority to Control the School Program, The Courts and American Education Law,* and *Understanding Supreme Court Opinions.* In addition, he is a contributor to a wide range of legal and educational journals.

Index